IMAGES
of America

WASHINGTON COUNTY REVISITED

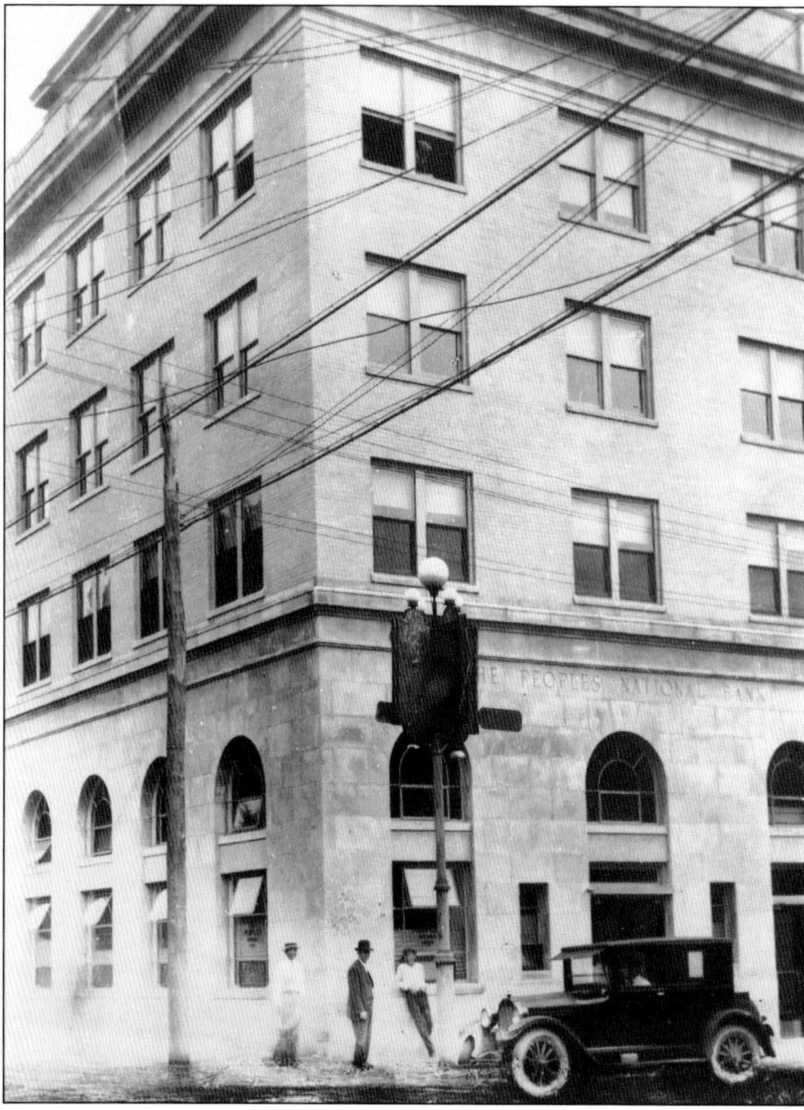

PEOPLE'S NATIONAL BANK. Completed in 1924, the People's National Bank building was the first four-story building in Abingdon and is still among the taller buildings today. The bottom floor was faced with limestone while the next three stories were of brick construction. Builders added a frame fifth floor on top by 1928. Abingdon residents still recall the parties held on the top floor during its heyday. The Depression put this bank out of business, but several other banks have occupied the building through the years. (Courtesy Lowry Bowman.)

ON THE COVER: This train is coming around the bend around 1910 with loads of logs near Damascus. Several brave men are perched atop the tall stacks of virgin timber. The Virginia-Carolina Railway extended a line from Abingdon to Damascus in 1900, and the Norfolk and Western Railway later bought the line and extended the system to Elkland, North Carolina. According to a 1912 lumber magazine, at that time, Washington County was producing more lumber than the entire state of Pennsylvania. After a boom of about 25 years, the northern timber companies finished taking the trees and left the mountains behind, bare of their foliage. (Courtesy Virginia Cornett Smith.)

IMAGES
of America

WASHINGTON COUNTY REVISITED

Donna Akers Warmuth

ARCADIA
PUBLISHING

ISBN 978-0-7385-5335-1

Published by Arcadia Publishing
Charleston, South Carolina

Printed in the United States of America

Library of Congress Catalog Card Number: 2007935231

For all general information contact Arcadia Publishing at:
Telephone 843-853-2070
Fax 843-853-0044
E-mail sales@arcadiapublishing.com
For customer service and orders:
Toll-Free 1-888-313-2665

Visit us on the Internet at www.arcadiapublishing.com

This book is dedicated to all those who have come before us in Washington County, the brave pioneers and our ancestors who settled the fertile Holston River Valley. I would like to especially thank my Akers, Davis, Hagy, Jameson, and McCulloch families of the Rich Valley community in Washington County and my husband, Greg, and sons, Owen and Riley, for their enduring support and understanding.

CONTENTS

ACKNOWLEDGMENTS

This book is only intended to be an informal assortment of historic images that shows the lives of the people and communities of Washington County, Virginia. Rather than a formal history of the area, this collection of images only provides a "snapshot" of the past. Many of the facts in the captions are based on verbal information or family stories from contributors, so minor discrepancies may exist. The author's best efforts were made to verify dates of major events and facts, but often there was scant information and conflicting data.

I wouldn't be able to compile these books without the generous help, interest, and support of citizens of Washington County. Many thanks for saving your family photographs, houses, schools, and buildings of this region. The Museum of Middle Appalachians (MOMA) and the Historical Society of Washington County are both major repositories of historical information and photographs, many of which are available for public viewing.

I would like to thank the following individuals who provided images, historic information, or contacts for this book: Harry Haynes with Museum of Middle Appalachians, Mary Jones Hardwick, DeAnna Akers Greene, Mike Hoback, Garrett Jackson, Susie Copenhaver Lang, Irene Johnson Meade, Luther Johnson, Peggy Johnson, Harry Minnick, Juanita Mock Neese, Doug Patterson, Lowry Bowman, Louise Fortune Hall, Marilou Hall Preston, Joe Smith, Jeff Weaver, Bobby Cuddy, Alberta Copenhaver, Susi Copenhaver Lang, Ruby Stovall Clark, Linda Orfield Crane, Patricia Leonard, Don Smith, Troy Taylor, Rick Rouse, Lois Snodgrass Shupe, Kathy Musick, the Jack Kestner family, Hayter's Gap branch of Washington County Public Library, Terri Collier McCroskey, Hobart M. McCall, Roy Rector, Doris Campbell Peters, Evelyn McThenia Hale, Virginia Cornett Smith, Dorothy Johnson Kelly, Helen Johnson Holliday, Sam Campbell, Blair Keller, Roger Brannon, Nellie and Ken Akers, Owen August Warmuth, Mark and Connie Simcox, Dr. and Mrs. John Johnston, Jane and Helen Bryan, Doris Musick, Lynda Campbell, Nancy Moore, Eleanor Arnett Blevins, Tammy Martin, Darlene Scott Hockett, Helen Wood, Damon C. Carroll Jr., Rich Valley Methodist Church, Marie Snavely Yeatts, and Judy Owens.

The assistance and advice of Brooksi Hudson and Courtney Hutton with Arcadia Publishing have been most helpful in the process of compiling and completing this book. Thanks to Greg, Owen, and Riley for understanding the time commitments with putting together these books.

As always, thanks to my mother, Nellie Hensley Akers, for childcare, encouragement, a genetic interest in history and writing, and a soft shoulder to lean on.

INTRODUCTION

Even though this is the second volume compiled about Washington County, please bear with the author for another history lesson. Washington County is a land of contrasts, from the wealthy red-brick houses with columns in Abingdon, to the simple vernacular farmhouses in the river valleys, to the mobile homes up lonely "hollers." Much of the different socioeconomic levels of residents can be traced to geography and soil types, early industries, and railroad lines, as well as the location of the Washington County courthouse. Few folks realize that money from exploiting salt deposits in nearby Saltville actually provided the funds for the early families like the Prestons and Kings to construct the fine houses and academies in Abingdon. As Harry Haynes at the Museum of Middle Appalachians puts it, "All roads lead to Saltville." In fact, in 1803, a toll road or turnpike was built between Abingdon and Saltville and was the best road in the entire region.

In order to gain a clearer understanding of the region, one needs to appreciate its geography. The area lies in the Great Valley region of Virginia. Three branches of the Holston River—the North, Middle, and South Forks—divide the valleys and provide fertile soils. Native Americans occupied this fertile river valley in the distant past, but only stone points (arrowheads) and tools, pottery shards, and traces of skeletons remain as proof. At the time of European exploration, the land was a hunting ground for the Cherokee, Shawnee, and Six Nations tribes. Thomas Walker and surveyors from the Loyal Land Company first surveyed land here in 1746. Settlers from Maryland, Pennsylvania, and the Shenandoah Valley soon were attracted to the resources of this land—mainly cheap land and abundant water sources and game. The Loyal Land Company quickly began surveying and selling parcels.

The time period between the 1750s and up to the late 1700s was a time of unrest in the region, with many conflicts between settlers and Native Americans. Settlers' fears resulted in 23 forts being built on the Holston and Clinch Rivers for protection against the Native American attacks. Black's Fort was built by Joseph Black in 1774 near today's Abingdon, and the first court for the area took place there in January 1777. Conditions were so serious that settlers fled back up the Valley Road, leaving their farms deserted. These brave settlers returned in large numbers to this territory only after the Revolutionary War and the French and Indian War ended.

In 1776, Washington County was formed from Fincastle County, and in later years, the counties of Buchanan, Dickenson, Wise, Russell, Scott, Smyth, Lee, and Tazewell were carved from this large area. In 1780, some 400 brave men, called the "Over the Mountain Men," volunteered in a militia under Gen. William Campbell and marched over the mountains to defeat the British at the Battle of Kings Mountain. The following recorded descriptions of Abingdon and Washington County demonstrate the historic growth and development. In 1782, the settlement of Abingdon included a log courthouse, Dunn's Hotel, a log jail, three taverns, hazelnut trees, chinquapin bushes, plum trees, and saplings. With plenty of cheap land, the area attracted settlers in droves. Between 1793 and 1835, Abingdon was the commercial center and post office for southwest Virginia and eastern Kentucky.

By 1835, Abingdon had grown to be a good-size town, with 150–200 houses, 2 academies, 2 hotels, 3 taverns, a flour mill, 9 mercantile houses, 3 groceries, 1 wool and 2 cotton factories, 4 tanyards, 10 blacksmith shops, 1 hat factory and store, 6 wheelwrights and wagon makers, 2 cabinet factories, and 2 boot and shoe factories. The town was a major stop on the Great Wagon or Valley Road into Kentucky and the West. In fact, historians estimate that 100,000 settlers traveled through Abingdon to Kentucky and points west just between 1780 and 1790. Travelers would stop to trade out their worn wagons for a new wagon from the Hagy Wagon Company or another wagoner and obtain cash for their trips at this last banking center.

In 1888, the following businesses were located in the county: 3 agricultural implements, 3 banks, 1 bookseller, 1 cigar manufacturer, 2 clothiers, 11 coach and wagoners, 39 general merchants, 10 grocers, 2 hardwares, 7 hotels, 1 lumber dealer, 8 milliners, 34 corn and flour mills, 10 saloons, 1 tinware manufacturer, 6 tanners, and 2 tobacco dealers.

Other communities, such as Damascus, Glade Spring, and Meadowview, also grew and prospered as trade locations, especially after connections to the railroad system were established.

The Civil War had a major negative affect on the economy and the region with two Union raids within the county and many buildings burned. Union troops attempted to destroy the salt mines in nearby Saltville and cut off the railroad lines. Many Washington County sons were sent to fight the Yanks and never made it back home.

Despite the geographic odds and Reconstruction, businesses and commerce thrived in this rural region, largely due to the construction and expansion of the railroad. The Virginia and Tennessee Railroad was built from Lynchburg to Abingdon by 1856 and extended to Bristol. In 1900, the Virginia-Carolina completed a line to Damascus. By 1911, the Norfolk and Western Railway had bought out the V-C company and extended rail lines to remote Elkland, North Carolina. Many of the stops, such as Hellena, Delmar, Creek Junction, Cant Work, and Franctionsville, have been all but forgotten today. Rail stations allowed passengers and goods to travel into and out of the region. Grocery stores in Abingdon shipped animal skins, farm produce, and household items to stores all over the eastern seaboard.

A few facts from the U.S. Census can help the reader develop a picture of today's Washington County: in the year 2000, the population was 51,103, with Abingdon having 7,780 residents, Emory and Meadow View area with 2,266, Glade Spring with 1,374 residents, Damascus with 981 residents, and Saltville with 2,204. Contrast those figures to those in Chataigne's 1888–1889 *Virginia Gazetteer*: Washington County population—25,203, Abingdon—2,500. As described in the 1888–1889 *Gazetteer*, "It is noted for its fine schools and colleges, bracing and salubrious climate, besides being a place of considerable importance as a manufacturing, commercial and shipping center."

According to this source, the following post offices were present in 1888–1889: Abingdon, Alum Wells, Benham's, Brumley Gap, Craig's Mills, Emory, Friendship, Glade Springs, Green Cove, Greendale, Hazel Spring, Holston, Hyter's (sic) Gap, King's Mills, Lee's Mills, Leplo, Lindell, Lodi, Love's Mills, Lowland, Mendota, Meadow View, Moab, Mock's Mills, Montgomery, Osceola, Raven's Nest, Saltville, Shortsville, Smith's Creek, Stump, and Wallace's Switch. Many of these community names don't appear on today's maps and live only in the memories of the older generation. In 1888–1889, there were 105 white and 21 "colored" schools in the county. However, a number of other private schools and colleges existed in the area, including Abingdon Male Academy, Academy of the Visitation, Barrack Institute, Emory and Henry College, Hamilton Institute, Jackson Female Institute, King College, Martha Washington College, Stonewall Jackson Institute, Southwest Virginia Institute for Young Ladies, and Sullins College (Bristol, Tennessee).

The excellent rail system attracted industrialists and capitalists from points north. The timber boom lasted almost 25 years and provided jobs and economic development to the communities. Woodworking plants, sawmills, extract plants, and other industries were developed near the rail lines, and they employed hundreds of men from the area. With the abundance of natural resources, industries also came to areas such as Saltville and Plasterco. However, as the trees were depleted, the main products for railroads disappeared, and mail and passenger train service was discontinued in 1962. In 1972, Norfolk and Western abandoned several sections of tracks. In 1982, the Town of Abingdon acquired the right-of-way for the railway to Damascus and up to Whitetop. Showing amazing foresight, the towns established the Virginia Creeper Trail for pedestrians and bicyclists.

Even though the economy has changed to more of a tourist and service economy, the individualistic and proud residents have remained in this land. This Appalachian community is trying to redefine itself so that younger generations don't have to leave for career opportunities elsewhere. Tourism and a growing service sector seem to be where the economies are turning. Economic development leaders are trying to recruit "clean," high-tech industries to replace the closed factories. Abingdon, Glade Spring, and Meadowview are all actively revitalizing their downtowns.

One

Recreation and Social Life

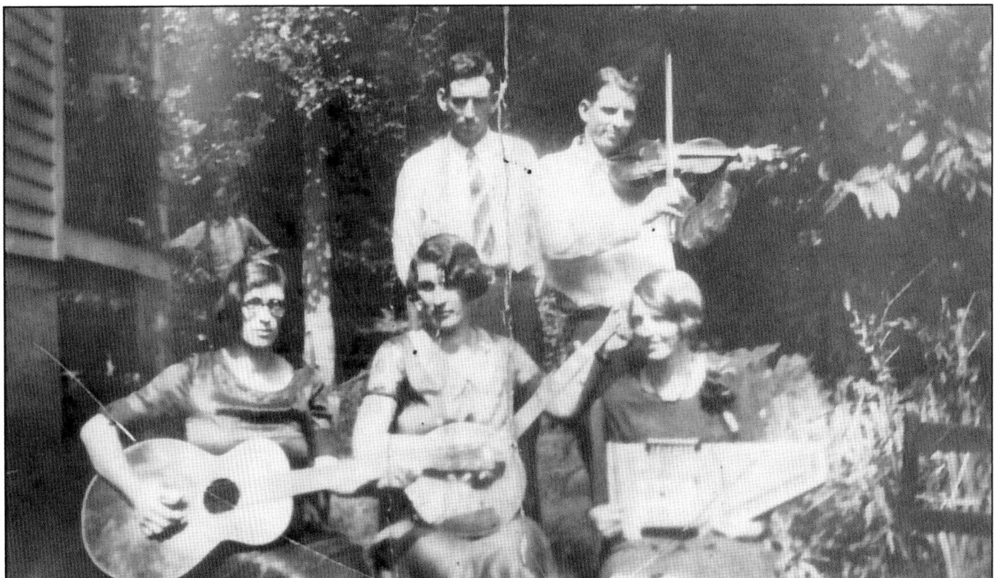

The Carter Family. The famous Carter Family from nearby Scott County often played informally at friends' and relatives' houses in the region. The legendary Carter Family is credited as beginning the commercial country music industry by recording their songs in nearby Bristol, Tennessee, in 1927. Lively bluegrass music performed each week continues the tradition at the Carter Family Memorial Music Center and the Carter Fold in Hiltons, Virginia. From left to right are (seated) Maybelle Addington (1909–1978), Sara Dougherty Carter (1898–1978), and Sylvia Ella Carter (1908–1991); (standing) A. P. Carter (1891–1960) and Grant Carter (1904–1964). (Courtesy Terri Collier McCroskey.)

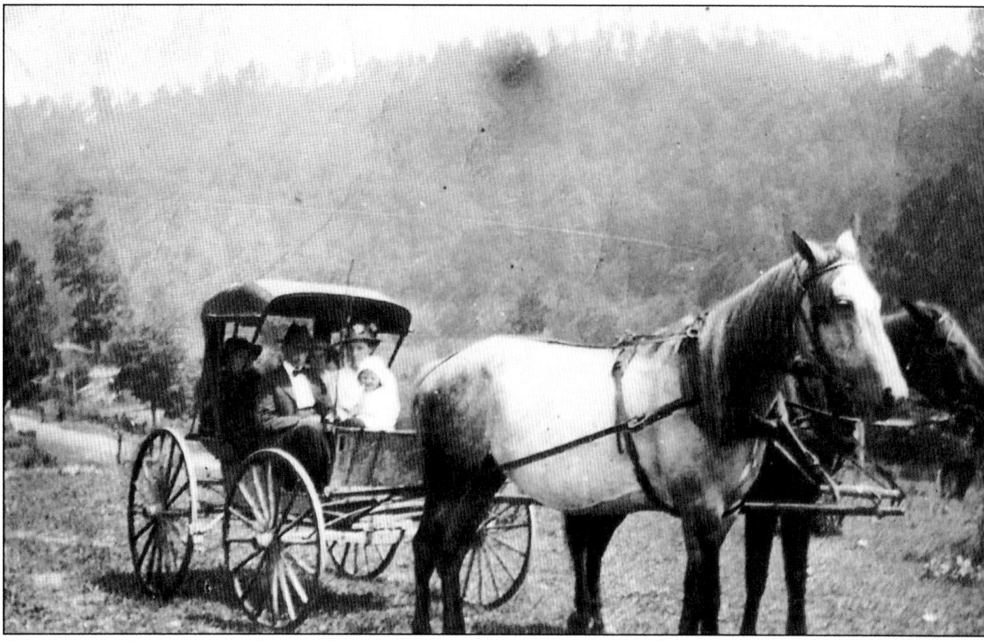

OUT FOR A DRIVE. Two horses lead a buggy on a fine summer day carrying Grover and Alberta Widener Buchanan and their children Lucille, Vivian, and Eileen. In the days of horse and buggy, any trip was an entertaining excursion. (Courtesy Susie Copenhaver Lang.)

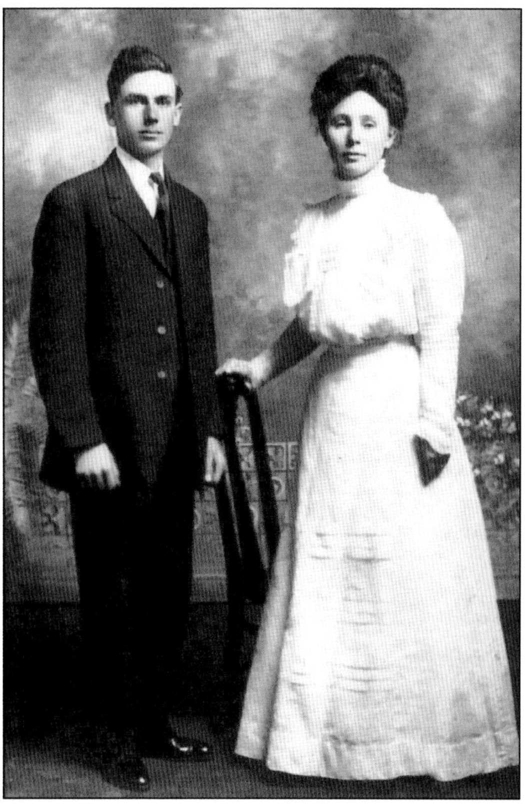

WEDDING, 1909. Grover C. Buchanan and Alberta Widener stand posed in their finest on their wedding day in 1909. Weddings were often large community affairs, with much food and socializing. In Appalachia, various tricks were played on the unwitting couple. Men would be "rode on a rail," which meant being carried astride a rail by a man holding each end. (Courtesy Susie Copenhaver Lang.)

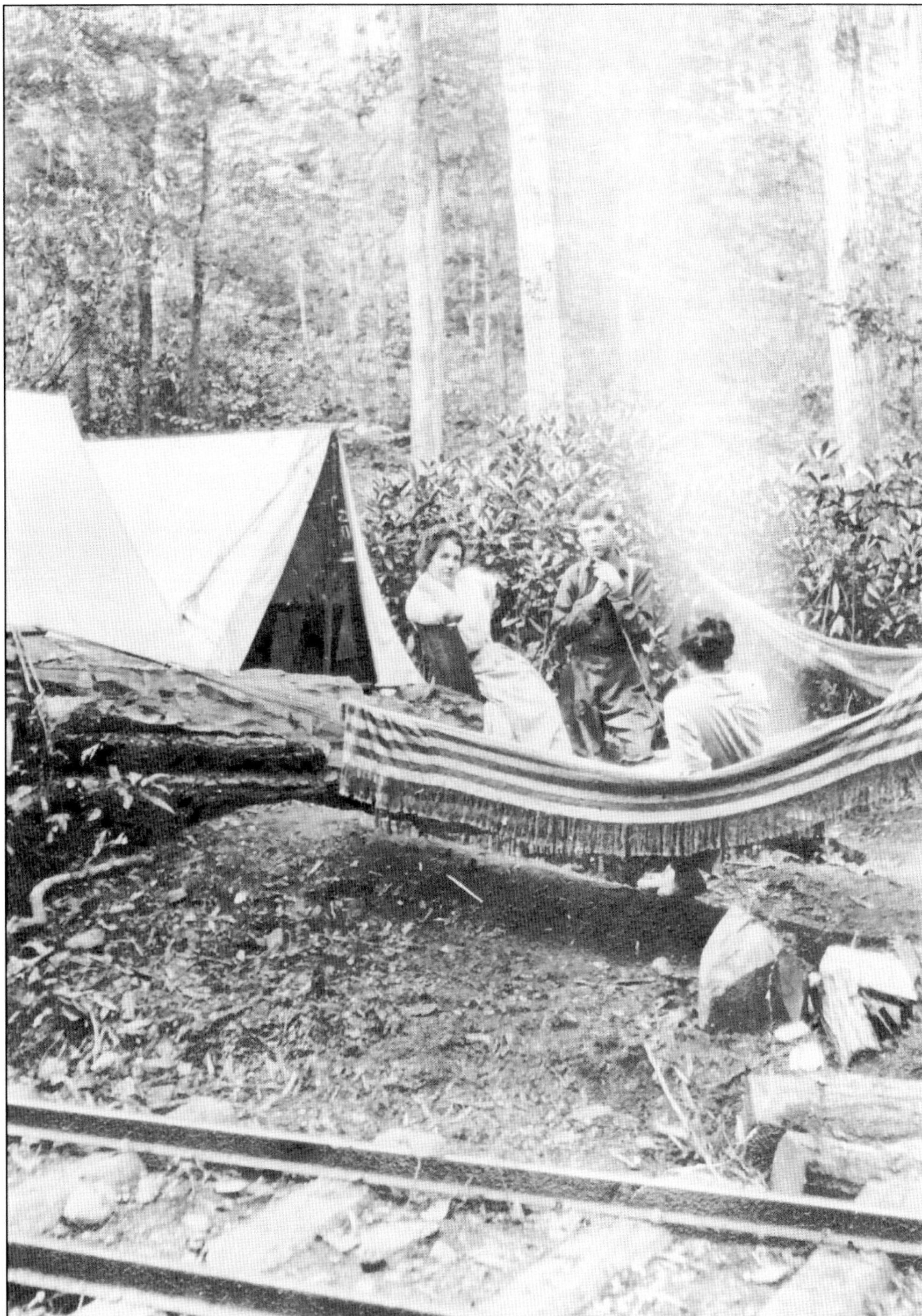

Campout at Whitetop. These campers are taking it easy now that the tents and hammocks are up. People would ride in on the narrow-gauge Laurel Railway and camp in the wilderness around Damascus and Konnarock for fun in the early 1900s. The fringed hammock adds a touch of luxury to the laurels. (Courtesy Virginia Cornett Smith.)

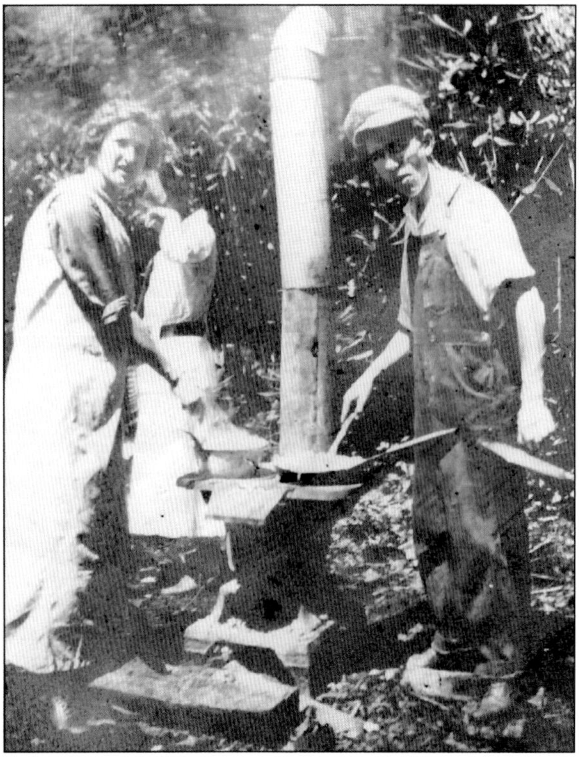

CAMP COOKING. Bess Rhea and an unidentified man are cooking over a stove in the outdoors. These youngsters were part of the camping group that enjoyed getting outside in the mountains around Damascus and Konnarock. Note the long apron that Rhea is wearing to protect her dress. (Courtesy Virginia Cornett Smith.)

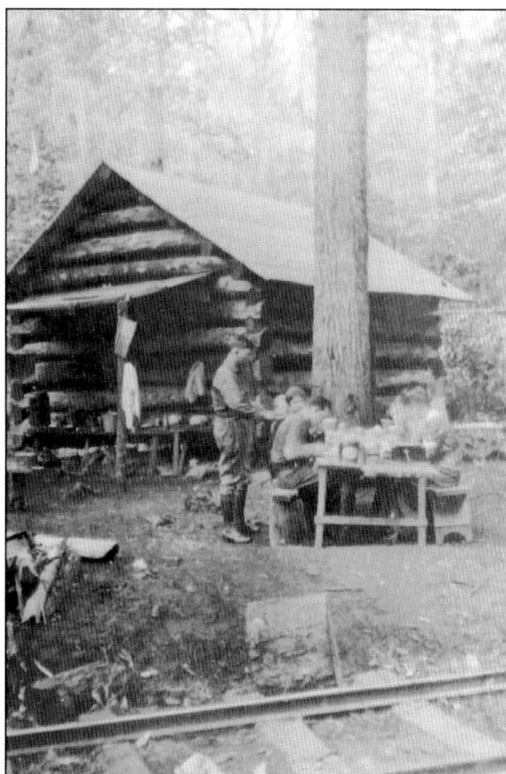

WILBURN WATERS CABIN. These folks are eating supper and camping at the Wilburn Waters cabin. Waters was a hunter and woodsman of the region and the subject of Charles Coale's book *The Life and Adventures of Wilburn Waters.* Robert Russell is serving while, from left to right, Karl Mock, Mareau Clement, Harold Baker, Lillian Mock, and Wilton Mock are dining al fresco. (Courtesy Virginia Cornett Smith.)

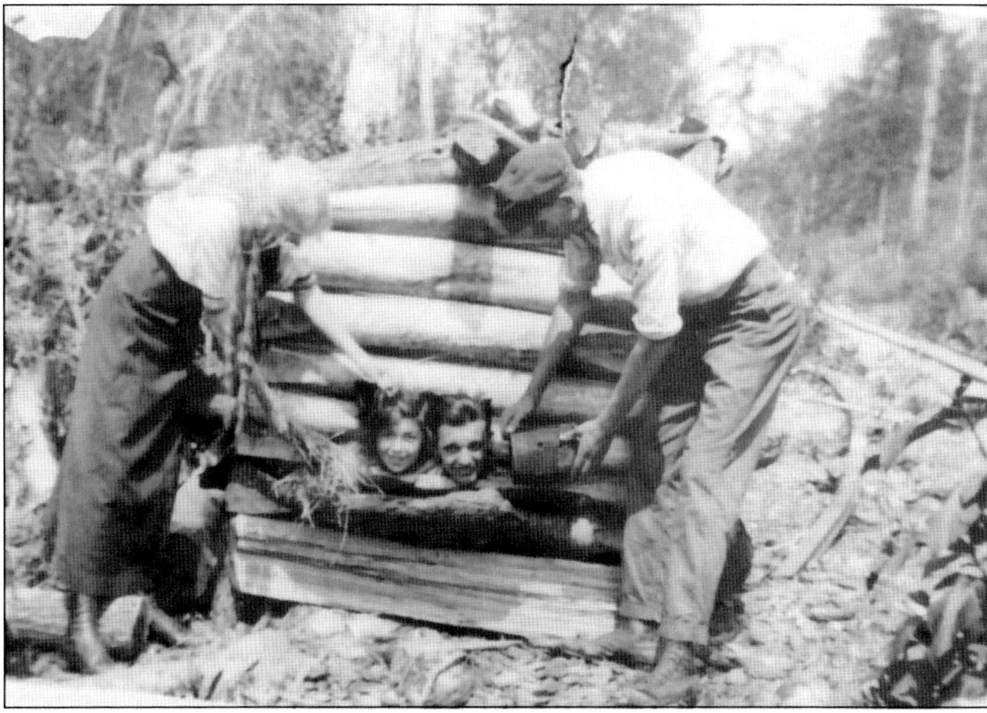

PEEK-A-BOO IN A PIGPEN. These Damascus campers are funning around about 1900 at the pigpen at the Wilburn Waters cabin. Note the railroad adjacent to the site. Elverene Clemments and Glen Elliott are inside the pen with their heads visible. On the outside are Mary Robinson and James Graham. (Courtesy Virginia Cornett Smith.)

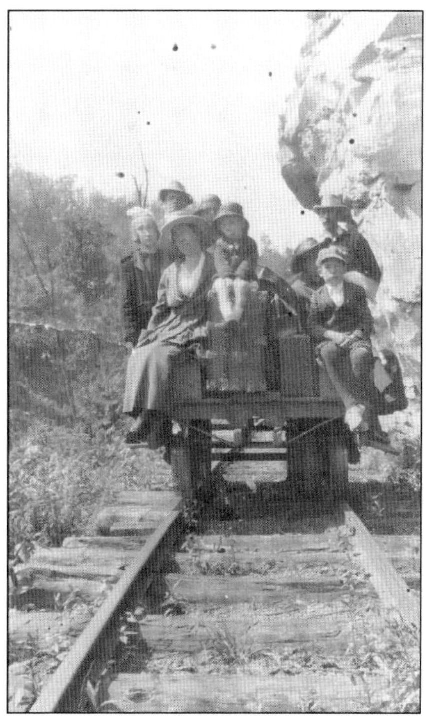

RAILROAD CART. This Damascus group is loaded with suitcases on a railroad cart with no engine in sight. Perhaps this is a handcart and the gentlemen in the back will be providing the muscle to move it. Area residents often rode along the tracks for speedy travel. (Courtesy Virginia Cornett Smith.)

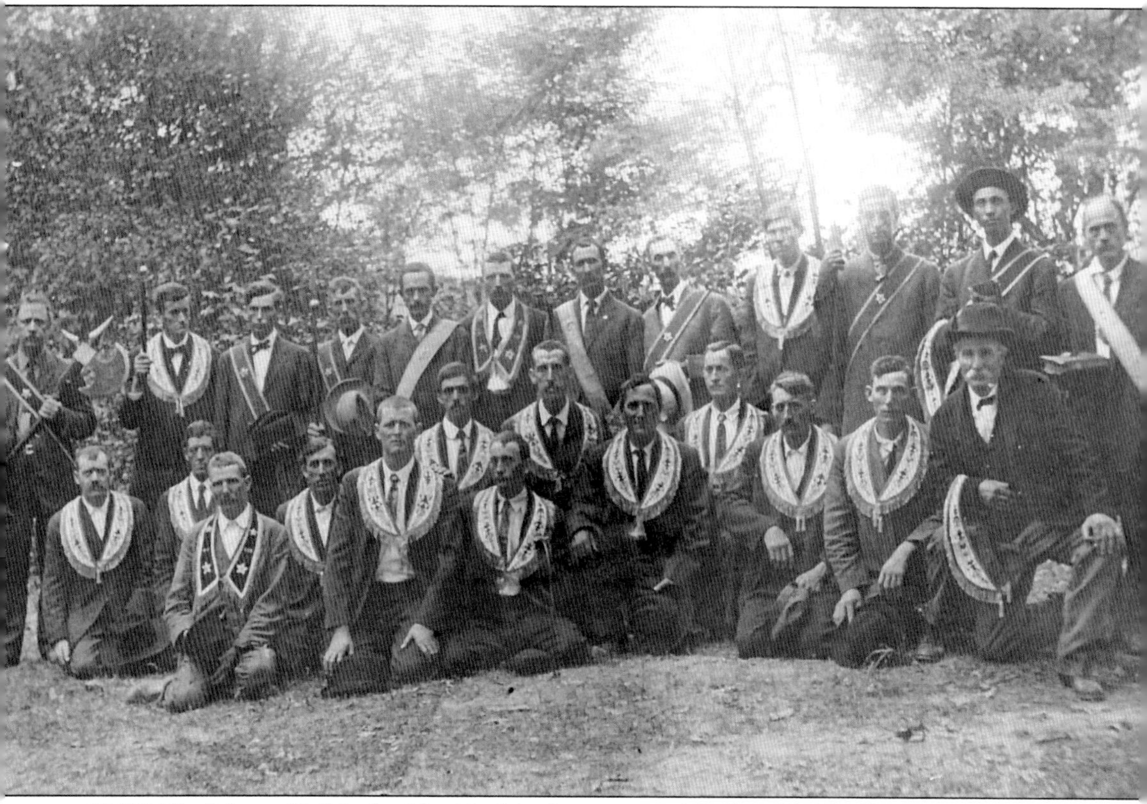

IOOF. The Liberty Hall Lodge No. 13 of the International Order of Odd Fellows was founded in Lodi at Liberty Hall Academy. The group received its unusual name in England because it was considered odd in the 17th century for a group to be organized for the purpose of providing aid to the needy. Pictured from left to right are (first row) Charles W. McThenia, Conley T. Palmer, William M. Bishop, Andrew E. Widener, Carmie Lewis, Sampson L. Doss, and William M. "Squire Bill" Widener; (second row) Shade Barr, J. Floyd Widener, William C. McCray, Zelia Hagy, William M. Wolfe, and Charles Bishop; (third row) J. Hughes Rouse, Samuel L. Kelley, Grover C. Buchanan, Frank Sheffield, Dave Blackburn, Robert M. Thomas, Smith Wagner, Thomas F. Jones, Ira E. DeBusk, Rush Floyd Fisher, Isaac B. Rouse, and Charles L. Greer. (Courtesy Evelyn McThenia Hall.)

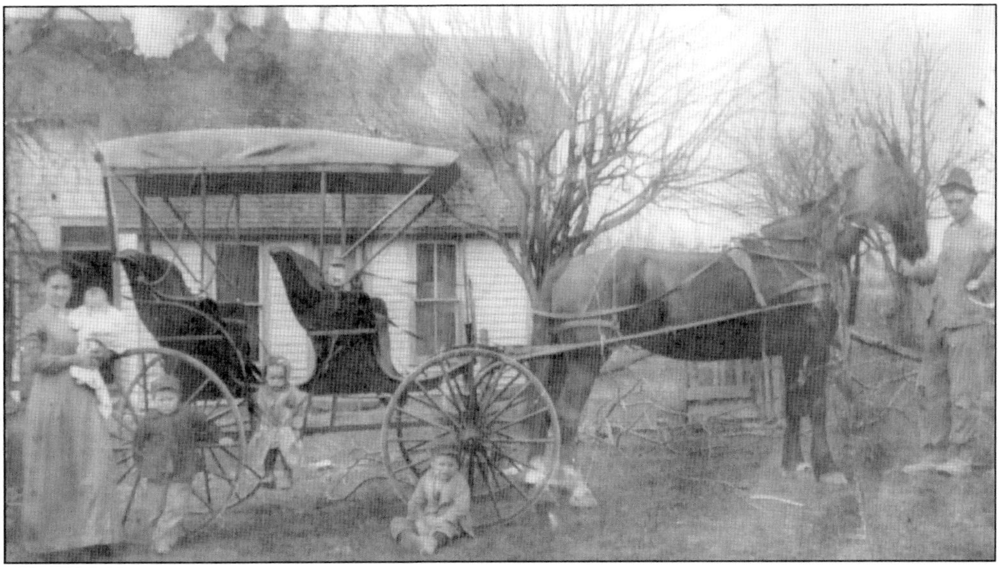

CAMPBELLS' SURREY. A graceful surrey led by a fine horse is ready to take the Campbell family on a ride in the Rich Valley community around 1915. Pictured from left to right are Willie Campbell holding baby James, Robert, Gladys, Earl, and George Washington Campbell (holding the horse). The house was located near White's Mill. (Courtesy Lynda Campbell.)

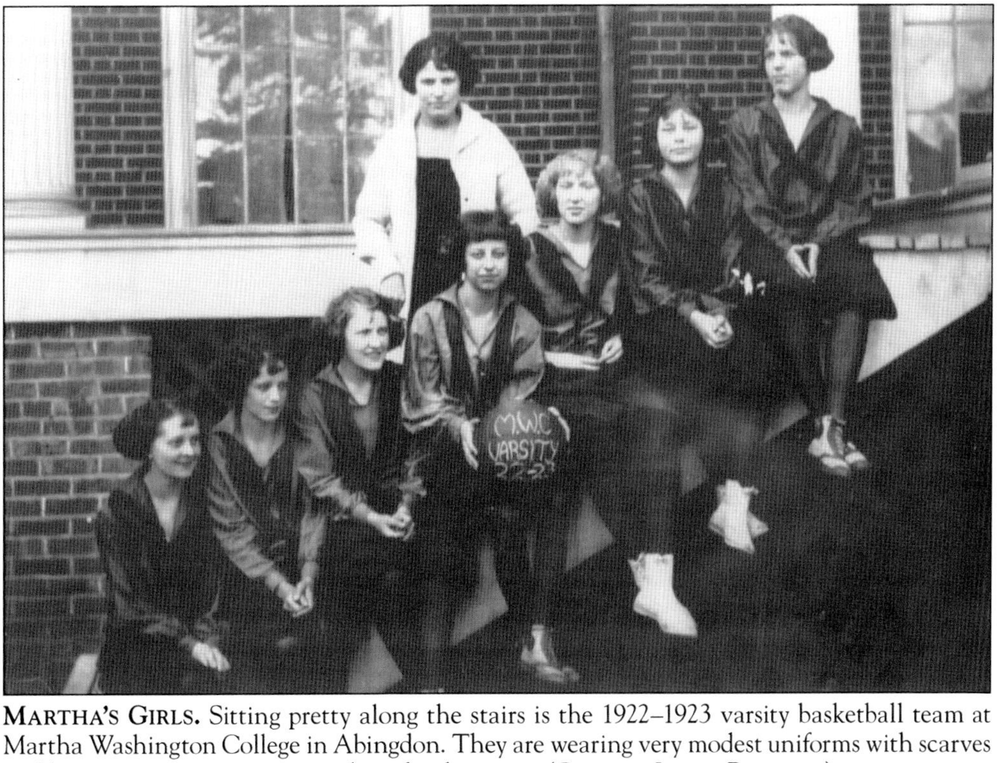

MARTHA'S GIRLS. Sitting pretty along the stairs is the 1922–1923 varsity basketball team at Martha Washington College in Abingdon. They are wearing very modest uniforms with scarves and boots, an appropriate sports dress for that time. (Courtesy Lowry Bowman.)

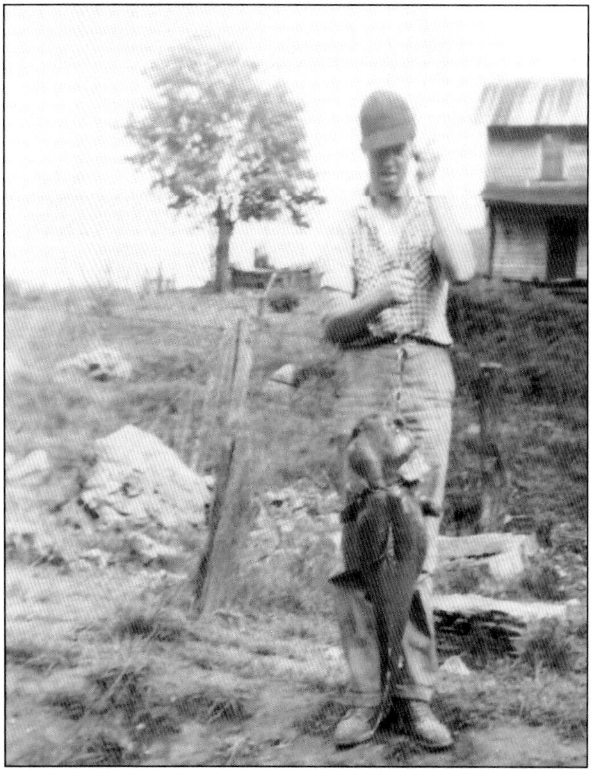

FISHING. Franklin Wagner poses proudly with his large catch in front of the Norris home place on Rambling Wood Road. The creeks and rivers of the region have always been good fishing locations. (Courtesy Ruby Stovall Clark.)

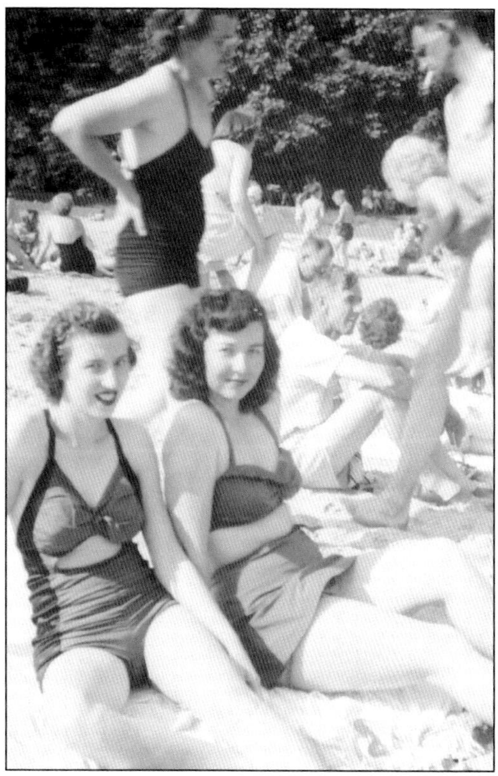

SWIMMING. Ruby Stovall Clark (left) and Betty Kid are sunning and considering swimming at Hungry Mother State Park in 1945. Clark later became a nurse and she and her husband lived on a farm near Meadowview. Several area lakes and swimming pools continue to provide recreational amenities to residents and visitors. (Courtesy Ruby Stovall Clark.)

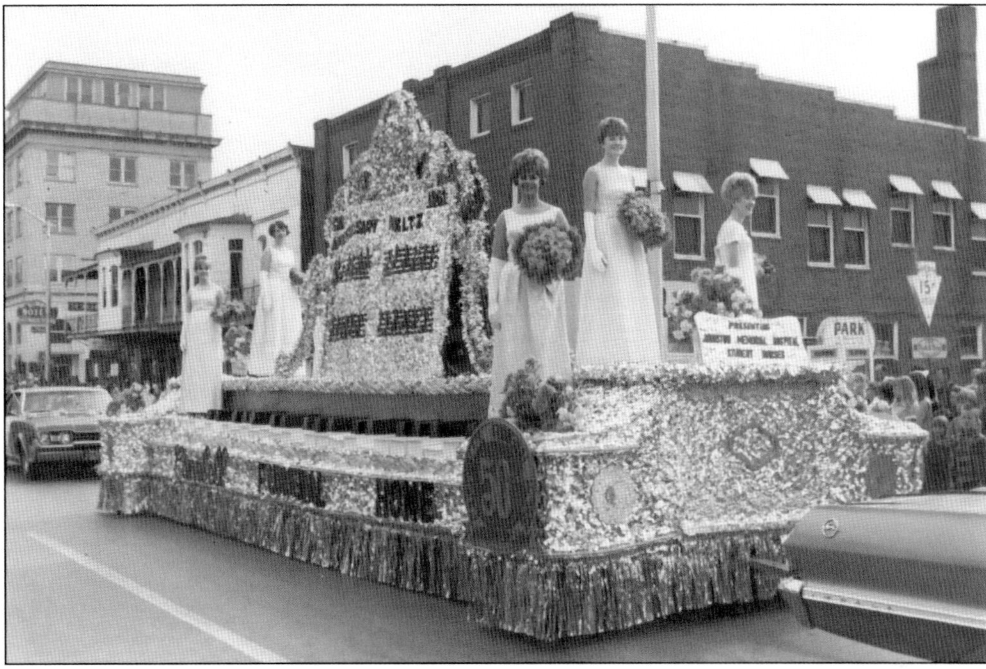

THE 1968 TOBACCO FESTIVAL PARADE. Several nurses from Johnson Memorial's School of Nursing pose on a float celebrating Campbell Funeral Home's 50th anniversary in downtown Abingdon. The Washington County Bank is the tall building; the Belmont and the Dollar Store are visible behind the float. Wanda Garland is the woman standing above the "50th" sign on the float. (Courtesy Sam Campbell.)

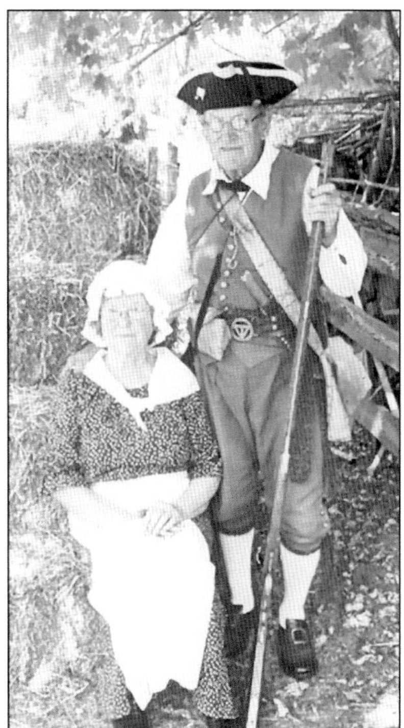

KELLERS REENACTING. The hobby of reenacting the Civil War and the Revolutionary War has become quite popular nationally and especially in this region because of its rich history. Walter "Blair" Keller and his wife, Gilda Mae Bower Keller, have been involved with the Washington County chapter of the Overmountain Trail Association and have celebrated the Revolutionary War victory at the Battle of Kings Mountain for many years. (Courtesy Walter B. "Blair" Keller Jr.)

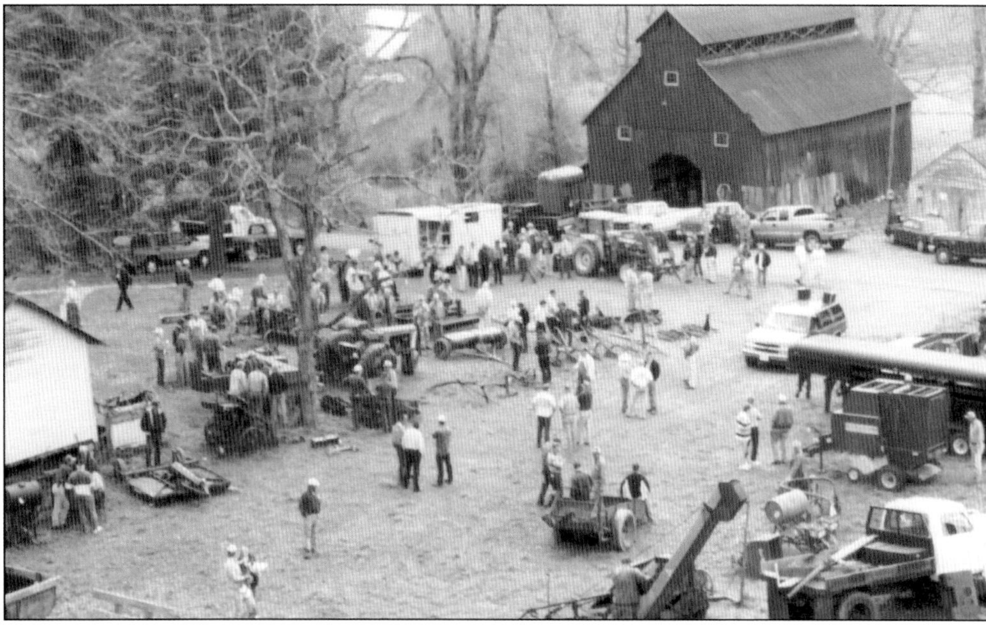

BRUMLEY GAP AUCTION. Meade Realty is conducting a farm auction in Brumley Gap. Auctions continue to be a place to meet and greet and perhaps get a bargain on some item. Several auction companies continue to work in the region. (Courtesy Irene Johnson Meade.)

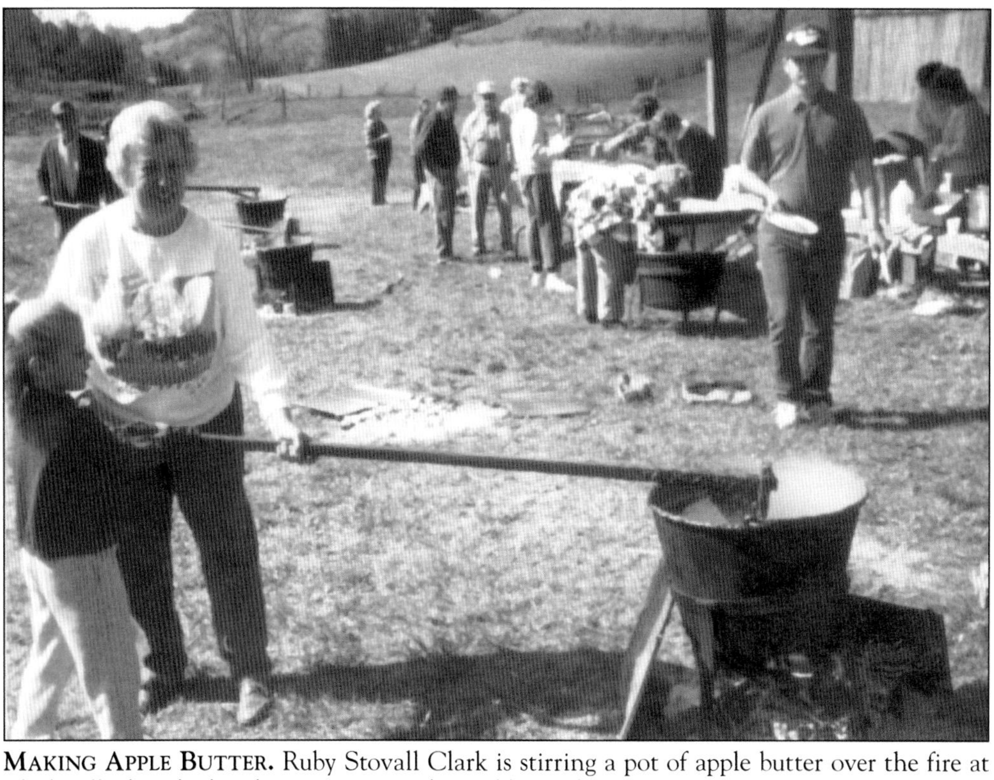

MAKING APPLE BUTTER. Ruby Stovall Clark is stirring a pot of apple butter over the fire at Blackwell Chapel Church. Maintaining these older traditions is a way to continue the rich and vibrant Appalachian culture here. (Courtesy Ruby Stovall Clark.)

Two

EDUCATION AND WORSHIP

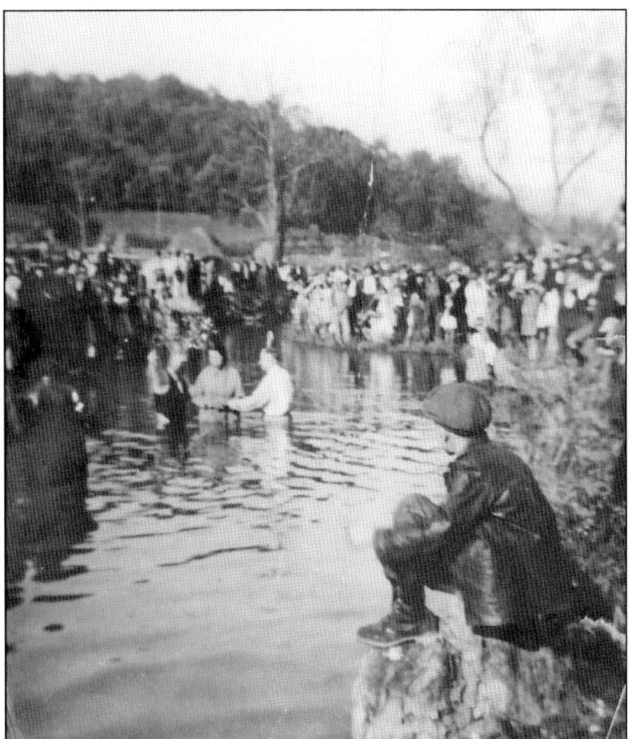

BAPTISM. This church group is gathered about 1940 for the baptism of Blanche McNew Litton in the Hayter's Gap community. Baptisms were frequent social events that bound the community together. (Courtesy Troy Taylor.)

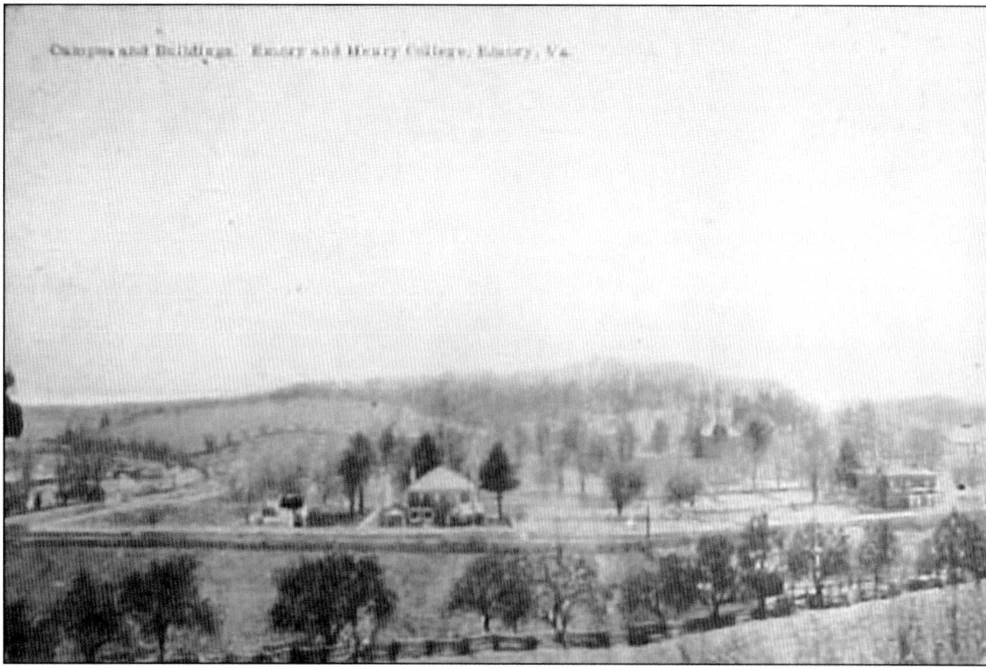

EMORY AND HENRY COLLEGE. This older view of Emory and Henry shows several buildings on the campus. Emory and Henry was established in 1838, and the campus is listed on the National Register of Historic Places. The college is always listed highly in the national private college rankings. (Courtesy Jeff Weaver.)

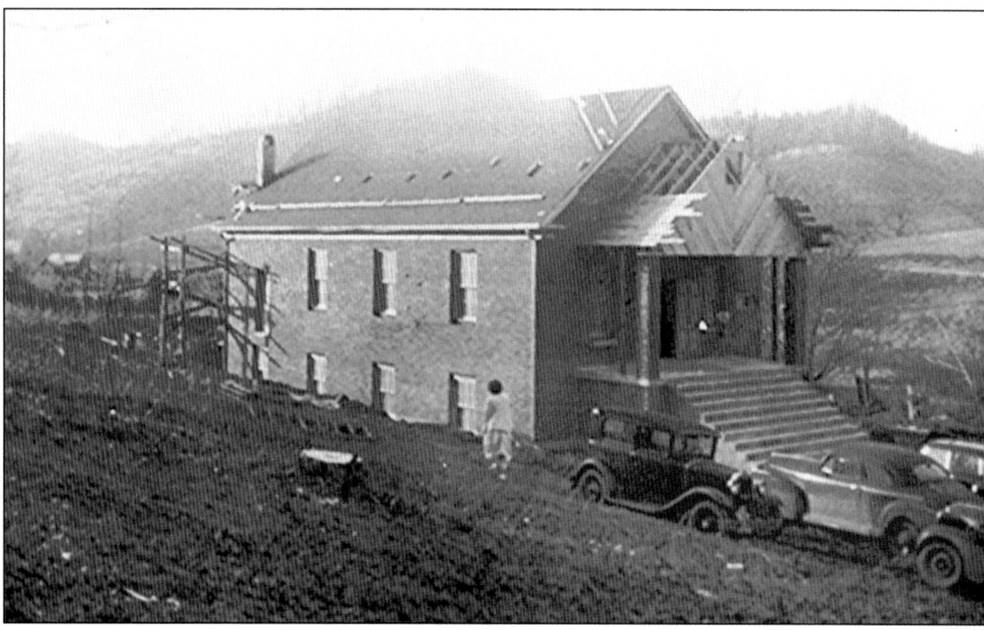

OLD CAMPGROUND CHURCH. This church obtained its name from the religious meetings held on the grounds. Circuit-riding preachers would conduct the assemblies, and folks would attend from miles around and camp out for the duration. The church is still located at S.R. 700 and Campground Road. (Courtesy Patricia Leonard.)

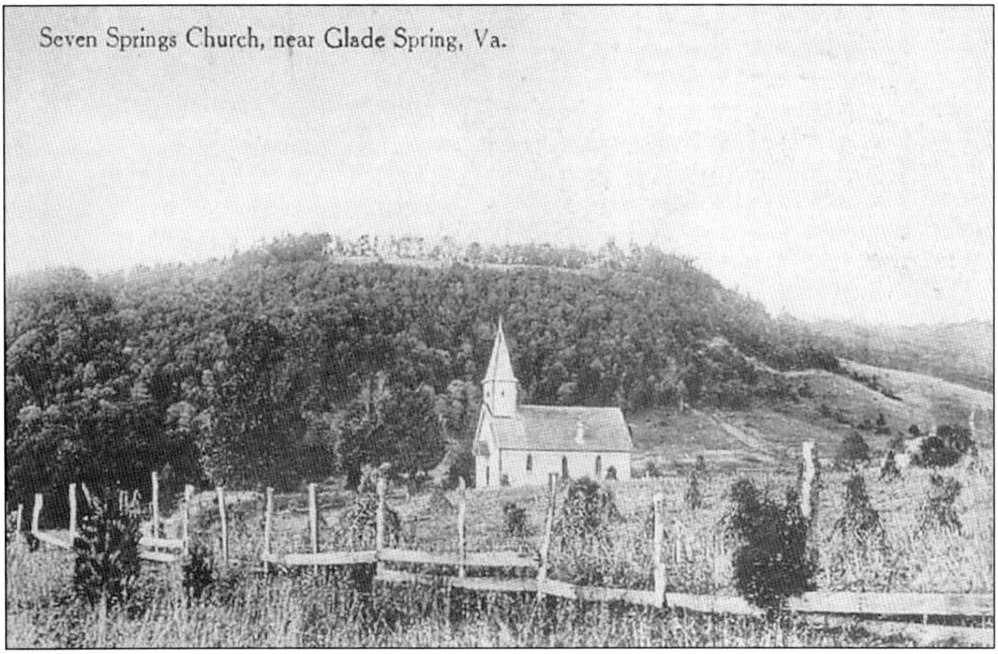

SEVEN SPRINGS CHURCH. This lovely white frame church is nestled in a valley near Glade Spring. It is located near the former site of the famous Seven Springs, a popular resort with decorative stone cathedrals covering each of its seven springs. (Courtesy Jeff Weaver.)

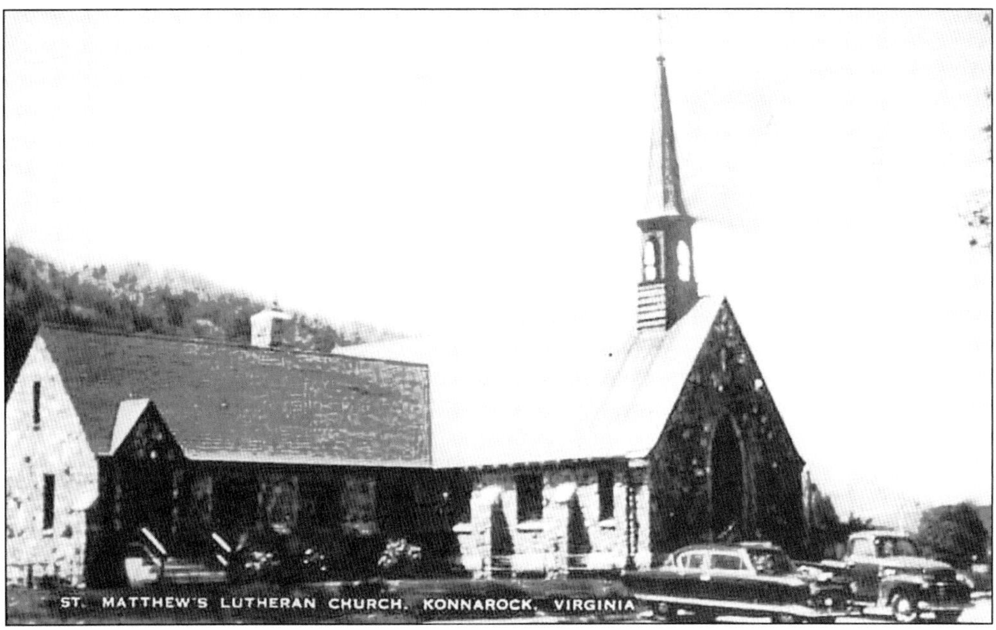

ST. MATTHEW'S LUTHERAN CHURCH. The lovely St. Matthew's Lutheran Church in Konnarock is shown in the mid-20th century. The stone construction and impressive design reflect the company town that briefly brought wealth to Konnarock. (Courtesy Jeff Weaver.)

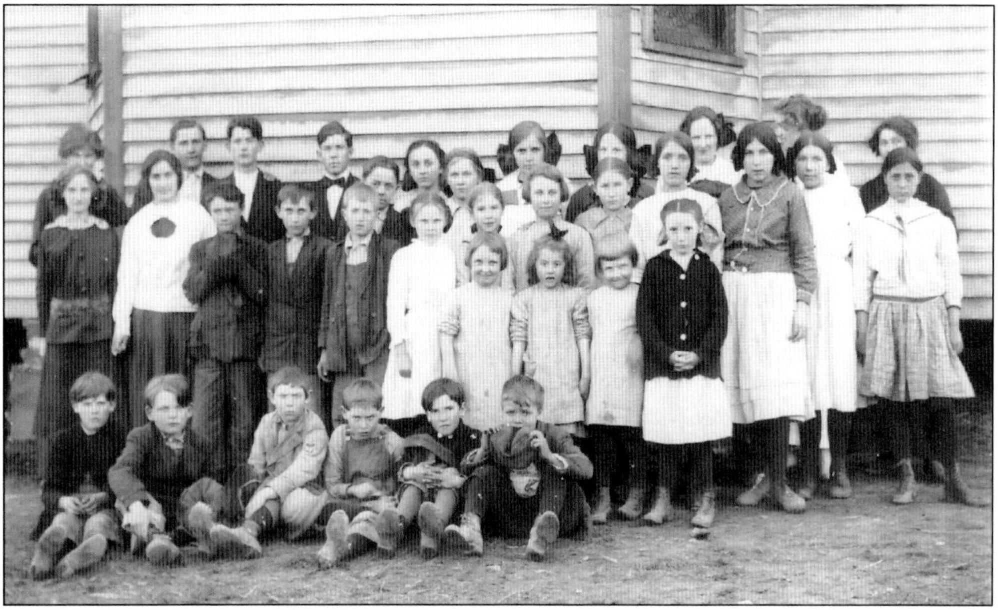

HAYTER'S GAP SCHOOL, 1912. Many students attended this school, and it was a landmark in the community for many years. The only identified children are (first row) far left, Earnest Little (1903–1942) and fifth from left, Howard Little (1906–1998); (second row) second from left, Floyd Kestner. Hayter's Gap School was located on a ridge just north of S.R. 80. (Courtesy Troy Taylor.)

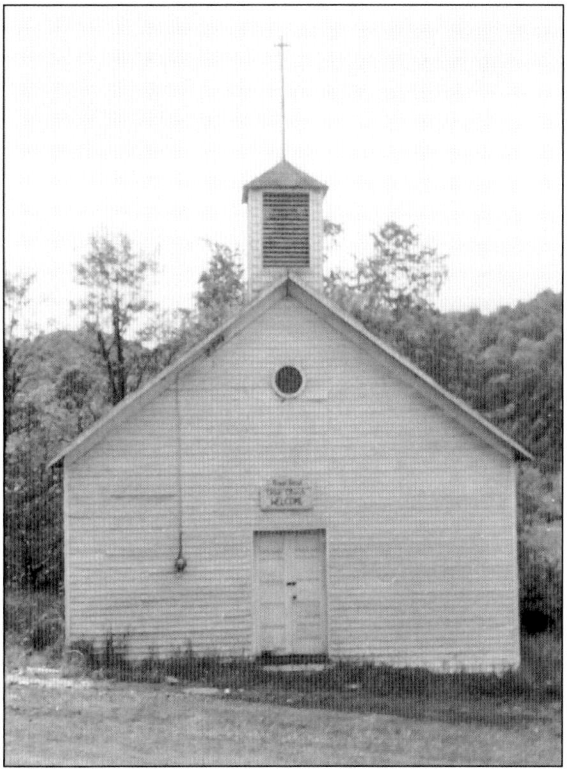

RIVERBEND UNION CHURCH. Built in 1925, this old country church is still standing on North Fork River Road. The lumber was sawed at the Snodgrass sawmill. Early pastors were Joe Johnson, Floyd Kestner, Luther Kestner, Vince Wilson, and Pat Snodgrass. It is now the Holiness Church pastored by Roger O'Quinn. (Courtesy Lois Snodgrass Shupe.)

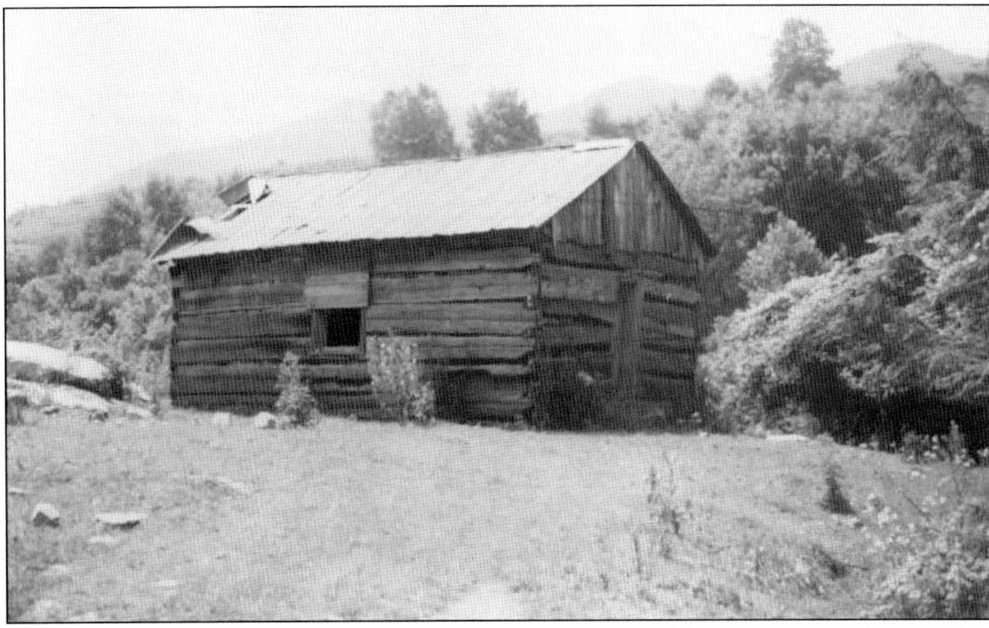

TUMBLING COVE SCHOOL. This one-room log cabin school stood for many years in the Tumbling Creek community near the Virginia State Checking Station, but it was burned down by the state years ago. (Courtesy Troy Taylor.)

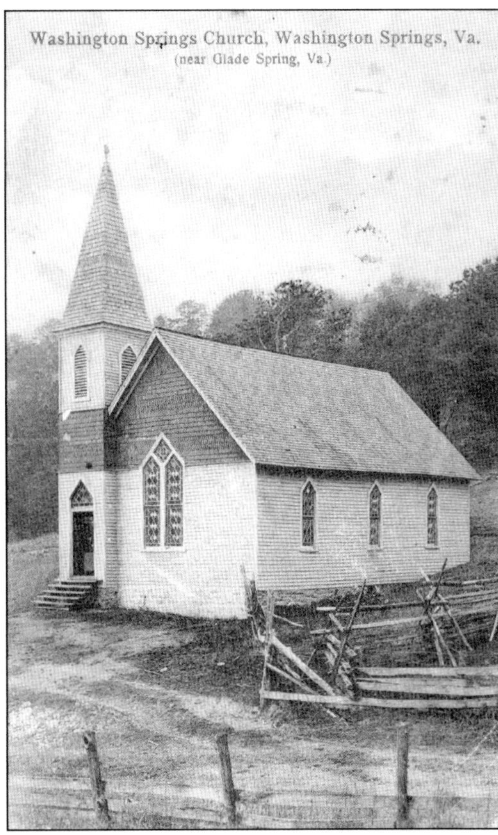

WASHINGTON SPRINGS CHURCH. Located in Washington Springs near Glade Spring, this church is featured on this early-1900s postcard. The ornate Gothic stained-glass windows and decorative shingles contrast with the primitive split-rail fence. (Courtesy Troy Taylor.)

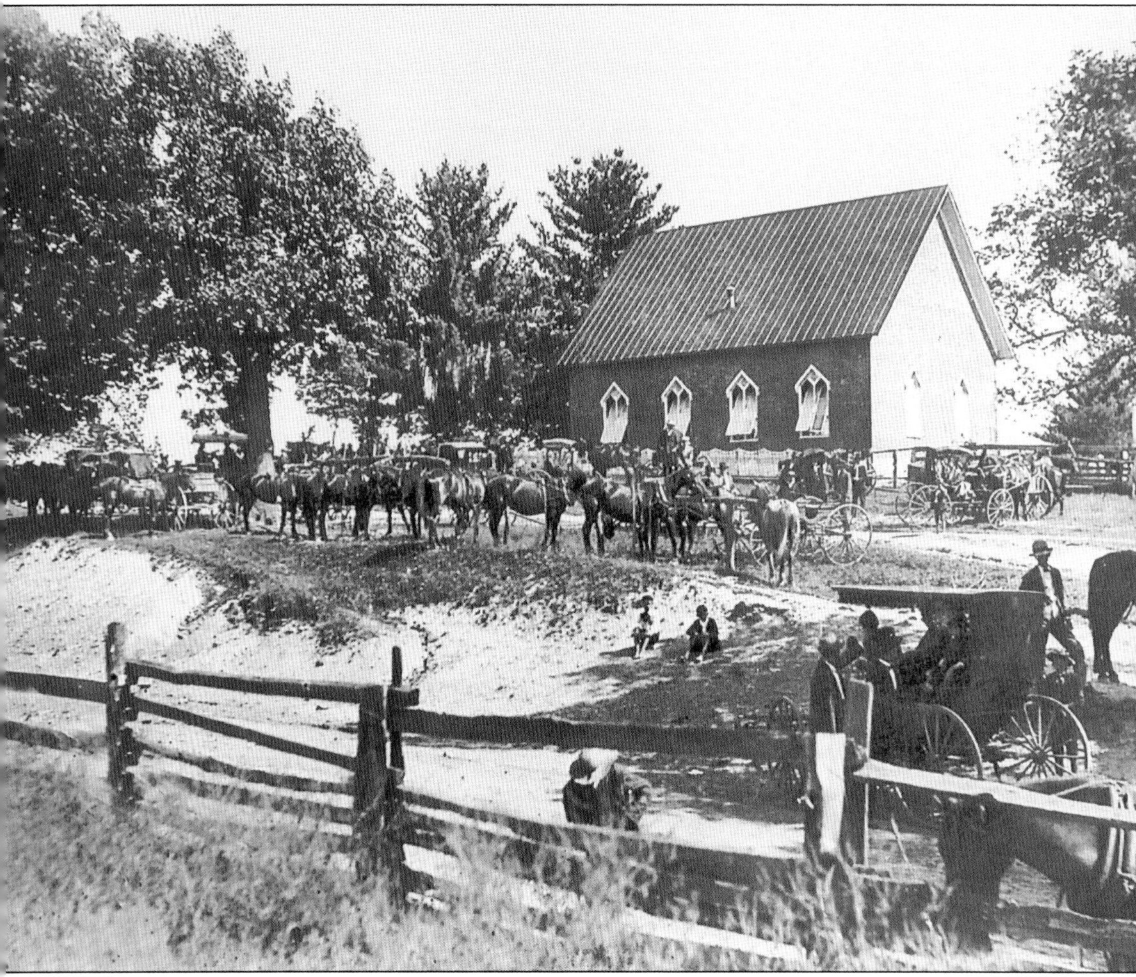

OLD GLADE PRESBYTERIAN CHURCH. This *c.* 1900 church gathering at the Old Glade Presbyterian Church was typical in this rural area. Horses pulling buggies and wagons were tied in the shade while the faithful gathered to worship, praise, and socialize. The young boys sitting in the foreground of the photograph are enjoying the sun. An early community cemetery is located on the church grounds, and the church is still active today. An earlier church was located on the site in 1795, and the current brick church was built in 1845. Additions have been constructed on this building over the years, but the lovely Old Glade Church still retains its historic integrity. (Courtesy Francis Darlene Scott Hockett.)

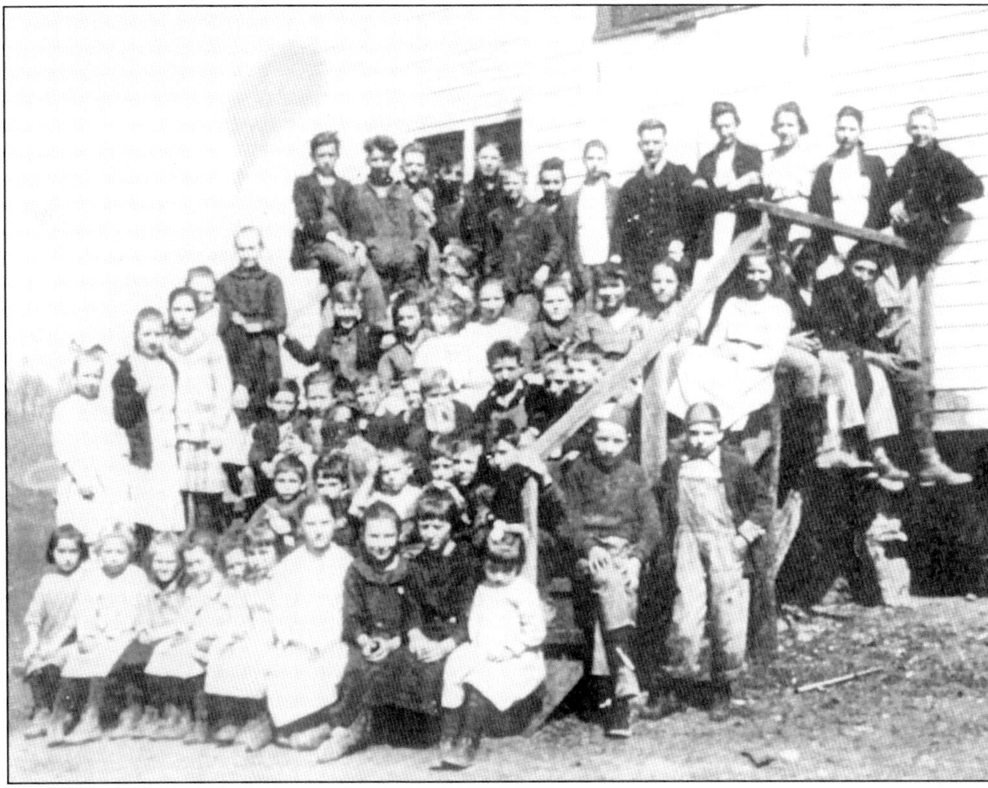

BLACKWELL CHAPEL SCHOOL, C. 1912. The Blackwell Chapel community school was originally two stories but today is only one story. It is used as a residence. The school hosted the famous Carter Family at a student assembly one year. (Courtesy Michael Hoback.)

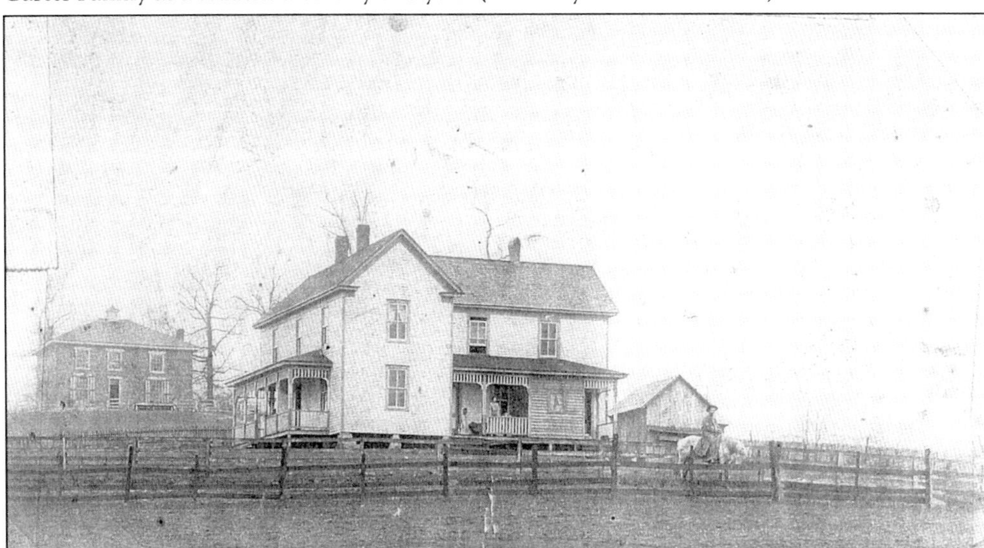

ROCK SPRINGS PRESBYTERIAN CHURCH MANSE. This lovely house was the manse for the Rock Springs Presbyterian Church in Lodi. Liberty Hall Academy, founded in 1866, is visible on the left of the photograph. (Courtesy Evelyn McThenia Hale.)

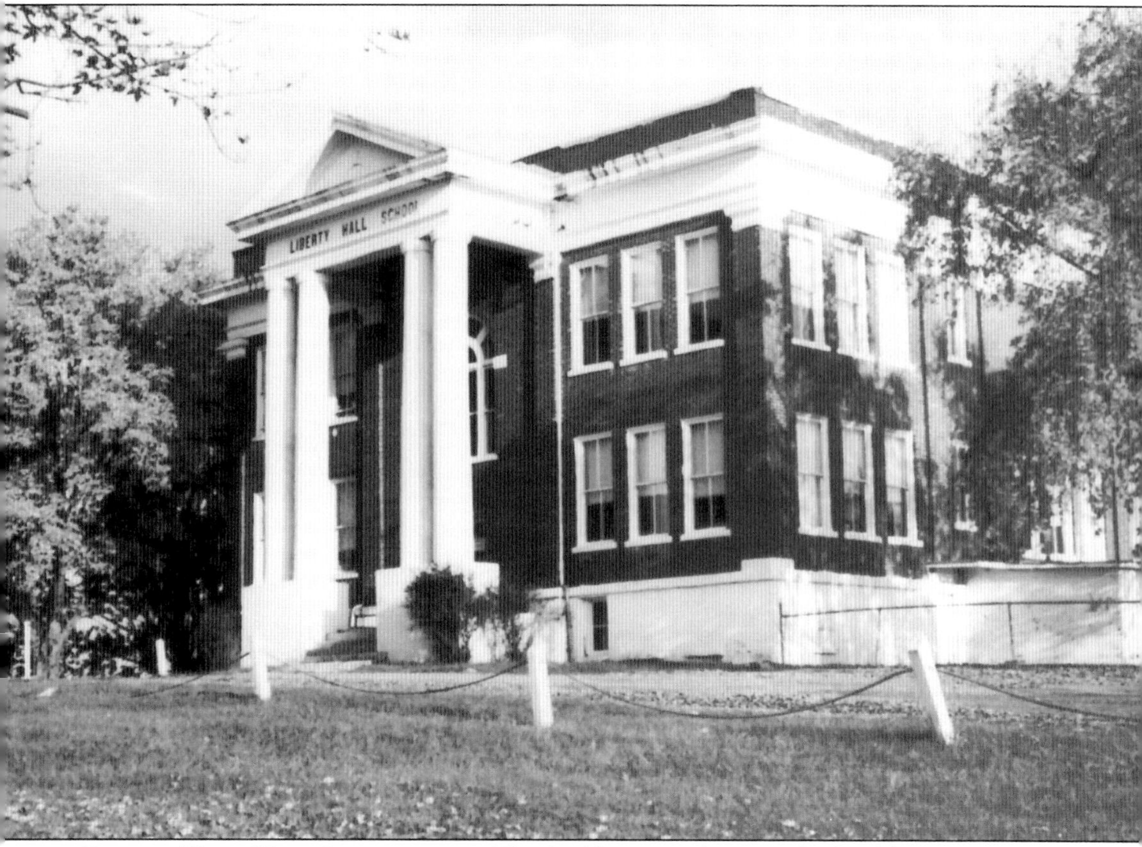

LIBERTY HALL HIGH SCHOOL, 1979. This building was the second school known as Liberty Hall in the Lodi community. Founded in 1866 by Rev. James Keys, the first school was a private school known as Liberty Hall Academy. The academy sponsored Liberty Hall Lodge No. 104, AF&AM, and Liberty Hall Lodge No. 13, IOOF. The Lodi crossroads community grew to include a post office, church, lodges, schools, and stores. In 1878, the Presbyterian Church bought the school and recorded that it should forever be used as a school. Principals included T. W. Hughes, Reverend McClure, W. J. Edmondson, W. G. Edmondson, and S. G. Edmondson. School in the original building was discontinued in 1915, and classes were moved to the new Liberty Hall High School. The community and private citizens helped to fund the costs for this building, originally a three-story building, with six classrooms, an auditorium, and basement. In 1951, an addition was built onto this building, which still stands, although in serious disrepair. This historic building needs to be restored for adaptive reuse, perhaps as a community center, by a committed property owner. (Courtesy Susie Copenhaver Lang.)

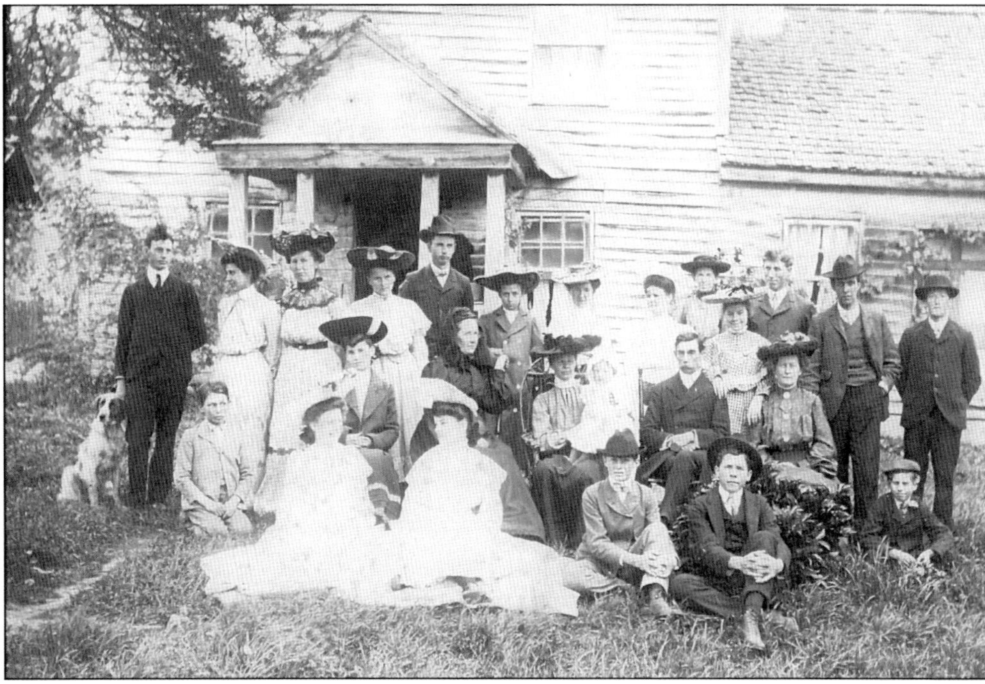

LIBERTY HALL COMMENCEMENT. The graduating class of Liberty Hall Academy in Lodi is shown posed outside the Moore home place on Monroe Road near the school. Pictured are Professor Carmack and Reverend Pittman along with their families and others. William and Elizabeth Steel Moore were the owners of the house. (Courtesy Evelyn McThenia Hale.)

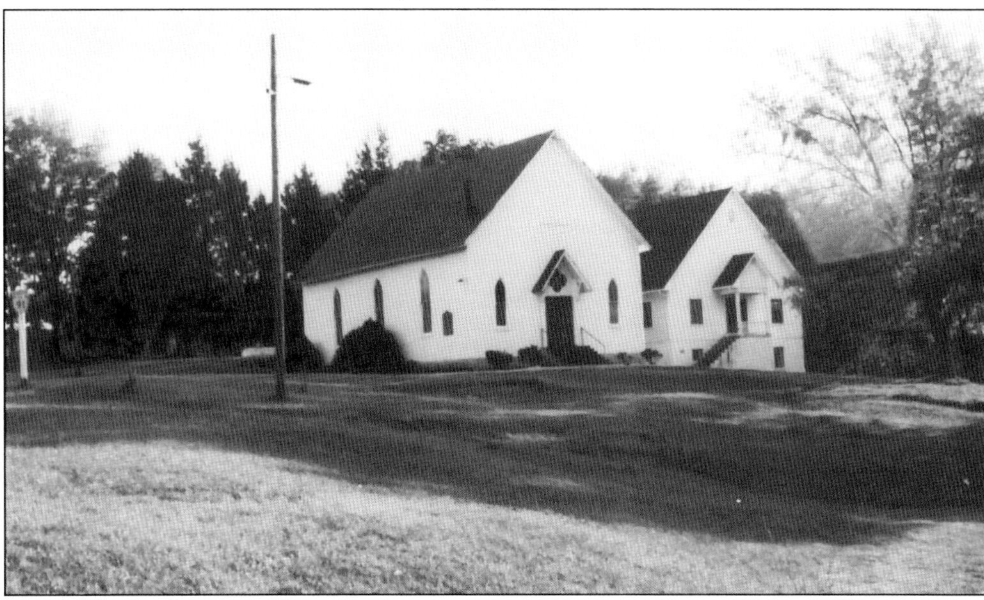

ROCK SPRING PRESBYTERIAN CHURCH. The Rock Spring congregation gathered as early as 1781. Built on land deeded in 1820 by Robert Edmondson and Matthew Brown, the current building was erected in 1884. Early pastors included the Reverends Edward Crawford, Stephen Bouelle, and ? Harper. The cemetery across the road is home for many of the local pioneering families as well as several veterans of the American Revolution. (Courtesy Susie Copenhaver Lang.)

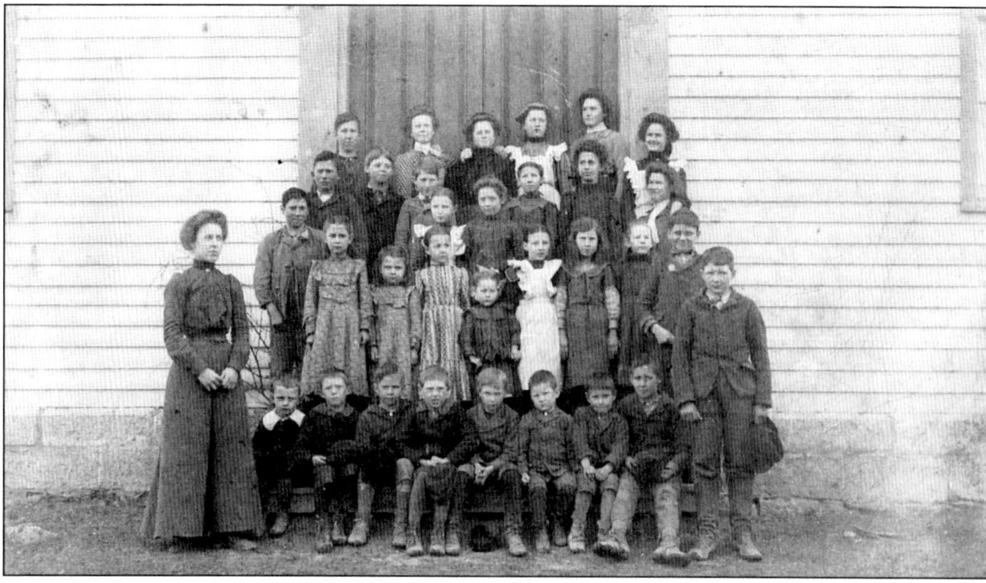

Rock Springs School. The students of Rock Springs School in Lodi pose here around 1904 with their teacher, Bertha Mast. The only identified children in the photograph are Andrew McThenia (first row, far left), Della McThenia (second row, fourth from left), Ollie McThenia (second row, sixth from left), and Lucy McThenia (third row, second child from left). (Courtesy Evelyn McThenia Hale.)

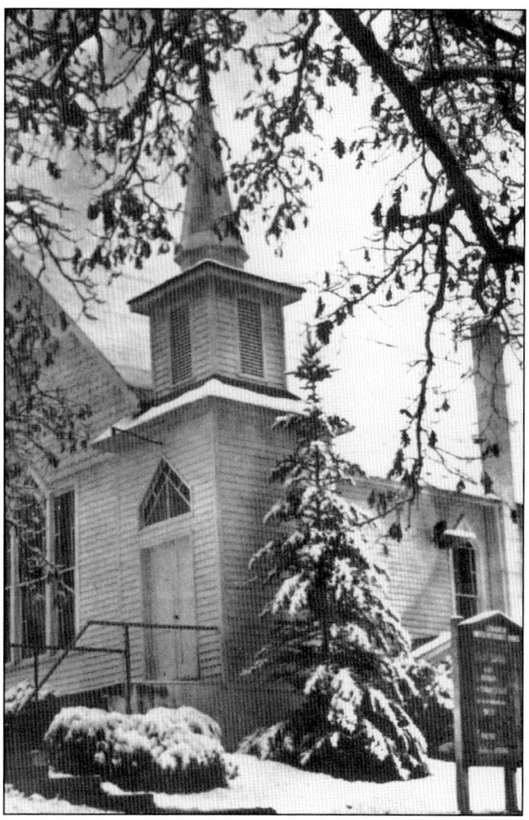

Lebanon United Methodist Church. This church was built on the site of an early campground meetinghouse dating to the early 1800s. The church register shows members as far back as 1888, but the building likely dates to about 1900. Land from the Clarks and Millers was donated for the church. The church has long been associated with Emory and Henry College, with many professors and students attending and providing sermons. (Courtesy Linda Orfield Crane.)

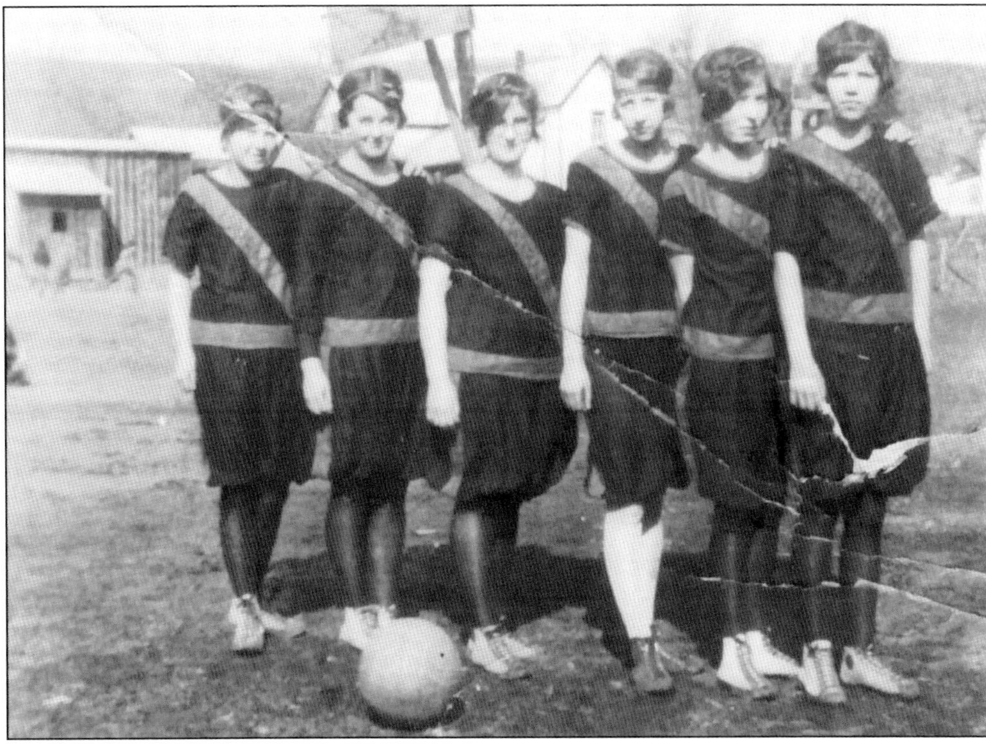

Girls' Basketball. The girls' basketball team from Bethel High School, dressed in the most fashionable uniforms of the day, is shown posed outside in the 1920s. The only identified person in the photograph is Grace Helen Stovall, on the far right. (Courtesy Ruby Stovall Clark.).

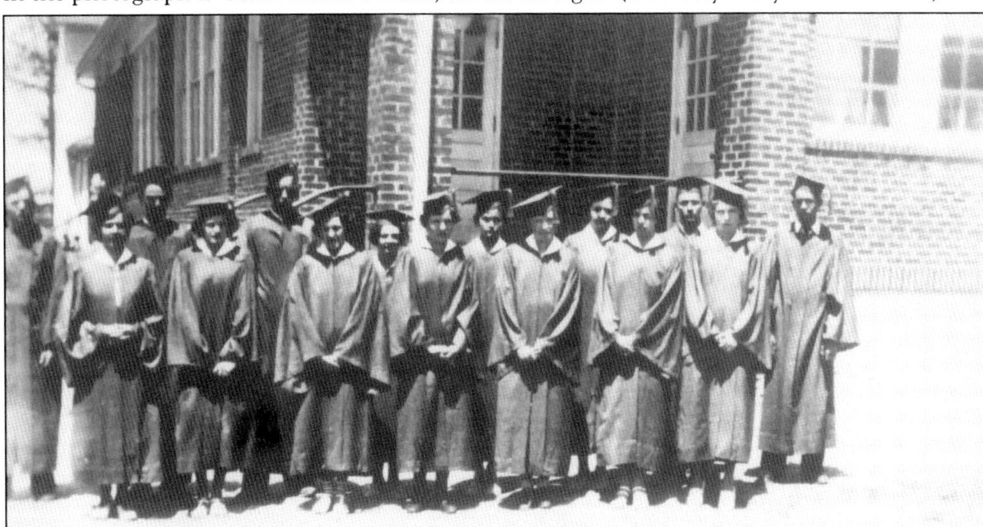

Bethel School Class. The brick Bethel High School can be seen behind this graduating class. From left to right are (first row) Elizabeth Wilkinson, Juanita Neal, Mildred Casteel, Hazel McCall, Virginia Millsap, Judith Rosenbaum, and Mary Lester; (second row) Eual Rambo, Beecher Price, Russell Rutledge, Eleanor Leonard, Ora M. Vanhuss, Grace McCann, Berl Millsap, and Harry Minnick. Today the building is used as an antiques store and residence. (Courtesy Harry Minnick.)

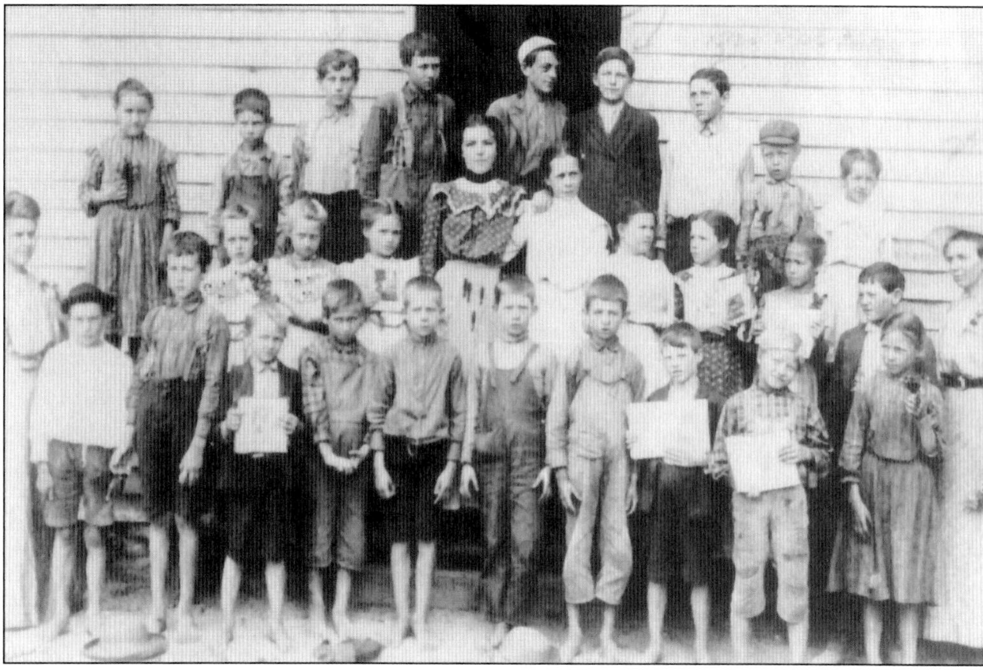

Good Hope School, c. 1905. Students at the Good Hope School, formerly located on Good Hope Road, stand for their picture to be made. The only identified students are as follows: (first row) third child from the left, Walter B. Keller; (second row) far left, Clara Duke, and far right, Naomi Keller; (third row) fifth from left, Dave Able, and sixth from left, Bob Duff. (Courtesy Walter B. "Blair" Keller Jr.)

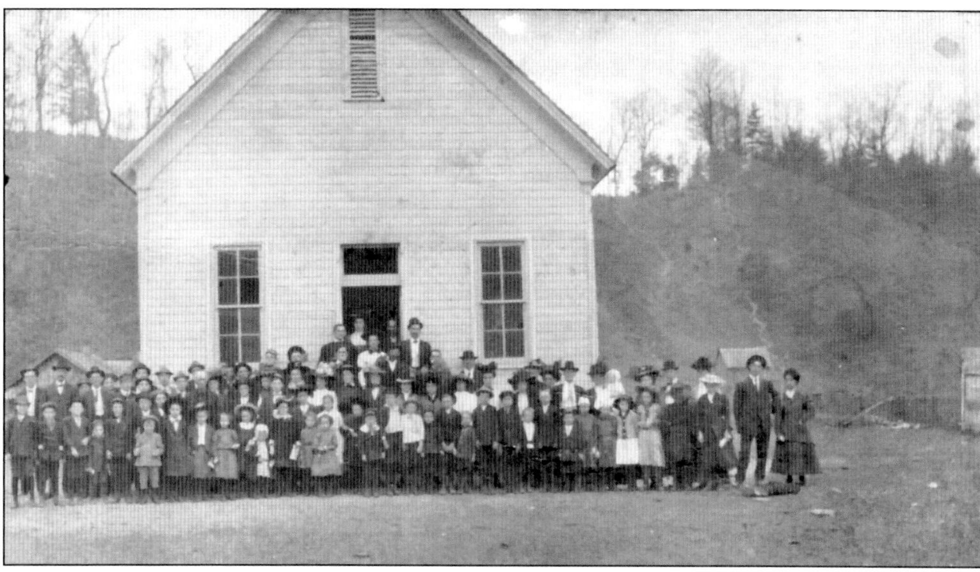

Laurel Community Church. This postcard is dated 1910 and lists Rev. J. M. McChesney as the preacher at Laurel Community Church. The church is still used and stands on Blossom Road. John F. Ramsey furnished the lumber to build this nondenominational community church. (Courtesy Virginia Cornett Smith.)

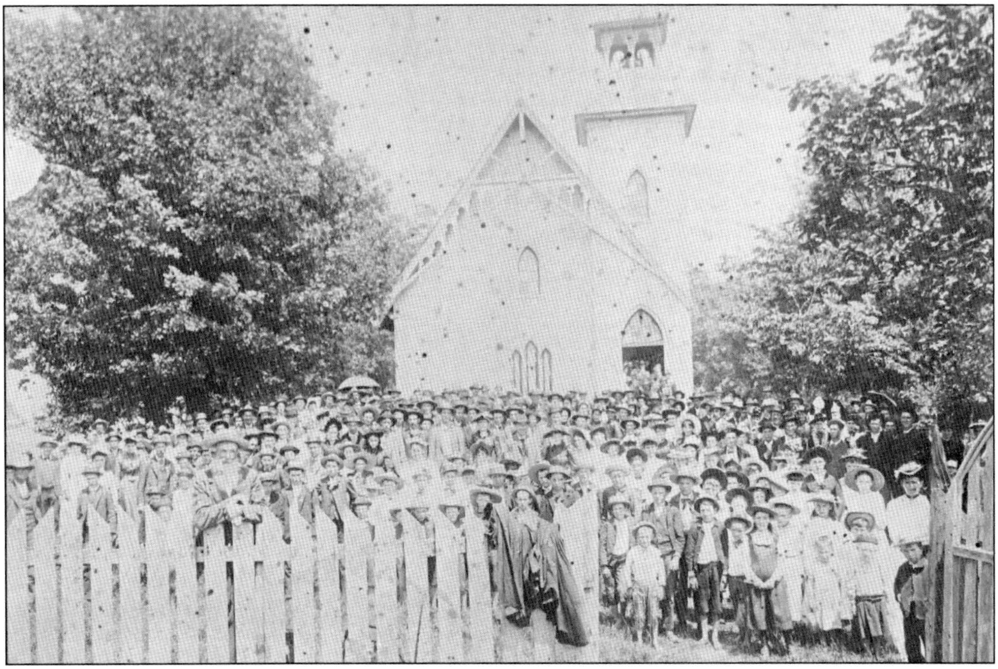

GREEN SPRING PRESBYTERIAN CHURCH. This early photograph of the Green Spring Presbyterian Church shows the congregation and the frame church, which burned in 1921. A brick church was built in 1923 for this active congregation, and it is still being used today. The congregation was first organized around 1781 and included many of the earliest settlers. (Courtesy Walter B. "Blair" Keller Jr.)

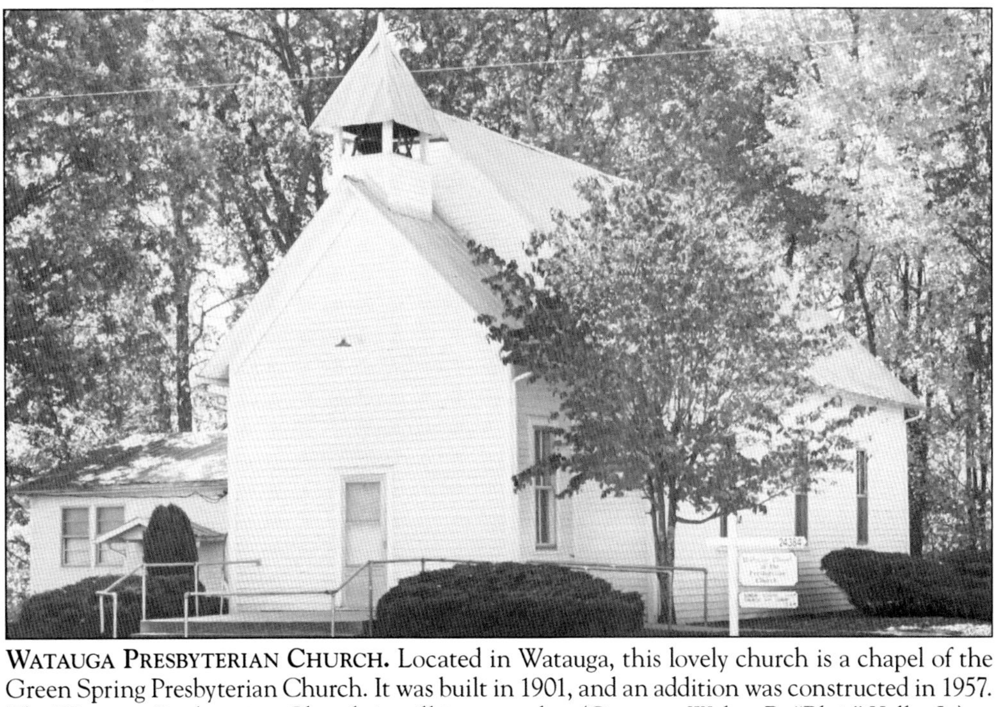

WATAUGA PRESBYTERIAN CHURCH. Located in Watauga, this lovely church is a chapel of the Green Spring Presbyterian Church. It was built in 1901, and an addition was constructed in 1957. The Watauga Presbyterian Church is still in use today. (Courtesy Walter B. "Blair" Keller Jr.)

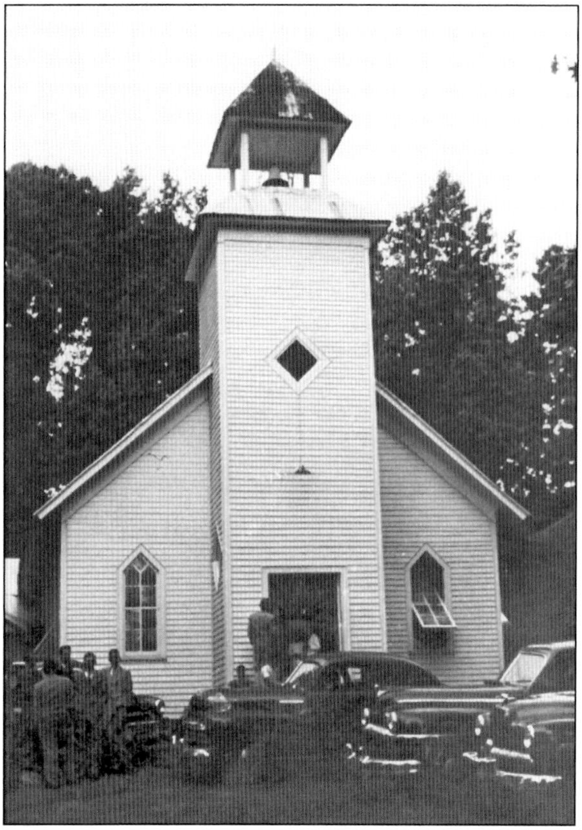

CLEVELAND PRESBYTERIAN CHURCH, C. 1950. Another chapel of Green Spring Church, the Cleveland Presbyterian Church was dedicated in 1912 and is still being used. Rev. James M. McChesney and Rev. T. J. McConnell preached early services here. After Robert Berry purchased the land for the church and cemetery, community members built the church. (Courtesy Walter B. "Blair" Keller Jr.)

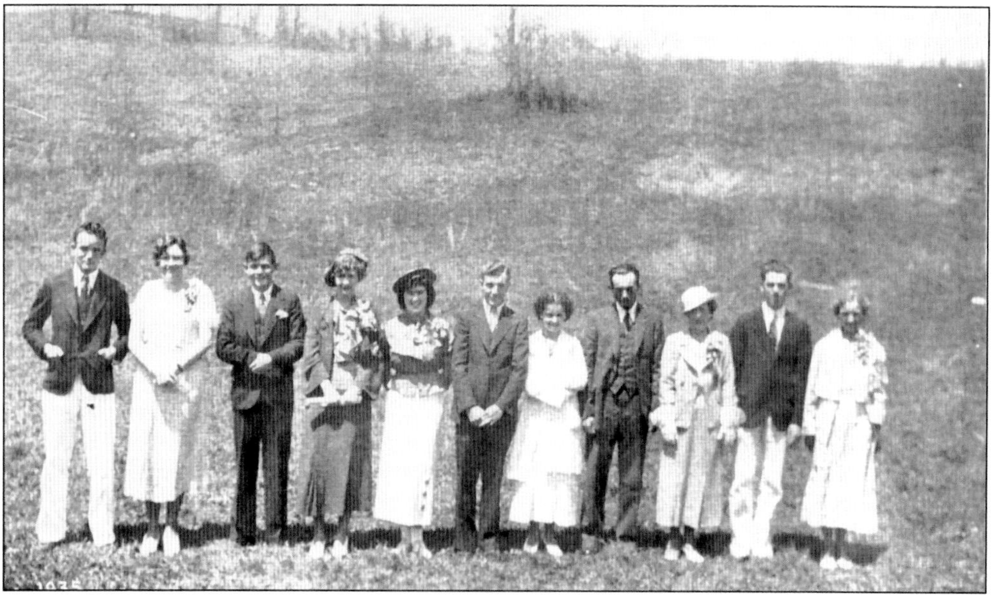

GREENDALE CLASS. Pictured here on April 22, 1935, is the graduating class of Greendale High School. The brick school building in Greendale is now used as a nursing home. The only person identified in the photograph is Mike Kelly, standing on the far left. (Courtesy Dorothy Johnson Kelly.)

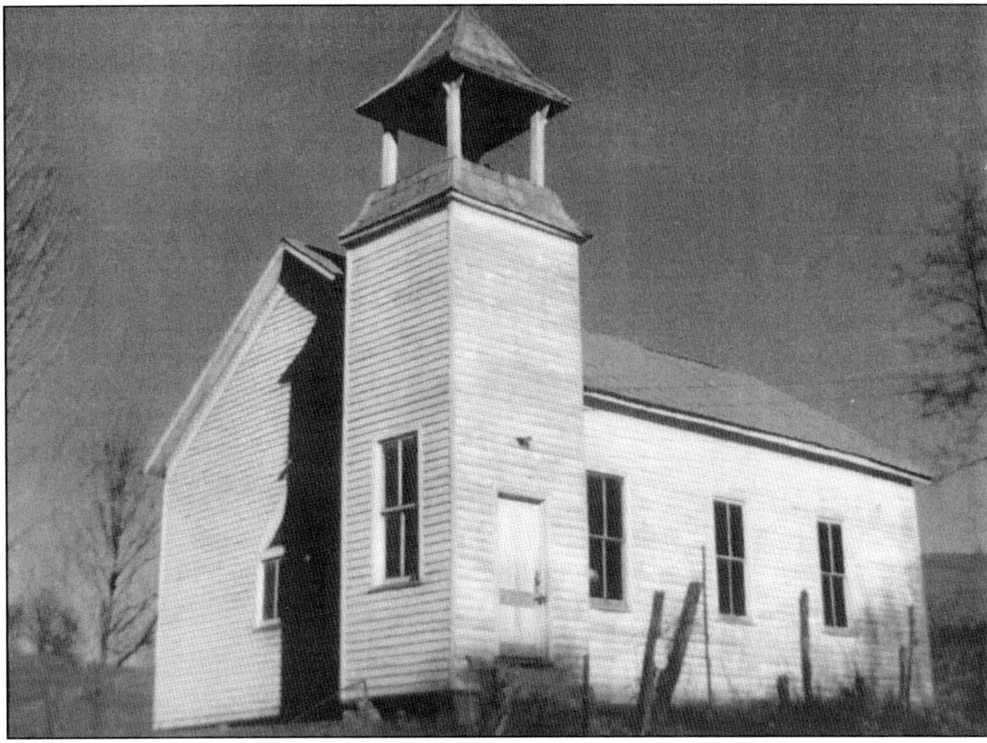

LOWLAND UNITED METHODIST CHURCH. This simple church served many families in Rich Valley through the years, including members of the Akers, Campbell, Sullins, and Dove families. The congregation was active in the singings and church meetings at Laurel Springs, just up White's Mill Road. Like many of the small country churches, the congregation eventually dwindled. The structure is still standing today on Toole's Creek Road, and its use has changed to a family dwelling. (Courtesy Rich Valley Methodist Church.)

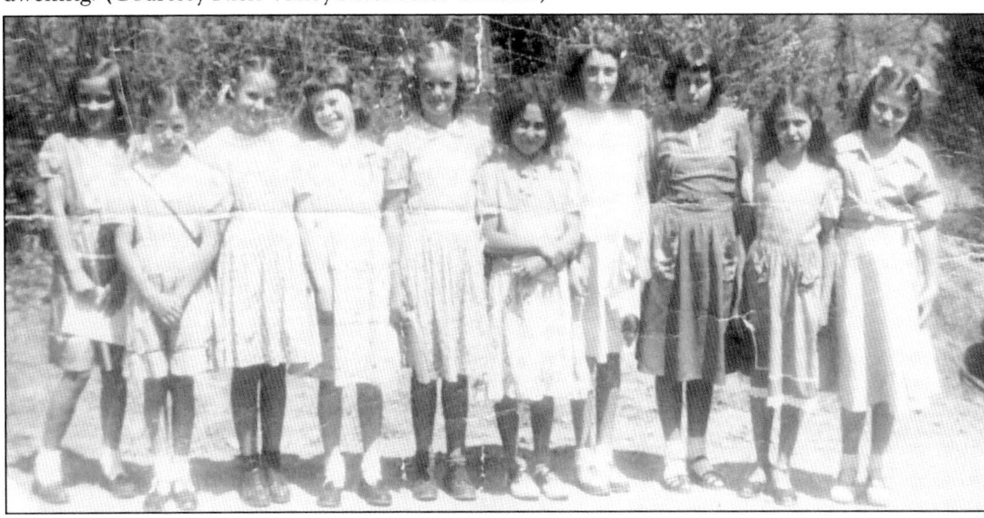

LOWLAND METHODIST SUNDAY SCHOOL, C. 1940. This girls' Sunday school class, taught by Pearl Kestner Akers, is pictured outside Lowland United Methodist Church on Toole's Creek Road. From left to right are Jean Sullins, Peggy Dove, Pearl Gilly, Annette Akers, Mary Gilly, Louise Sullins, Betty Jane Sullins, Jean Pierce, Betty Marsh, and Gladys Dove. (Courtesy Ken and Nellie Akers.)

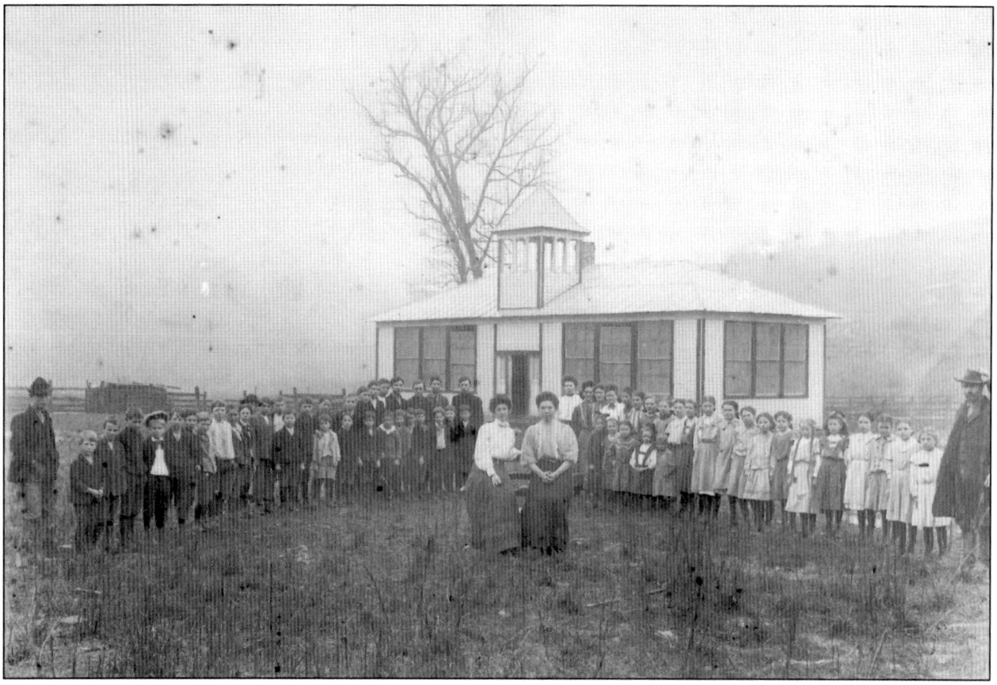

YELLOW SPRINGS SCHOOL, C. 1900. Located in the Yellow Springs community, this two-room schoolhouse served the community children for many years. The building is still standing but is in disrepair. (Courtesy Harry Minnick.)

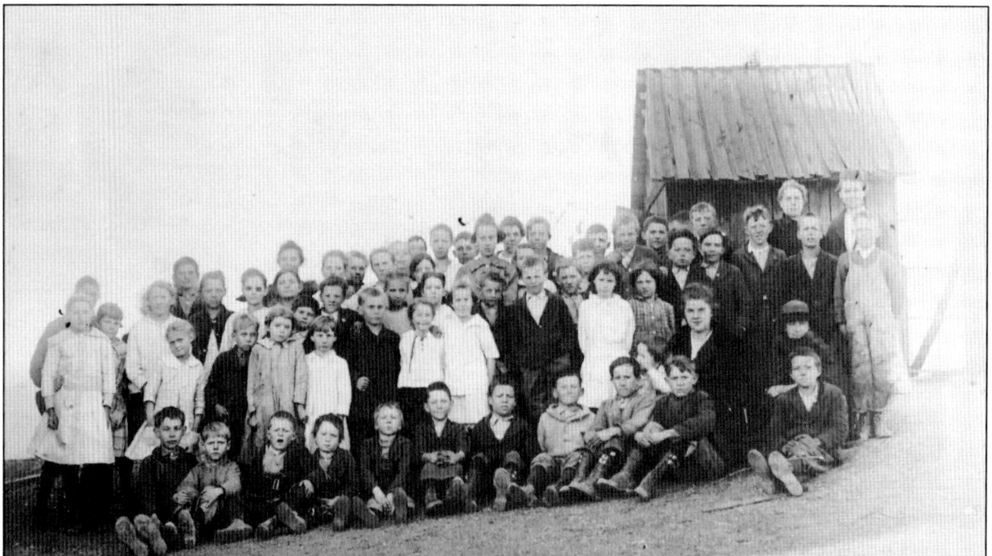

LIBERTY HILL SCHOOL. The class from Liberty Hill School in the Hankel community is shown in this early photograph. Notice the high buckled boots of the boys in the first row. (Courtesy Eleanor Arnett Blevins.)

Three

Work and Industry

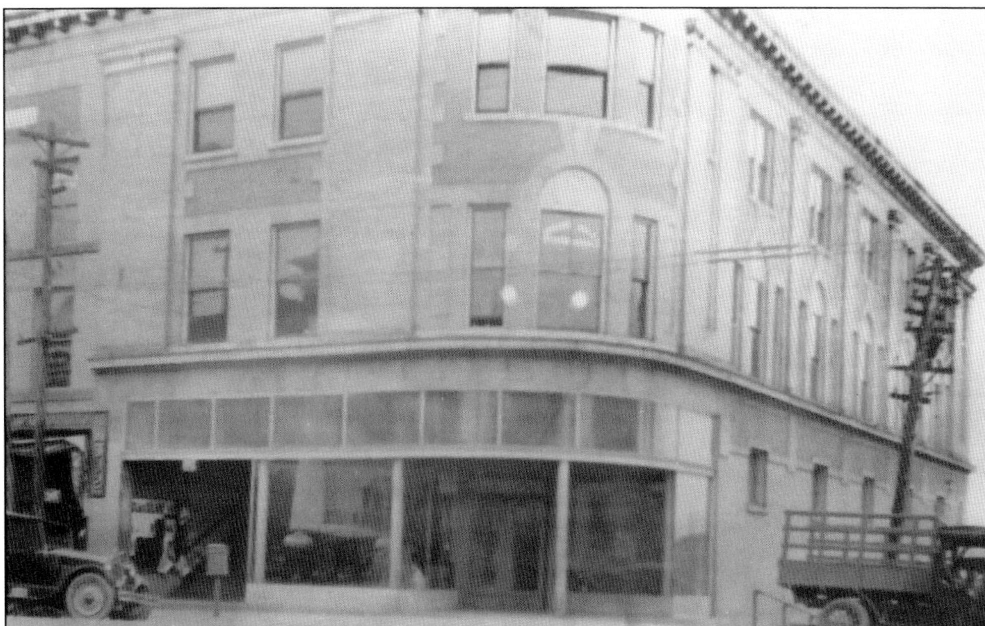

Dagmar Hotel. This *c.* 1930 photograph shows the Dagmar Hotel building, located on the corner of Court and Main Streets in Abingdon. Lewis Preston Summers began construction on the building in 1910, and it contained a barbershop, a billiard hall on the first floor, a lobby and dining room on the second floor, and hotel rooms on the third floor. The building has been served various uses, including as a dorm and classroom space for Stonewall Jackson College, a furniture store and undertaking business, and different law firms. The eastern section of the building was the location of a popular soda fountain called the Corner during the 1930s–1950s. Today this graceful building houses attorneys' offices and Congressman Rick Boucher's offices. (Courtesy Lowry Bowman.)

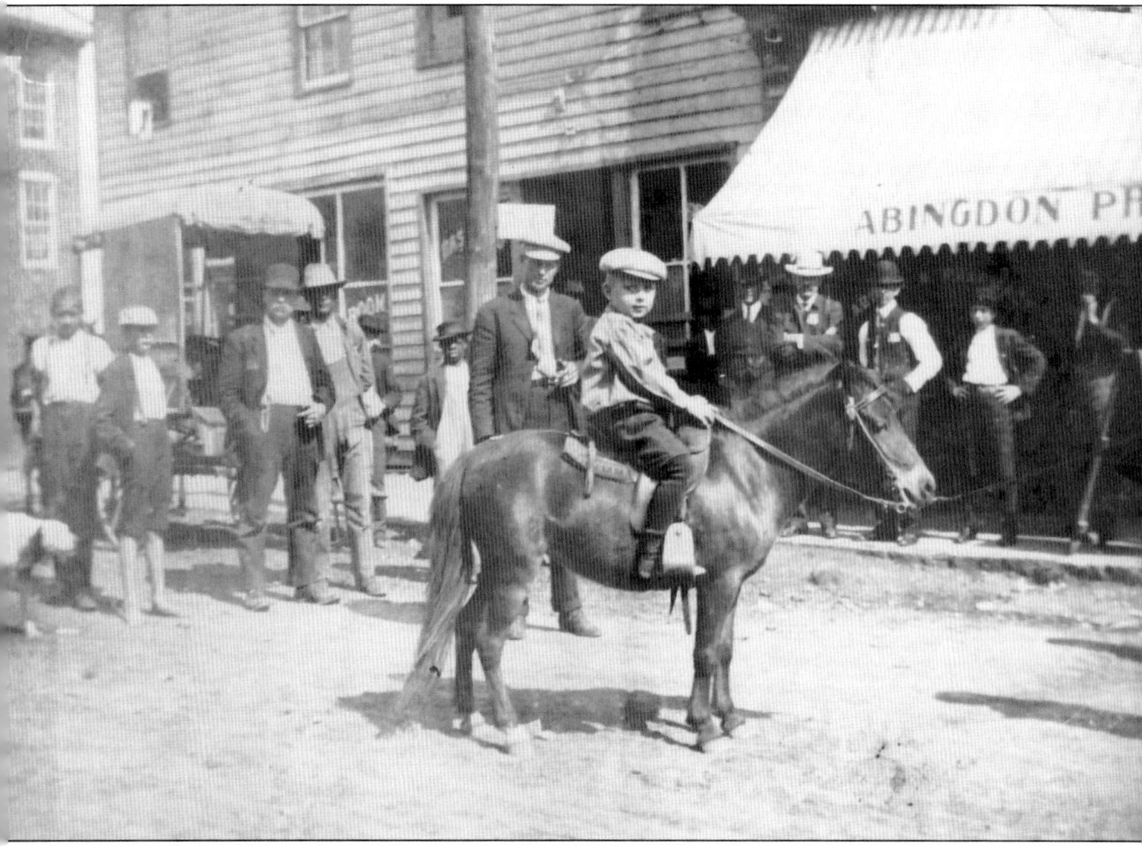

ABINGDON'S MAIN STREET, C. 1900. Various men are posed outside the Colonnade Hotel and the Abingdon Pharmacy on Main Street opposite the courthouse. The Abingdon Pharmacy was operated by Dr. George F. Grant and sold the famous springwater of the nearby Seven Springs Resort. Several of these men appear to be wearing badges, perhaps on break from work at the Washington County courthouse across the street. On the left of the photograph is the horse-drawn omnibus, made by the Hagy Wagon Company, which brought travelers from the train depot to the Colonnade Hotel. The hotel provided lodging with 70 rooms and meals to travelers and locals for almost 30 years. Thomas G. McConnell was the original owner of the Colonnade Hotel, and subsequent proprietors included Minter Jackson (1876–1913), James C. Campbell and James Armistead (1877), I. F. Jones (1878), and Charles Harris (1896). Several African American men are also standing along the left and in the background of the photograph. The young boy is astride a pony, and a tether line can be seen, held by someone outside the camera's eye. In 1910, the construction of the Dagmar Hotel building to the east of the pharmacy caused the collapse of the eastern wall of the store. Bottles of medicine fell from the shelves and were unearthed years later when construction once again took place on these lots. (Courtesy Virginia Cornett Smith.)

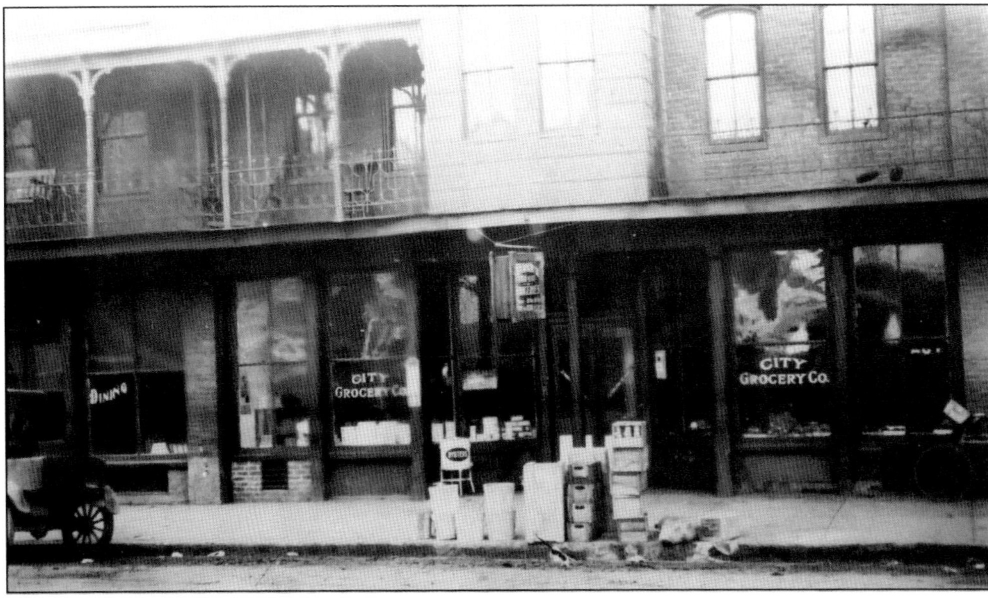

BELMONT HOTEL. The City Grocery Company was once located on the ground floor of the Belmont Hotel at the corner of Wall and Main Streets in Abingdon. The Belmont Hotel was built in 1887 but was demolished in 1981 to construct a new post office. Many locals mourn its destruction. (Courtesy Lowry Bowman.)

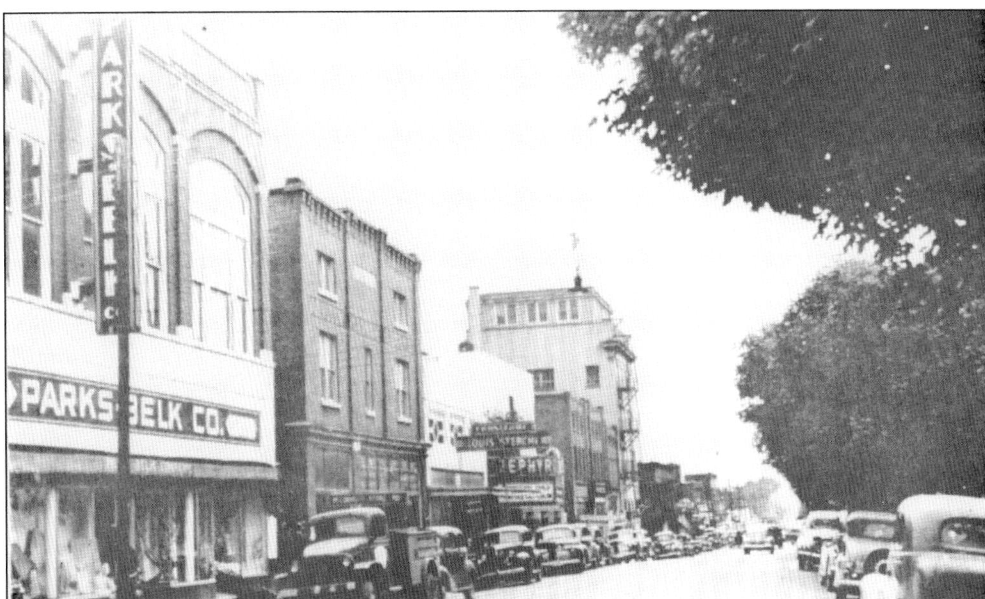

MAIN STREET, ABINGDON. This view of Main Street in Abingdon dates from about 1936. From left to right, signs can be seen for Parks Belk Company, Louis Sterchie, and the Zephyr Theatre. These commercial buildings have been preserved in Abingdon, and today a downtown revitalization group is being formed to bring new life to downtown. (Courtesy Roger Brannon.)

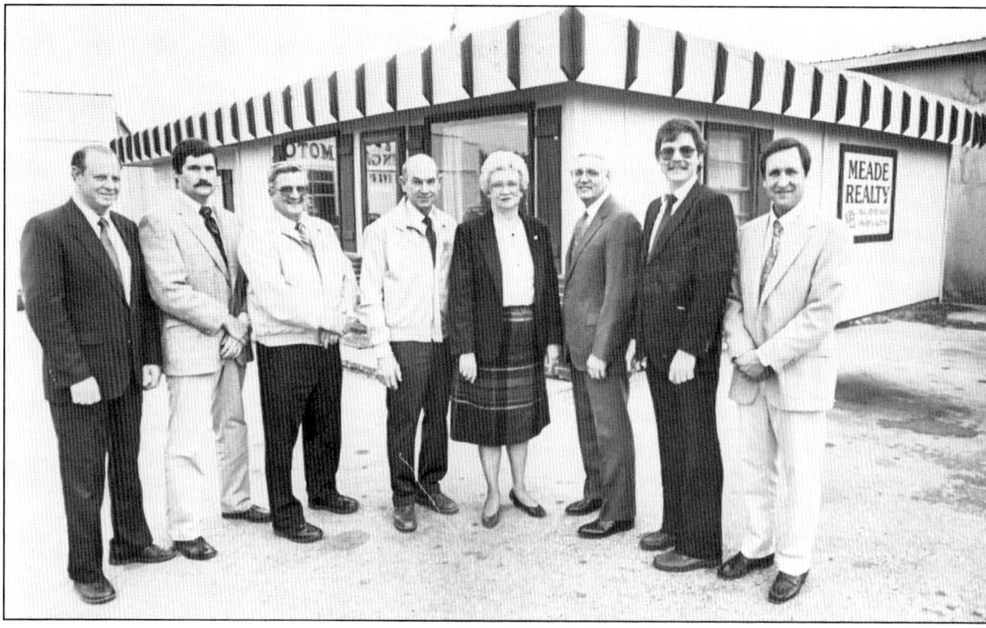

Meade Realty Auction Services. The Meade Realty Auction Service has served the region since 1982. Charles and Irene Meade, the owners, are active in a number of civic groups and events in the area, including the Washington County Fair. From left to right and standing outside their original office are Charles Meade, Michael Brillhart, Johnny Crigger, James Jones, Irene Meade, Ken Johnson, Fred Tweed, and Mike Anderson. (Courtesy Irene Johnson Meade.)

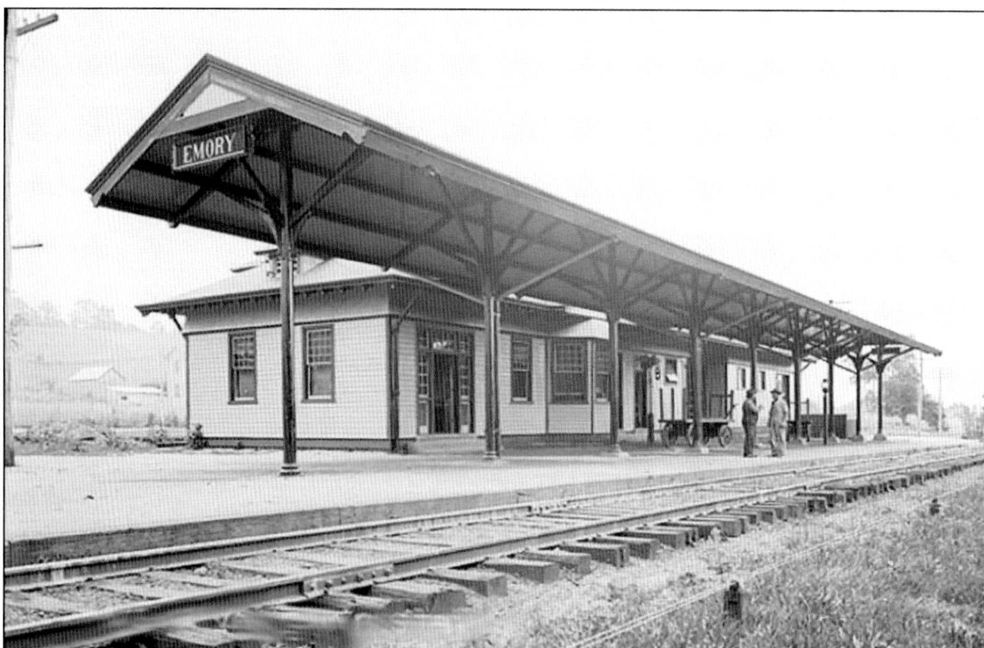

Emory Combined Depot. Two men talk outside the combined depot at Emory while waiting for a train to arrive. The historic building has been restored and preserved and functions as the 1912 Art Gallery for nearby Emory and Henry College. (Courtesy Jeff Weaver.)

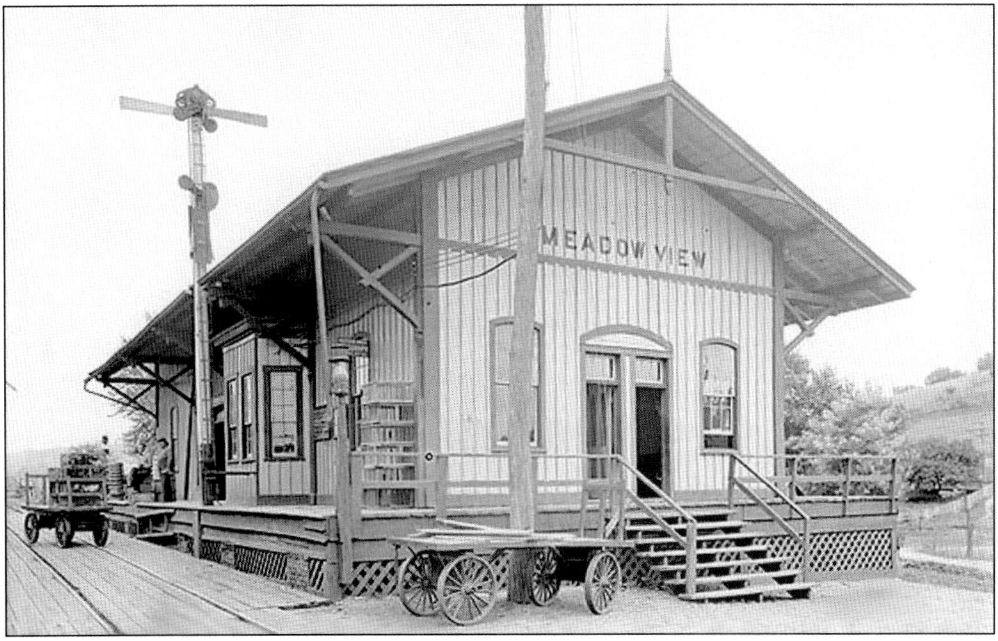

MEADOWVIEW DEPOT. Once the busy center of commerce, the Meadowview Depot was built in 1833. The design is identical to those depots along the Norfolk and Western railroad line running into Ashe County, North Carolina, and to Abingdon. Meadowview became a quiet residential community after rail service decreased. However, a civic group and citizens are restoring the Meadowview town square and have opened a general store, health clinic, and restaurant to help the local economy. (Courtesy Jeffrey Weaver.)

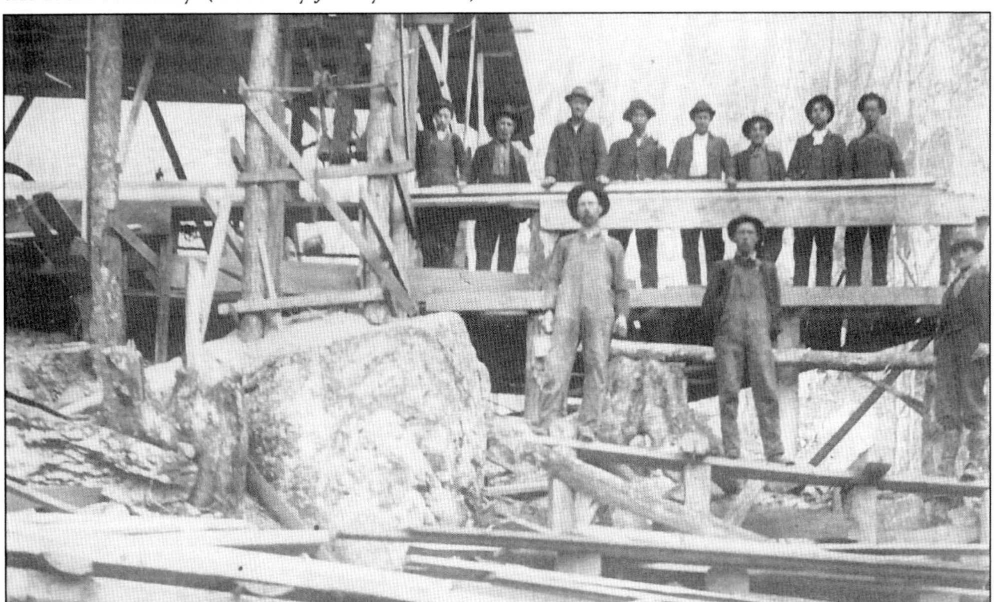

MCCRAY AND WALKER COMPANY SAWMILL. The McCray and Walker Sawmill was located in Tumbling Cove. The only persons identified in the photograph are (second row) second from left, Rufus F. McCray (c. 1851–1926), and sixth from left, Jasper McCray (1891–1974). Both McCrays owned the logging and sawmill operation. (Courtesy Troy Taylor.)

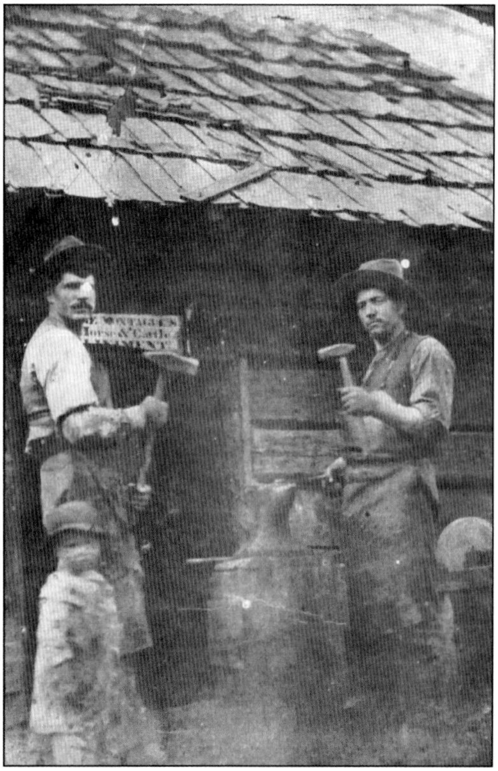

BLACKWELL CHAPEL BLACKSMITH. This c. 1870s photograph shows the local blacksmith shop of Blackwell Chapel community. Elbert S. Blackwell is standing on the left. The advertising sign in the background reads, "Mr. ? horse and cattle ointment." In the days of horse and buggy and hand tools, the neighborhood blacksmith shop was a necessary and busy place for horseshoes, farm-equipment repair, and metal items for home, work, and agricultural use. (Courtesy Michael Hoback.)

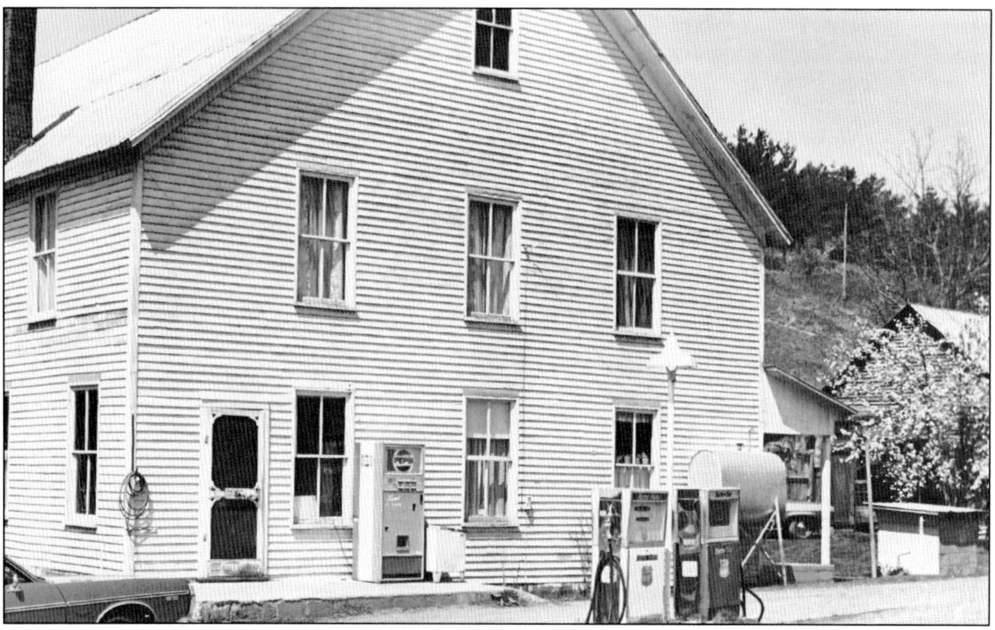

CRABTREE GROCERY. The William H. Crabtree store is located on S.R. 700 in Blackwell Chapel. Originally built by George Herndon in 1910, it only closed in 1988. It was purchased in 1946 by William Crabtree, who operated it until its closing. When the road was relocated in the 1950s, the back door was reoriented to become the front door. The building still stands today and hopefully will be restored by a committed property owner. (Courtesy Tammy Martin.)

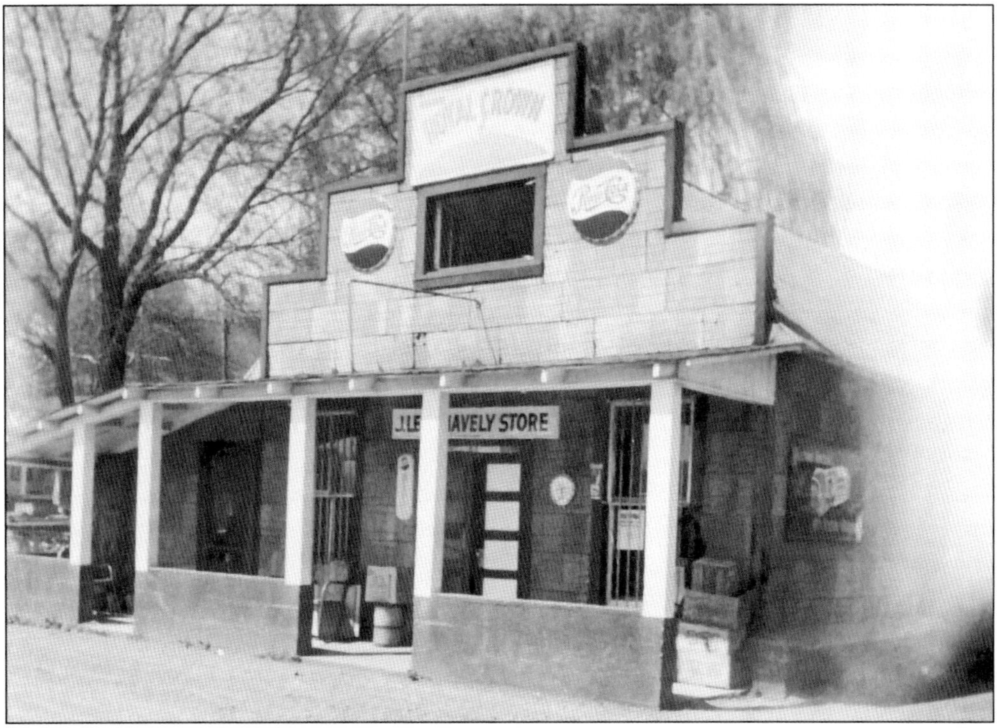

SNAVELY STORE. Lee and Eva Snavely opened the Snavely Store in about 1930, and it became a community gathering place. This *c.* 1960 view of the store shows a typical country store of that time period. (Courtesy Marie Snavely Yeatts.)

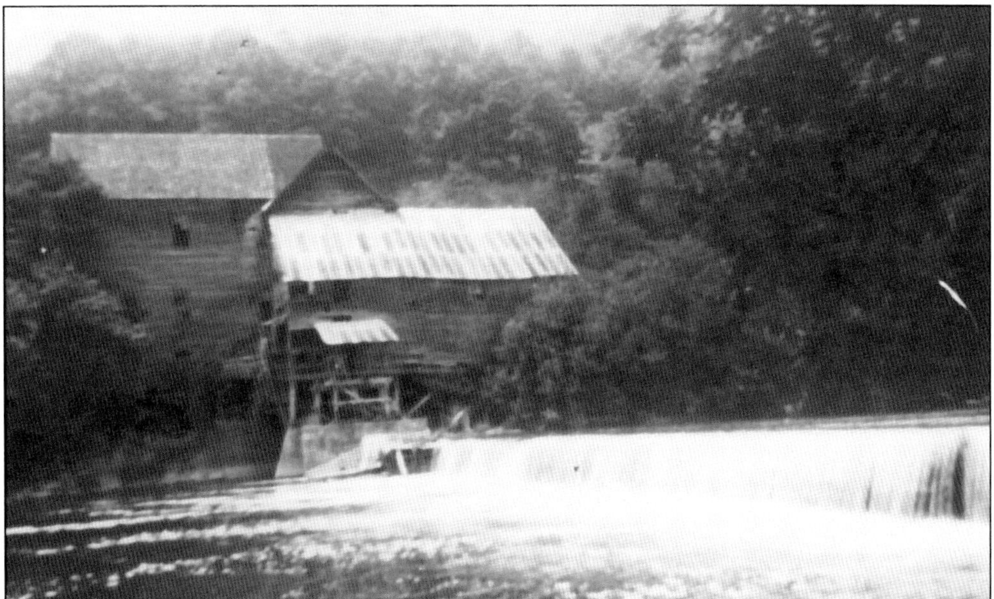

MENDOTA MILL, 1947. This gristmill was located on the North Fork of the Holston River in Mendota. Two mills were shown on the 1890 Boyd's Map on the North Fork near Mendota: J. M. Barker's Grist and Saw Mill and Bales Saw Mill. (Courtesy Terri Collier McCroskey.)

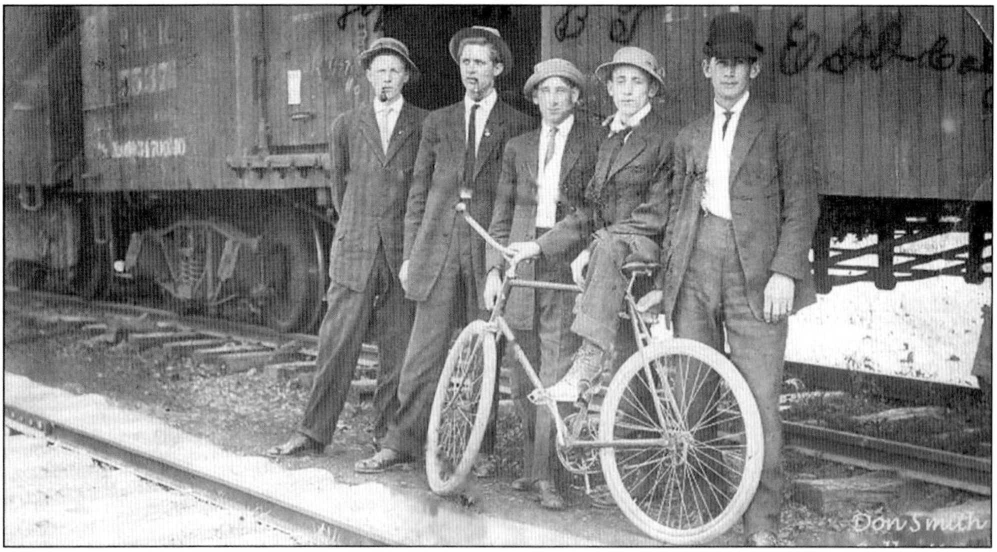

N&W AT PLASTERCO. These five young gents are posed with a bicycle in 1911 in front of a Norfolk and Western train along the branch line in Plasterco. This line connected Plasterco to Glade Spring and was installed to facilitate transportation of the gypsum from Plasterco. The only person identified in the photograph is Gifford Campbell, on the far left. (Courtesy Don Smith.)

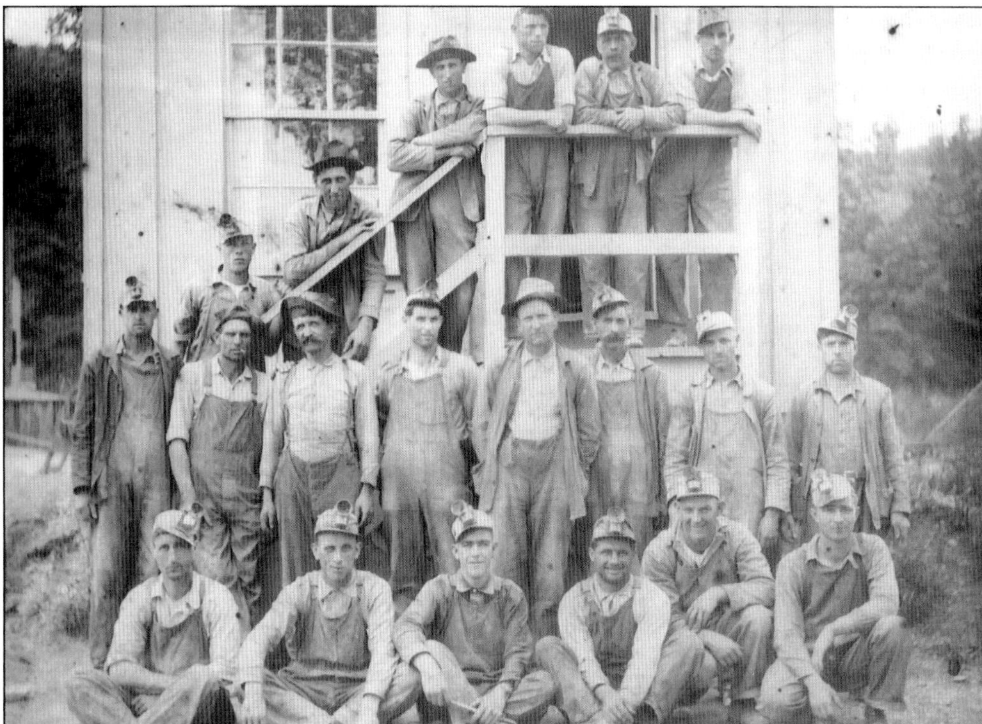

PLASTERCO MINERS. U.S. Gypsum employed many local workers, including miners, mechanics, and fabricators. This mine was considered to be the deepest gypsum mine in the world. The company was an early industry in the area and provided many jobs in the community. (Courtesy Bobby Cuddy.)

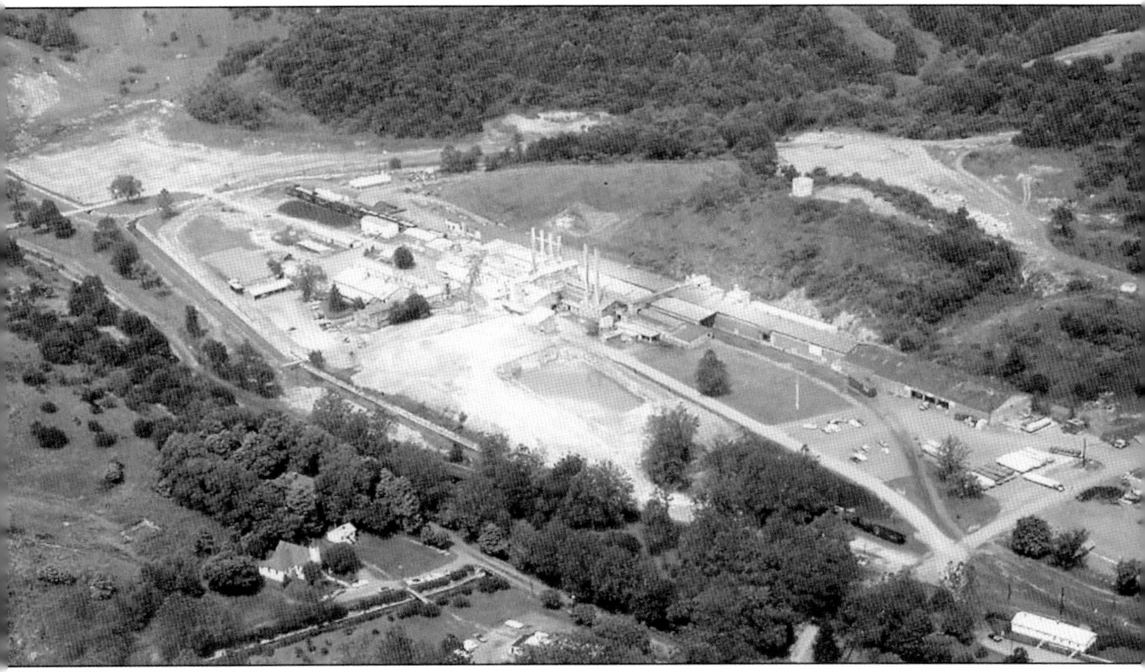

PLASTERCO, 1973. This 1973 aerial, taken by Don Smith, shows the dominance of the U.S. Gypsum plant in this small town. Plasterco was put on the map by Col. Francis Smith's Buena Vista Plaster Mining Company, which operated from 1808 until 1908. Gypsum removal has always been labor intensive, requiring miners to hand-dig it. Company housing was built adjacent to the main factory. After 1908, U.S. Gypsum took over and mined gypsum from open pits to produce wallboard until 2000. The industry did pollute the environment, as did others in the Saltville area, but it also helped the local economy. The years of intensive mining have made much of the Plasterco area unstable, and cave-ins have occurred. Today fenced areas with warning signs are all that remain of this industry and town. (Courtesy Don Smith.)

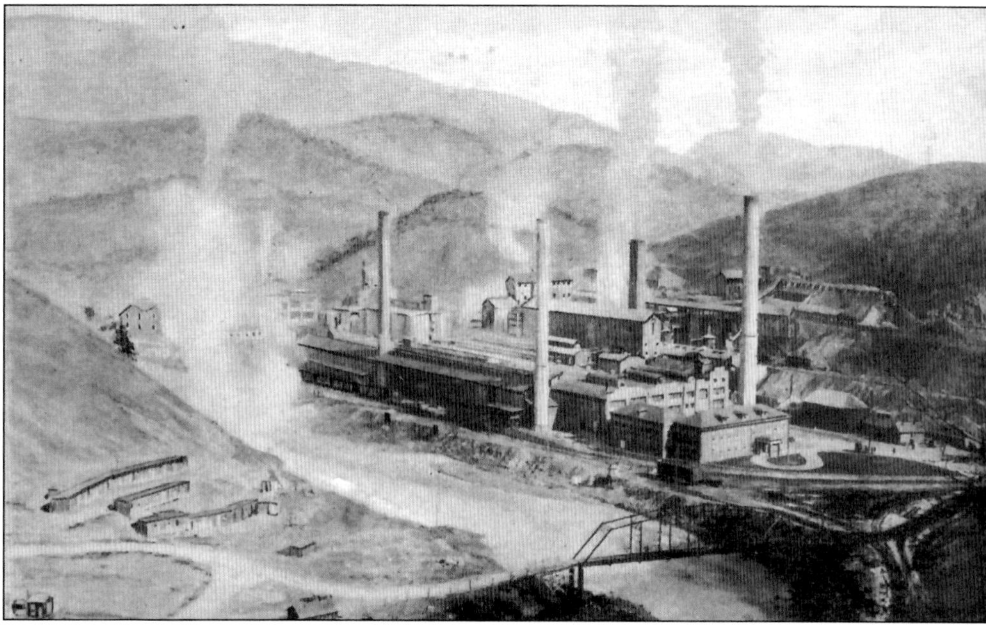

MATHIESON ALKALI WORKS. Established in Saltville in 1892, Mathieson created one of the nation's first company towns. The facility produced soda ash, a necessary ingredient in glass, detergent, and other chemicals. In the 1950s, the company merged and became Olin-Mathieson. Jobs at the company were very desirable, and the company provided employment. The factory closed in the 1970s, which hurt the local economy. (Courtesy Roy Rector.)

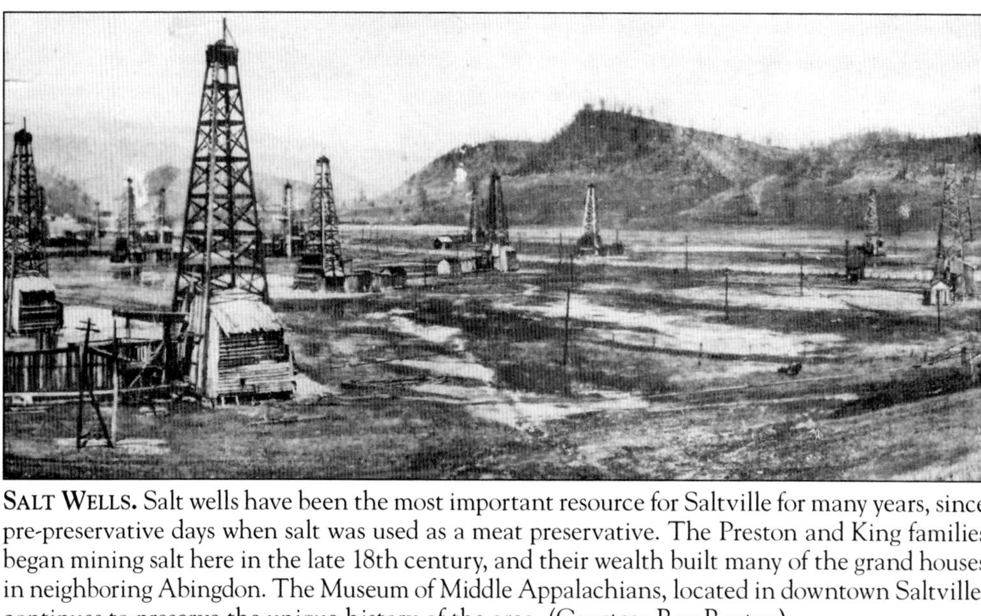

SALT WELLS. Salt wells have been the most important resource for Saltville for many years, since pre-preservative days when salt was used as a meat preservative. The Preston and King families began mining salt here in the late 18th century, and their wealth built many of the grand houses in neighboring Abingdon. The Museum of Middle Appalachians, located in downtown Saltville, continues to preserve the unique history of the area. (Courtesy Roy Rector.)

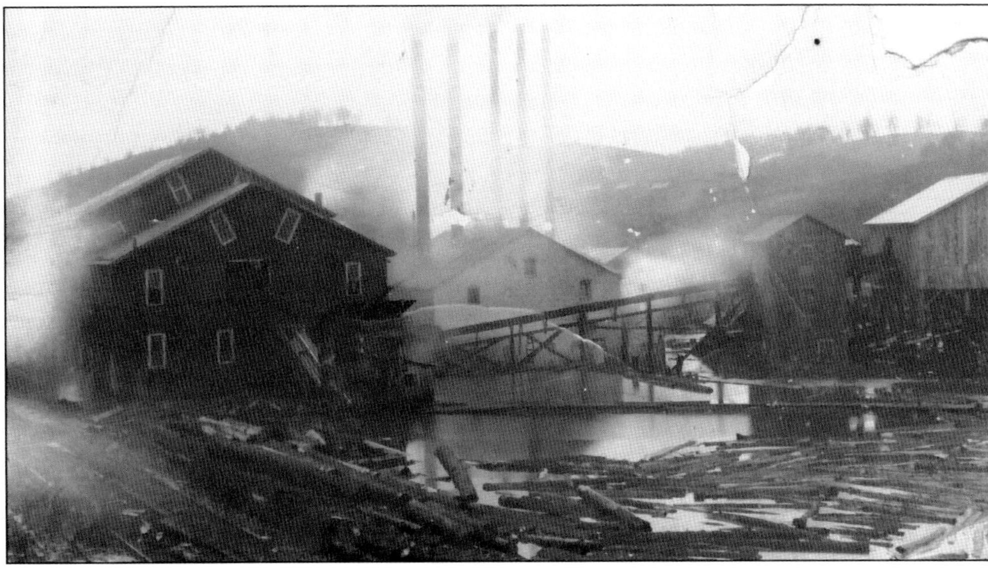

HOLSTON RIVER LUMBER COMPANY SAWMILL. Pictured around 1920, the Holston River Lumber Company was a large operation in Clinchburg. The Salt Branch Line ran from Clinchburg into Glade Spring to bring out the timber and industrial products. The railroad is visible on the left, and numerous logs are floating in front of the mill. (Courtesy Roy Rector.)

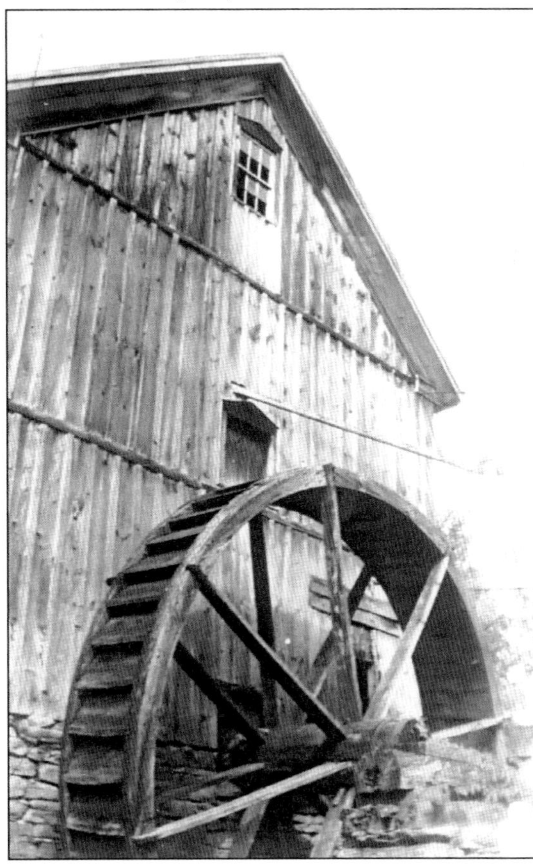

WIDENER'S MILL. Widener's Mill, with its wooden wheel, was located on Rush Creek in the Widener's Valley community. The mill was probably built by William "Squire Bill" Meek Widener in the 1870s. Christopher DeBusk may have operated an earlier mill in that same location. The mill was the center of the Rush Creek crossroads community of Masada and served as a meeting place and post office. (Courtesy Evelyn McThenia Hale.)

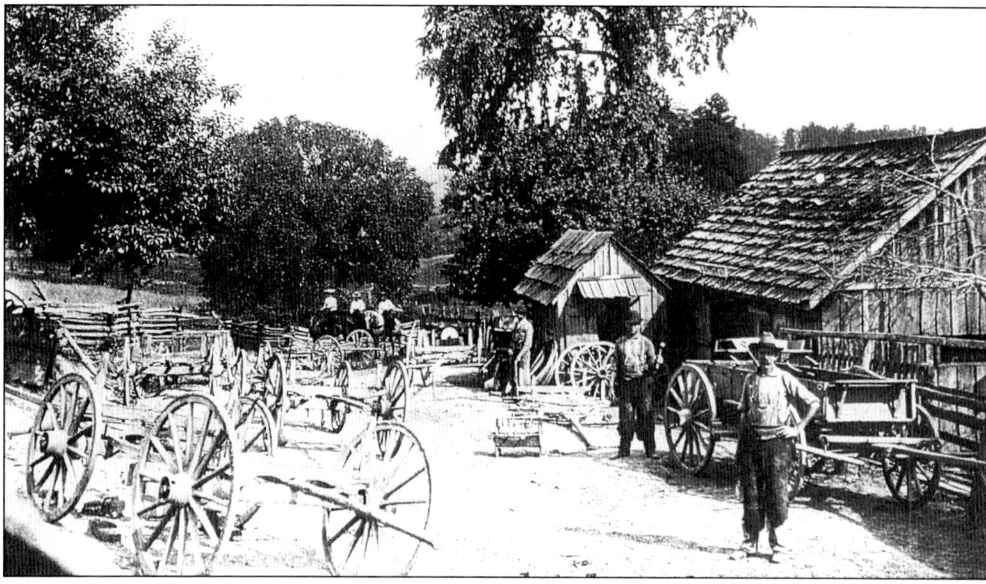

McThenia Blacksmith Shop, 1891. Today's peaceful Lodi was once a bustling community center, with at least two stores, a post office, Liberty Hall, and a blacksmith shop located along S.R. 91. The McThenia Brothers Blacksmith Shop, owned by Charles and Andrew McThenia, was a major destination for a population dependent upon horse and wagon transportation. In the top c. 1891 photograph, Andrew Patterson McThenia is standing in front. One of the ladies in the back is Belle Fisher Kelly. Note the wagon carriages awaiting metal work, the stacked wheels waiting for metal rims, and the ladies astride horses in the background. In the lower photograph, taken in 1899, the men on horseback are John McGee (left) and William C. Widener. Charles Wheeler is standing behind the farrier's tool box. Charles W. McThenia is holding the horse in the doorway. The man on the right is Andrew Patterson McThenia (brother to Charles), while the boy on the horse-hitching rail is John Alex McThenia. Note the horseshoes on the sign on the shingle roof. The small building on the left was a cobbler's shop run by R. L. Brown. A sign advertising Red Bird Chewing Tobacco is posted on the wall of the shop. (Courtesy Evelyn McThenia Hale.)

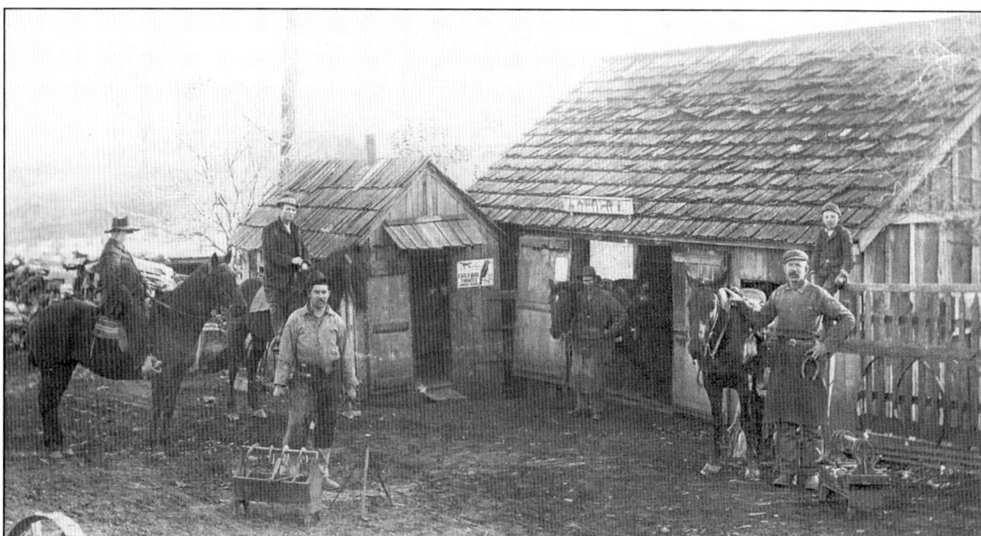

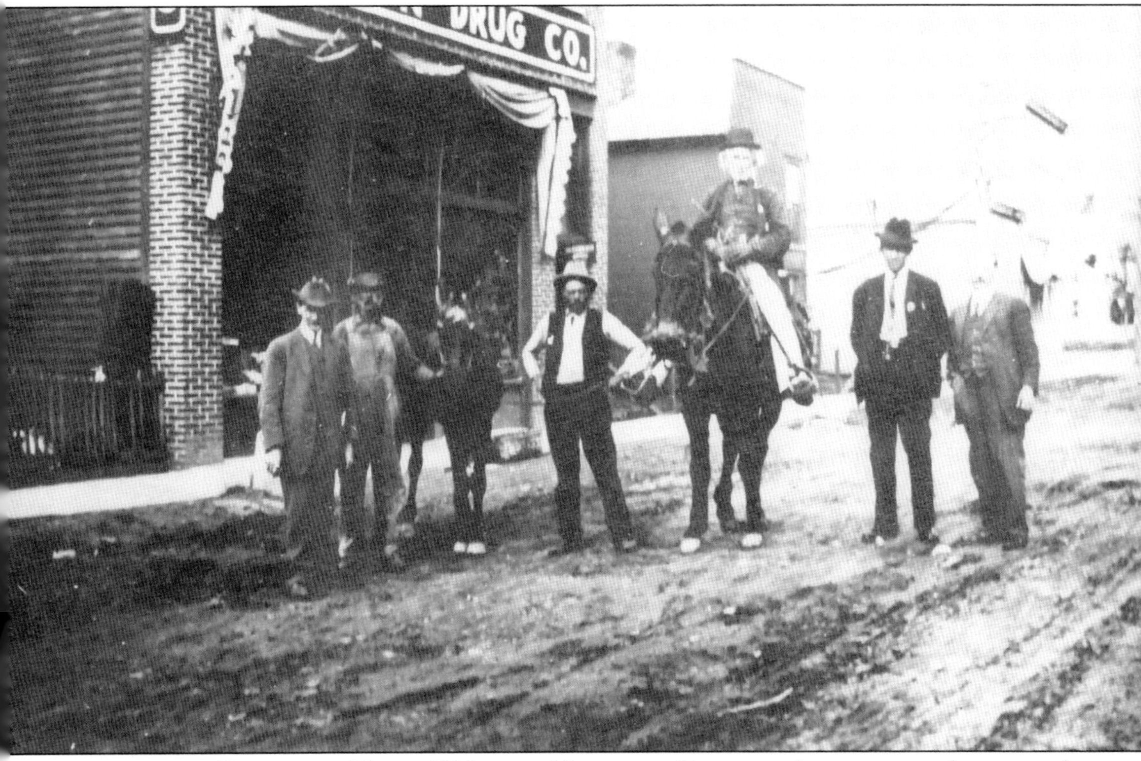

Downtown Damascus. This *c.* 1900 view of downtown Damascus shows a group of men posed on Laurel Avenue in front of what appears to be the Wingfield Drug Company, opened by Dr. J. L. Wingfield in 1901. (Rollins Grocery store later occupied the lot.) In front of the store there appears to be a boardwalk, which was built in 1902 or 1903 and made the street passable for pedestrians. At this time, Laurel Avenue was still a dirt road with no improvements. Posed in front of Wingfield's Pharmacy are the following, from left to right: unidentified, W. A. Minton, William Hand, ? Sprole, "Sleepy" Tom Clark, ? Parner, and J. L. Wingfield. Sleepy Tom Clark was a local character and itinerant preacher who traveled far and wide in his old wagon operating a side business of dog and horse trading. He could lie down and sleep anywhere and anytime, thus the name. Clark insisted that he had died once and handed out his printed cards reading "to Heaven, Hell, and Abingdon, Virginia." The town was first known as Mock's Mill after a nearby mill built by Henry Mock. Damascus was planned by J. D. Imboden to be a center for steel production, but it wasn't economically feasible to extract the manganese. The railroad reached the town in 1901 and facilitated a massive timbering business in the early 1900s. Several industries, such as American Cyanamid, Thayer Company Dimension Plant, and the Acme Bark-Extract Company, came to Damascus, flourished, and are now gone. (Courtesy Virginia Cornett Smith.)

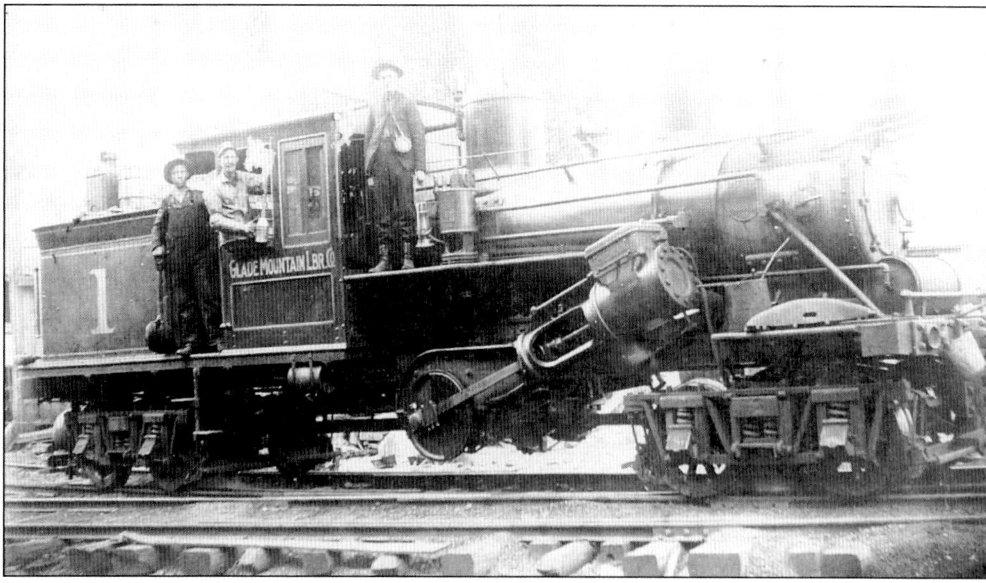

GLADE MOUNTAIN LUMBER COMPANY. Here's Engine No. 1 with the Glade Mountain Lumber Company, a smaller timber company that owned 10,000 acres in the Atkins area. Their band mill had a capacity of 35,000 feet of lumber. Note the man on the far left holding the shovel, with face and overalls darkened by shoveling coal into the hungry engine. (Courtesy Virginia Cornett Smith.)

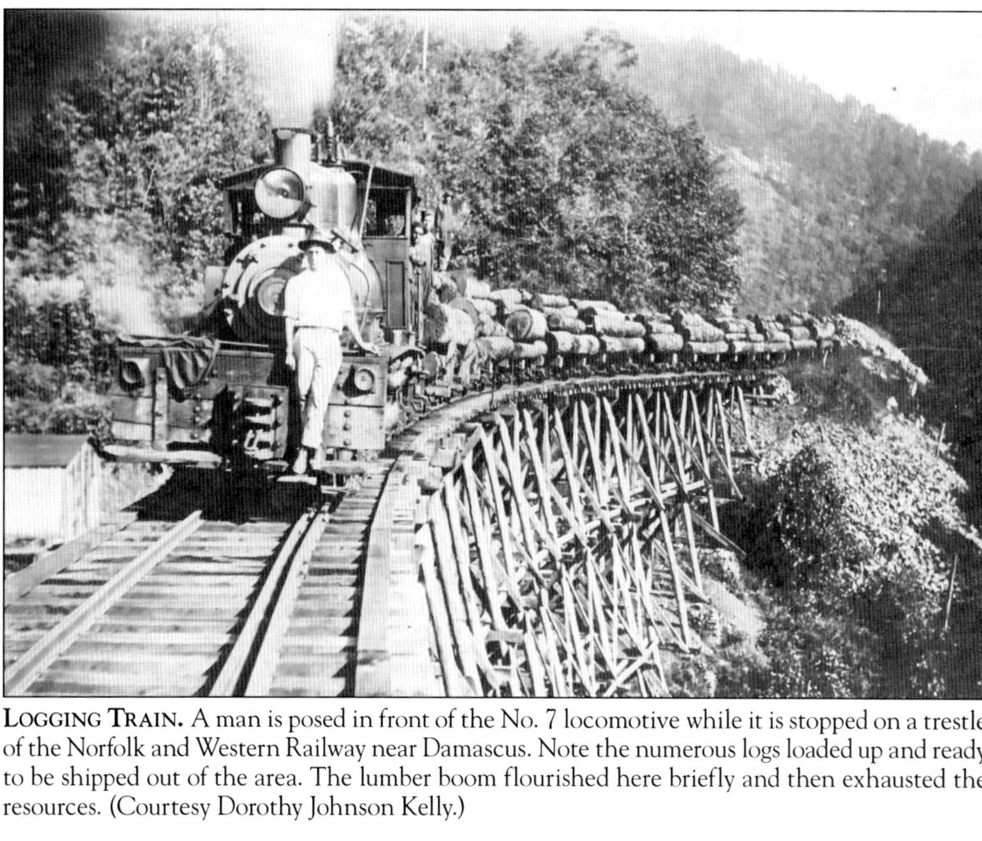

LOGGING TRAIN. A man is posed in front of the No. 7 locomotive while it is stopped on a trestle of the Norfolk and Western Railway near Damascus. Note the numerous logs loaded up and ready to be shipped out of the area. The lumber boom flourished here briefly and then exhausted the resources. (Courtesy Dorothy Johnson Kelly.)

Four

LANDSCAPE AND AGRICULTURE

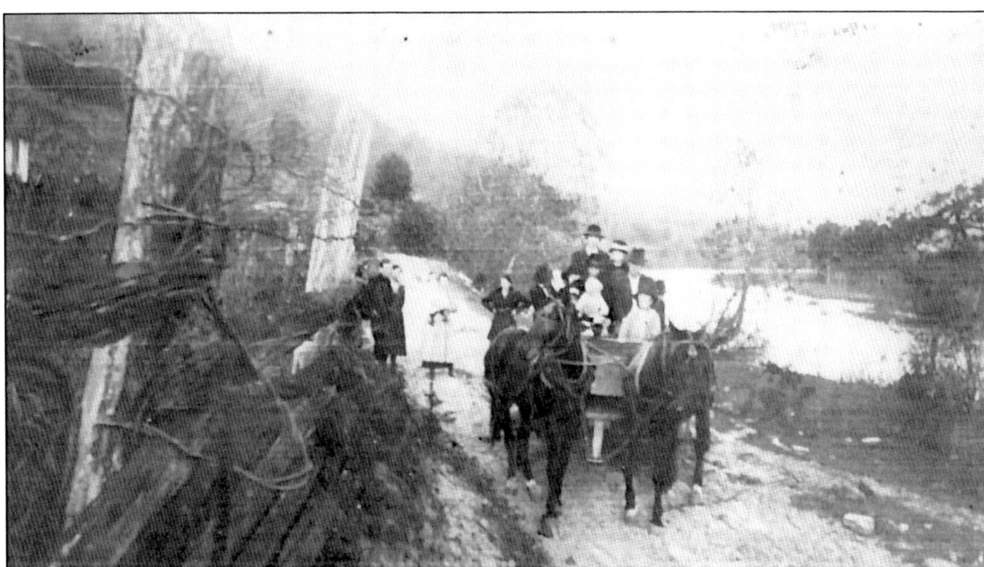

RIVER ROAD. The Taylor family is traveling down North Fork River Road in about 1920. Hiram Taylor is driving, and in the wagon are his wife, Rebecca Galliher Taylor, and several of their children, including Claude, Ocie, and Stuart. Note the wide North Fork of the Holston River running alongside the road. (Courtesy Troy Taylor.)

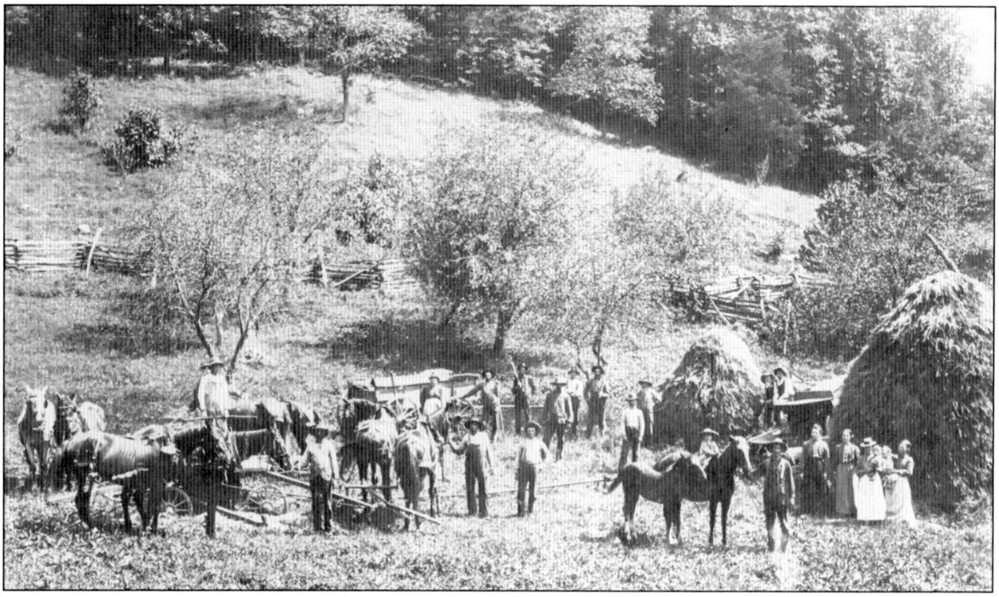

NORTH FORK FARM. This farming scene was photographed by Graham Roberts, a local farmer/photographer in the North Fork community. Wortie Phelps is astride the horse, with Herbert Phelps holding it. Alice, Ester, and Nannie are among the women holding the two children on the right of the photograph. Note the tall haystacks, as well as the pitchforks and horse-drawn equipment used to farm the land in those days. (Courtesy Dorothy Johnson Kelly.)

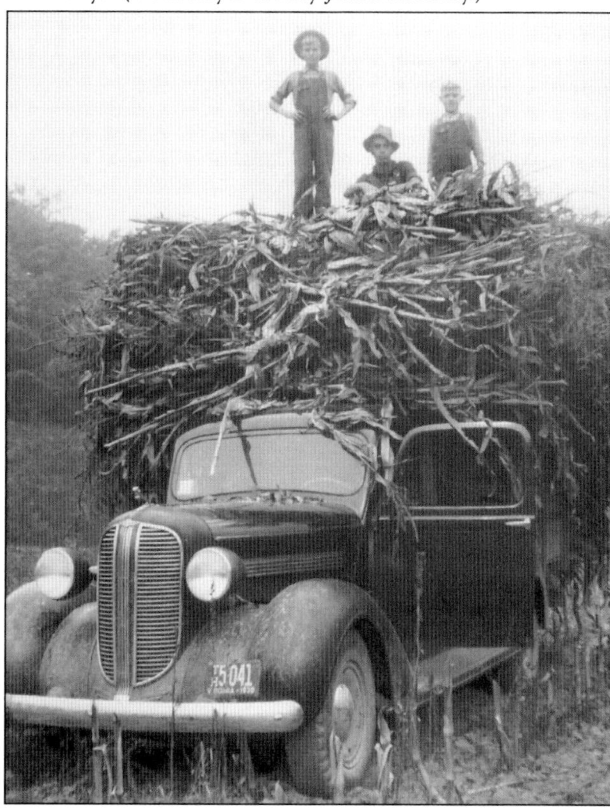

CORN HARVEST. The farm truck is loaded up with corn in Hayter's Gap in this c. 1939 photograph. Corn has long been a necessary crop and mainstay here. From left to right are Branson McCray (born 1926), Stuart Taylor (1915–2006), and Roy McCray (1930–1975). (Courtesy Troy Taylor.)

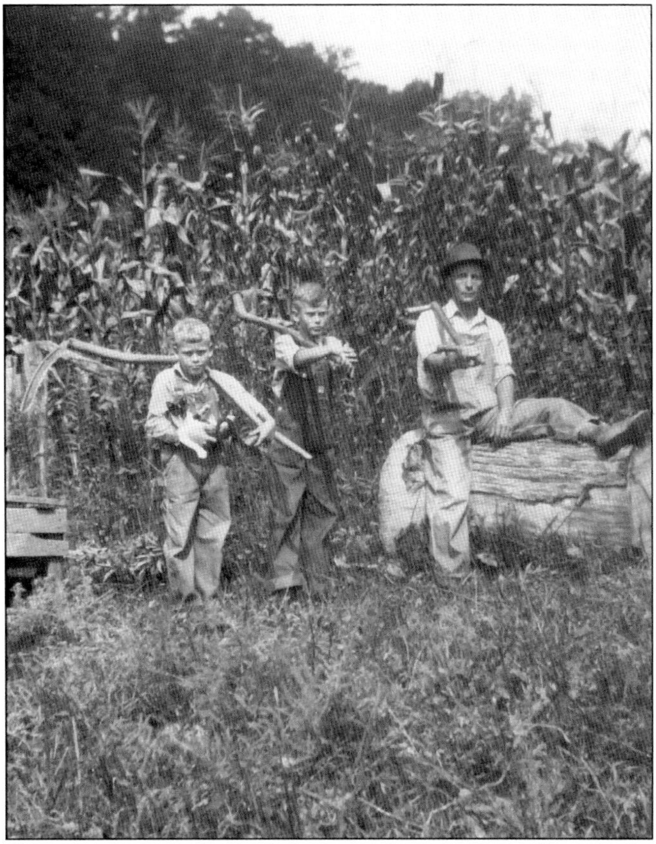

Cutting Corn. These men and boys have scythes in hand, ready to do the hot work of cutting corn in Hayter's Gap. Roy McCray (1930–1975) sits with his sons Branson McCray (left) and Carl McCray (right). Note the large log that Roy is sitting on. (Courtesy Troy Taylor.)

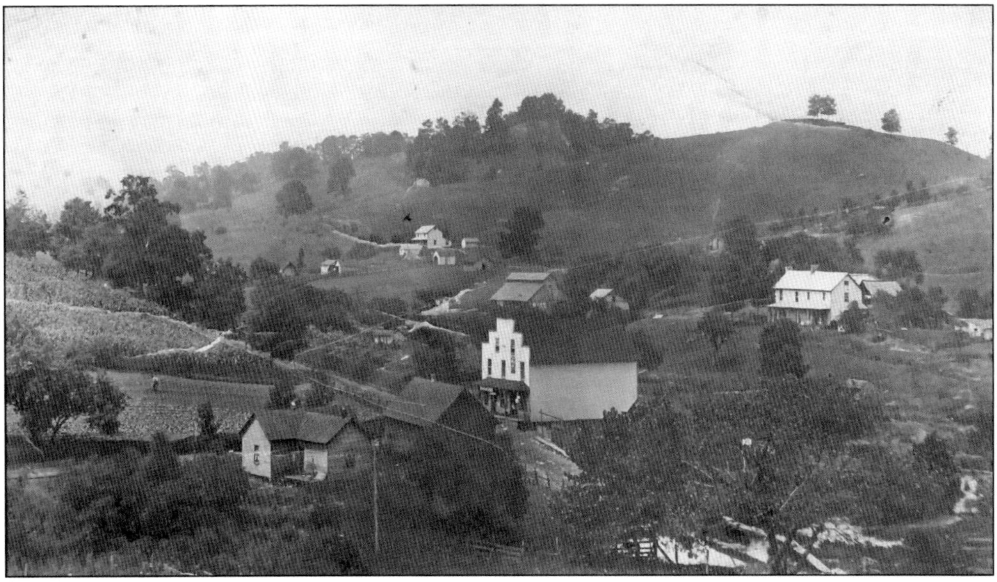

Lindell. This postcard, dated 1915, shows the Lindell community, which is still located at the intersection of Rich Valley Road and Lindell Road. The Rich Valley is noted for fertile farming and grazing land. The Lindell grocery store is near the center of the photograph, and a post office was once here, too. Several of the older houses still stand at this crossroads. (Courtesy Roy Rector.)

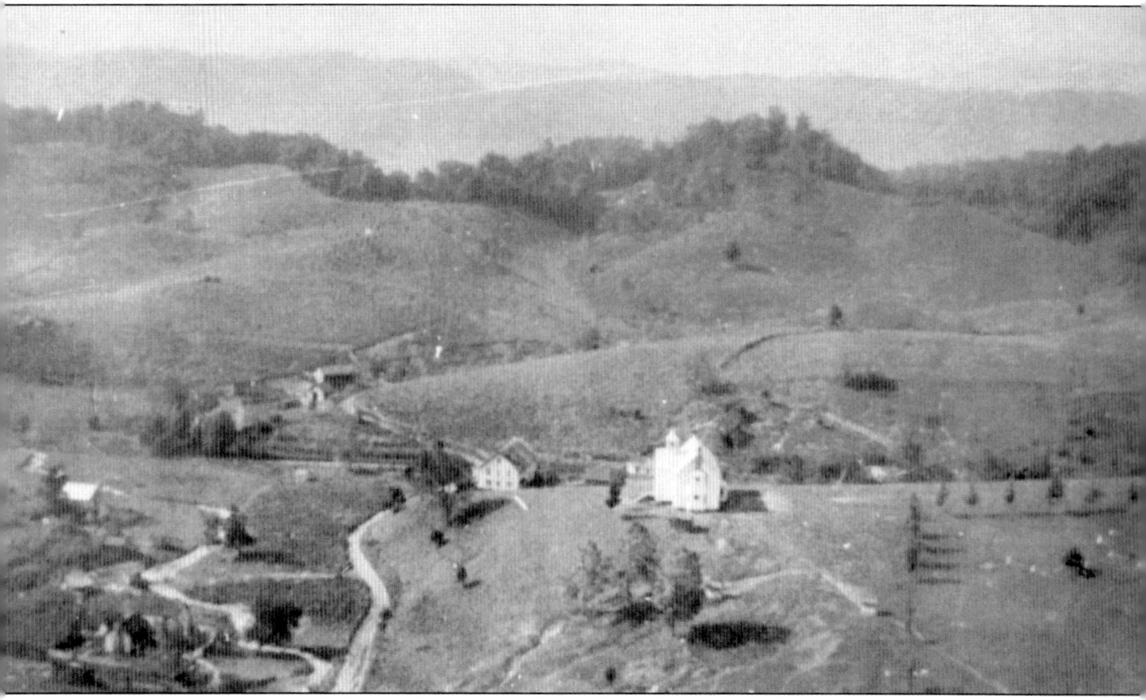

BLACKWELL CHAPEL. This *c.* 1910 aerial view of Blackwell Chapel community was taken from the top of the mill hill looking north. In the lower right-hand corner a cleared area for the cemetery can be seen, in the center is the Blackwell Chapel School, and to the left of the school is Herndon's Store (later Crabtree). In 1902, Joseph D. and Elizabeth Blackwell provided the land for church construction for $1. Blackwell Chapel Union Methodist Church was built in 1903 and stands back from S.R. 700. The church has a small but active congregation that is working to preserve the community's history and culture. Little Mountain of the Clinch Mountains is looming in the background. Note how much of this valley was cleared for agriculture and grazing. (Courtesy Michael Hoback.)

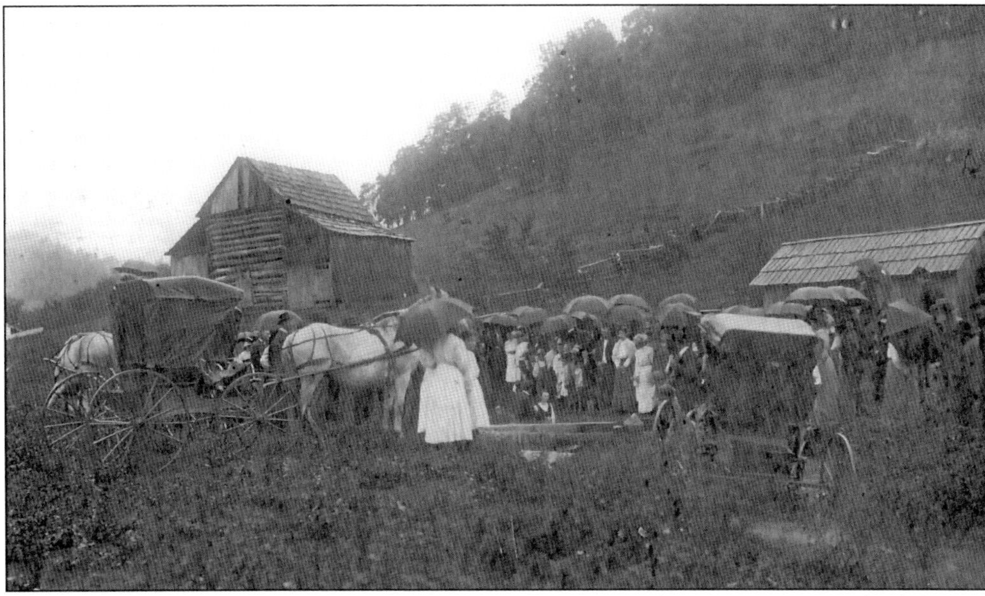

MAIDEN CREEK BAPTISM. Baptisms were, and continue to be, community and celebratory affairs at the local waters. This *c.* 1900 scene at Maiden Creek shows a gathering of that time, with the person being baptized in the center of the photograph. Note the log barn/granary building on the left. The enclosures on the buggies and the many umbrellas suggest that it was raining. The photograph was taken by Graham Roberts, a local farmer/photographer. (Courtesy Roy Rector.)

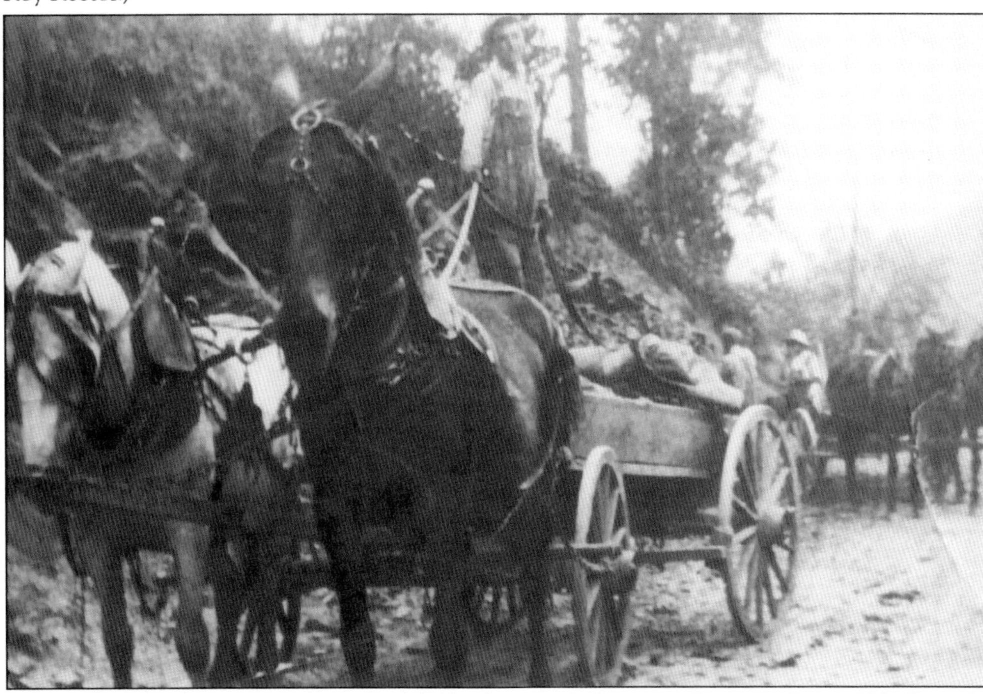

LOGGING TOOLE'S CREEK. James Campbell is logging by horse and wagon about 1929 along the dirt Toole's Creek Road. Scenic waterfalls, a popular picnic destination in the past, cascade down the creek as it runs into the North Fork of the Holston River. (Courtesy Lynda Campbell.)

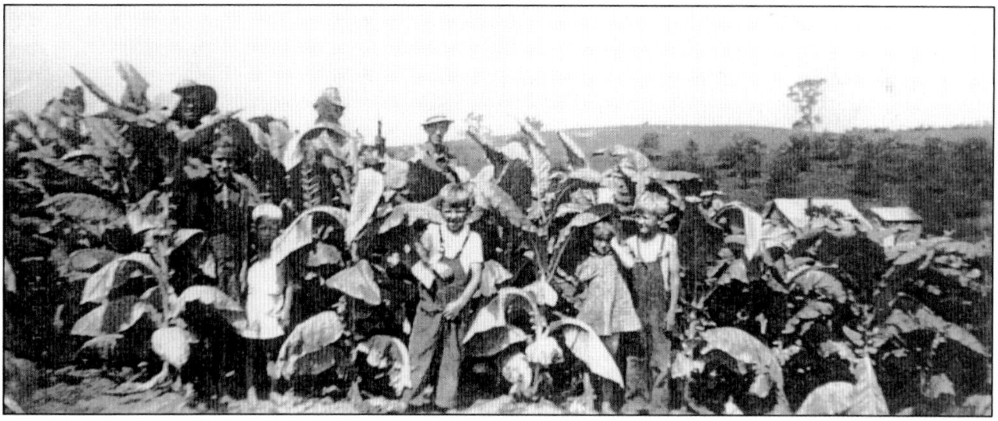

TOBACCO CROP. These tobacco plants are growing tall in this *c.* 1930 photograph. Tobacco was an early crop in Virginia and was grown in this region in the 19th century. Burley tobacco was introduced in the 1930s and quickly became a major part of the farming economy. Since the government stopped the allotment system, few folks grow tobacco anymore and small farmers have lost important cash crops. The two boys in front are Ernest (left) and Junior Copenhaver. This scene is now part of the past, as many tobacco farmers have joined the government program to reduce tobacco production. (Courtesy Susie Copenhaver Lang.)

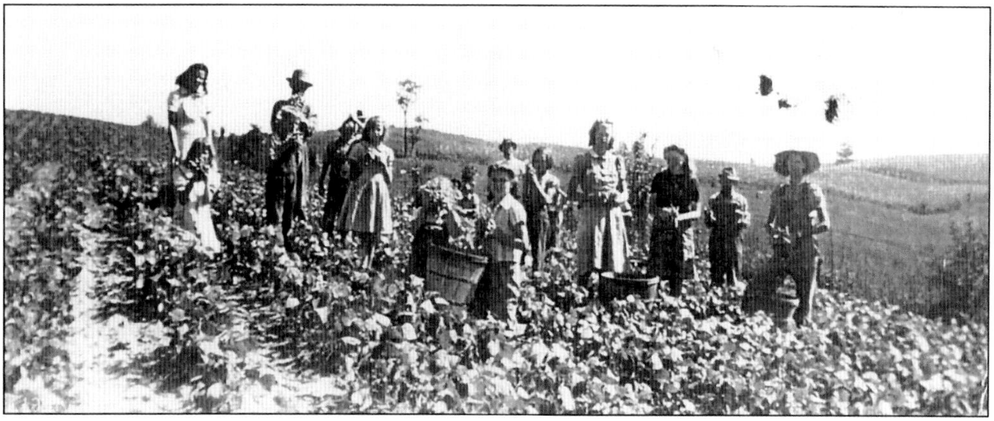

RUTABAGA HARVEST. These folks are picking rutabagas or yellow turnips in this field about 1930 on the farm of Steward and Goldie Copenhaver in the Lodi area. Few farmers grow rutabagas today, but they were once a common crop. (Courtesy Susie Copenhaver Lang.)

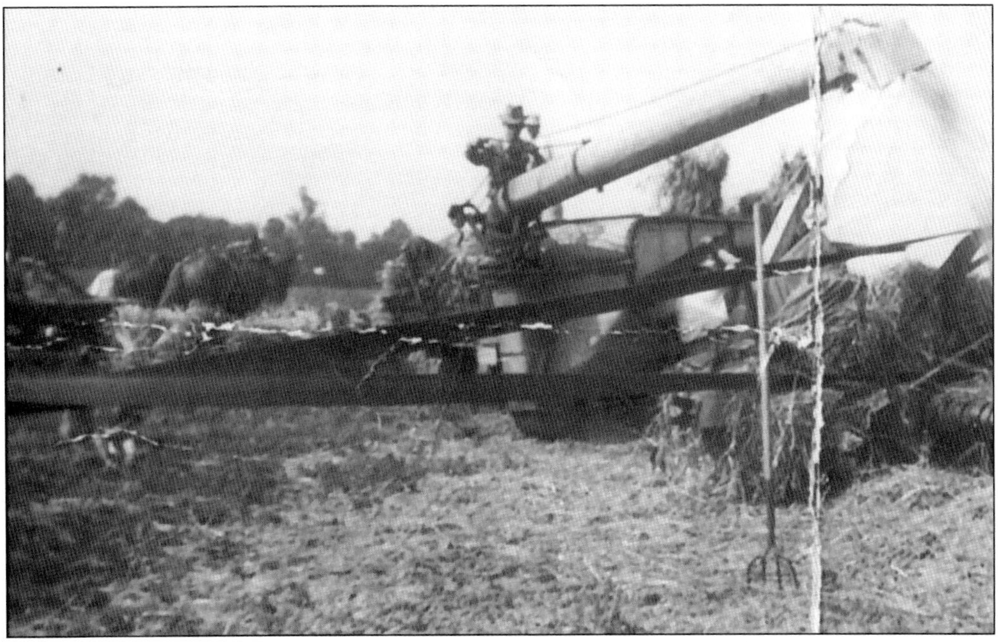

THRESHING WHEAT. The threshing machine is in action in this *c.* 1940 photograph at the John A. and Lucille Buchanan McCall farm on Monroe Road. Men from the community would pitch in to help one another, and women would spend the day cooking for hungry workers when the threshing machine from the area came to thresh their grains. (Courtesy Susie Copenhaver Lang.)

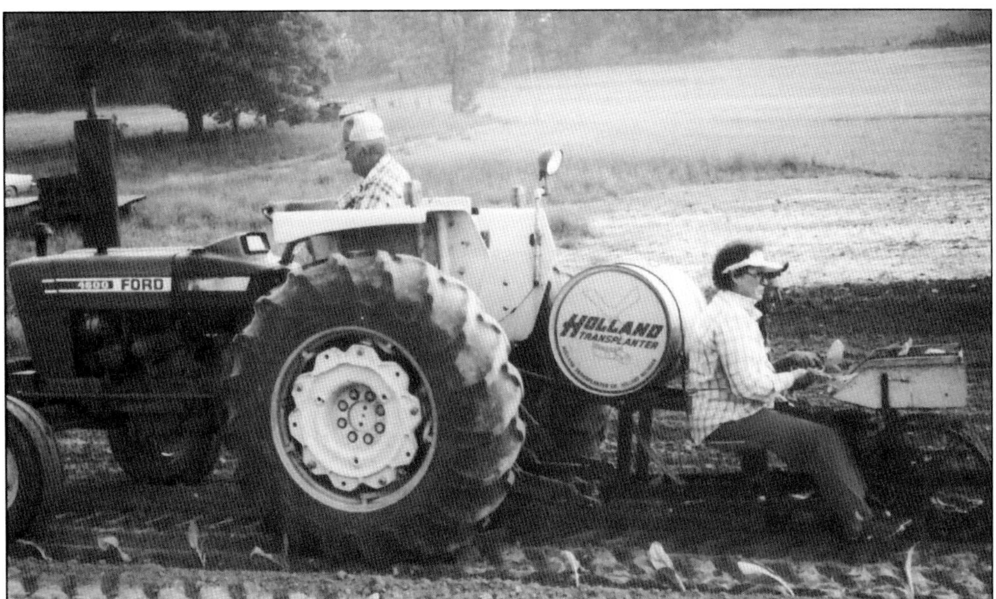

SETTING TOBACCO. Once a common scene in almost every field, today tobacco setting, or planting the young plants, has nearly disappeared from the landscape because of the tobacco buy-out program. Many farmers now miss the seasonal activity. Ernest Copenhaver drives the tractor while his wife, Alberta McCall Copenhaver (right), a master tobacco-setter, and another person are placing the seedlings in the setter. (Courtesy Susie Copenhaver Lang.)

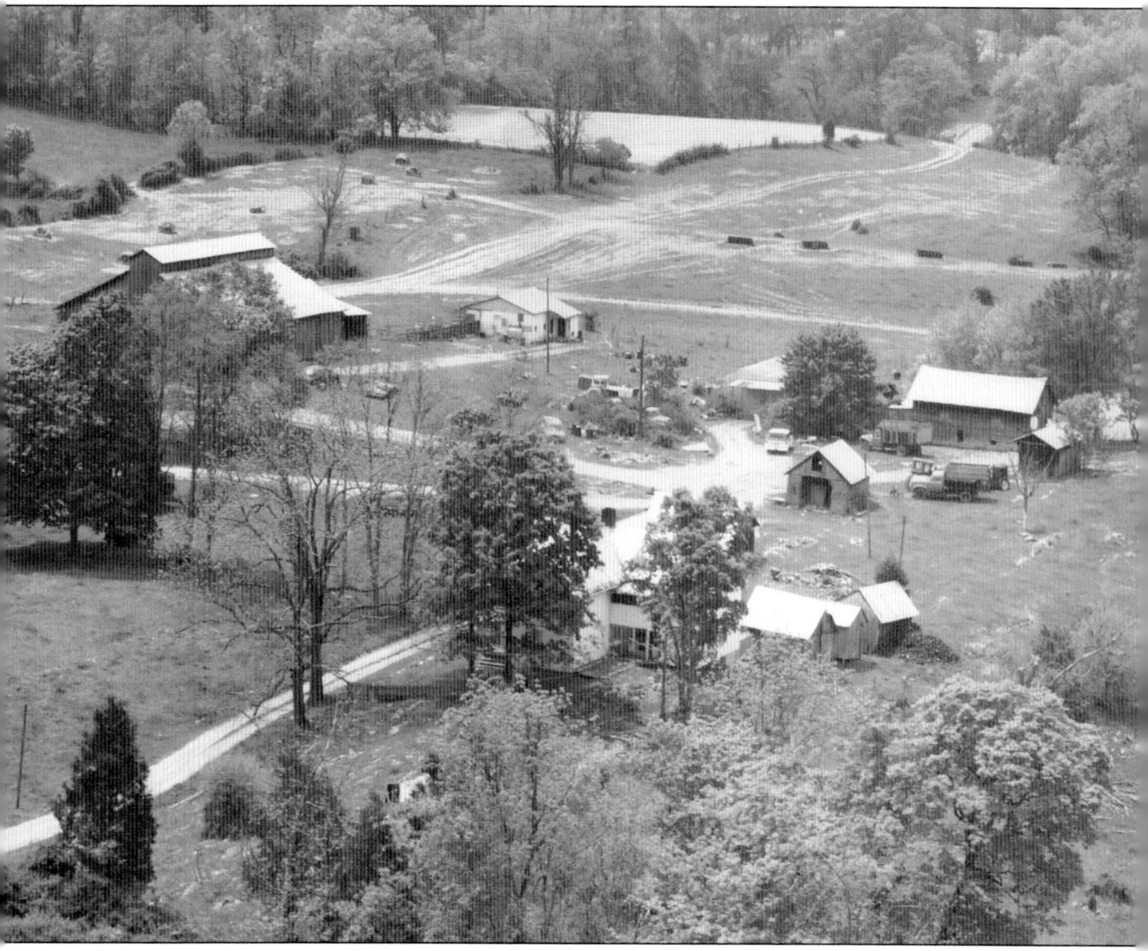

GRANT FARM. Sections of the Grant farm still remain in the family today. At one time, the farm included over 1,000 acres. This section is part of the land deeded to Dr. James Lewis Grant by his father, Dr. Robert G. Grant. The original farm extended to the Shallow Ford Bridge and was a land grant to Dr. Robert G. Grant and his wife, Jennie Scott Grant. The existing house was built in 1901 for about $800. A windmill was used in the 1930s to pump water to the house. This arrangement of farm buildings, with a granary, shop, milk house, barn, and surrounding fields, is typical of that time period and the region. The family struggled to hold onto this working farm and operated a dairy farm here until 1988. Grant descendants still live on and farm the land today, continuing a family tradition that is rapidly disappearing. In order for the area's rural landscape to be preserved in this region, a land trust needs to be formed to obtain easements preventing development that doesn't preserve the rural nature of this place. (Courtesy Irene Grant.)

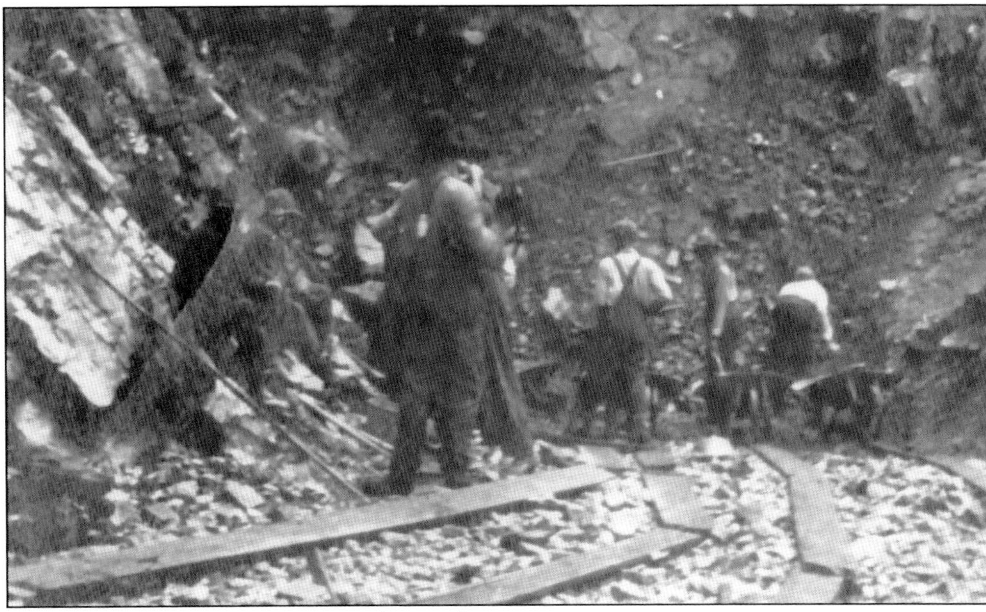

Backbone Rock Construction (Above) and Railroad Coming Through (Right). These two early photographs document the 1901 construction of the tunnel through Backbone Rock, just outside Damascus in Tennessee. The Empire Mining Company encountered the 20-foot-thick ridge when they were laying railroad track for the Beaver Dam Railroad to connect to the Virginia-Carolina line. The company blasted a short tunnel through the rock, and men had to hand-chisel it even higher to accommodate the smokestack of the train engines. The Tennessee Wildlife Agency later developed the area for camping, hiking, fishing, and picnicking. This regional park is a lovely recreational asset to the area. (Above and below courtesy Virginia Cornett Smith.)

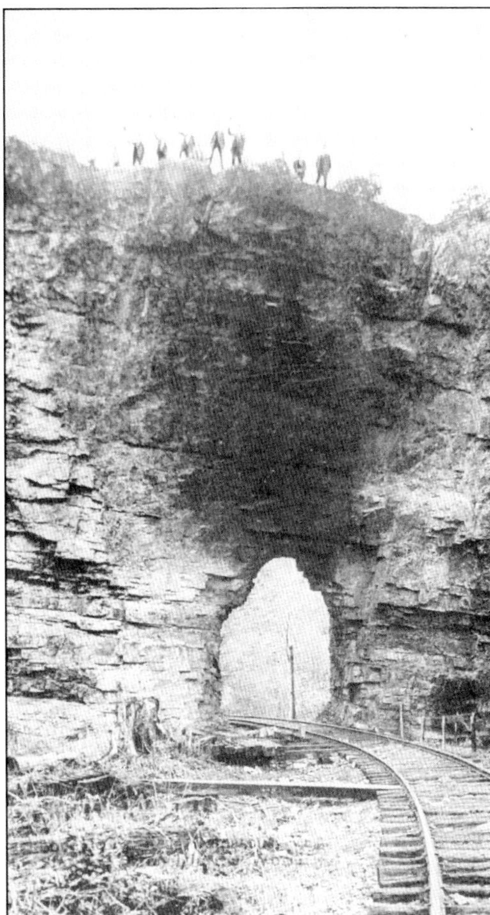

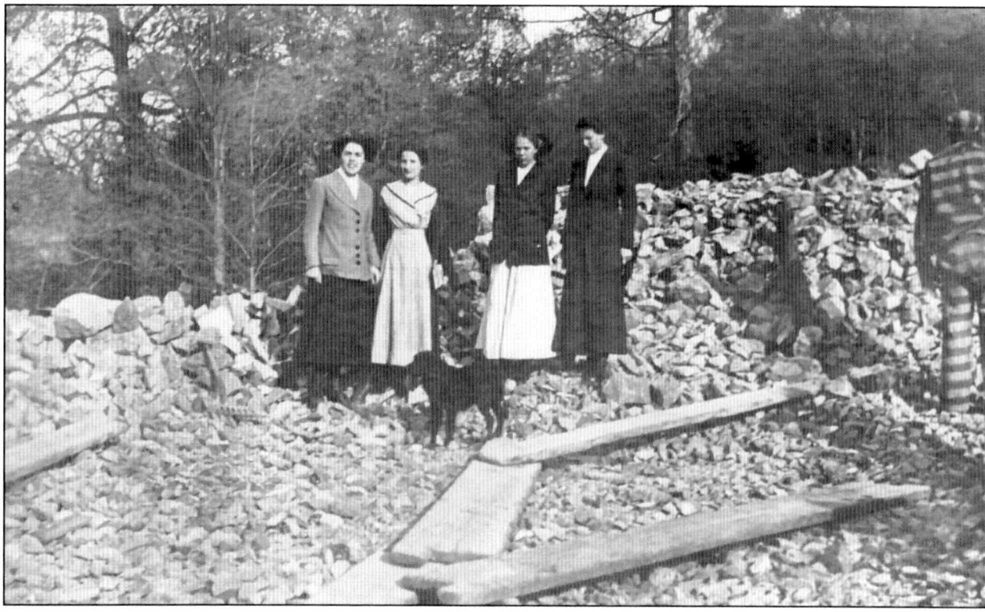

RAILROAD CONSTRUCTION NEAR DAMASCUS. Four young ladies, identified from left to right as Ora Hand, Bess Rhea, Rebecca Ramsey, and May Blackburn, as well as their dog are posed in front of a rocky construction area, which was likely being cleared for a rail line. Note the prisoner in the striped uniform on the right of the photograph carrying rocks. Convict labor was commonly used for railroad construction. (Courtesy Virginia Cornett Smith.)

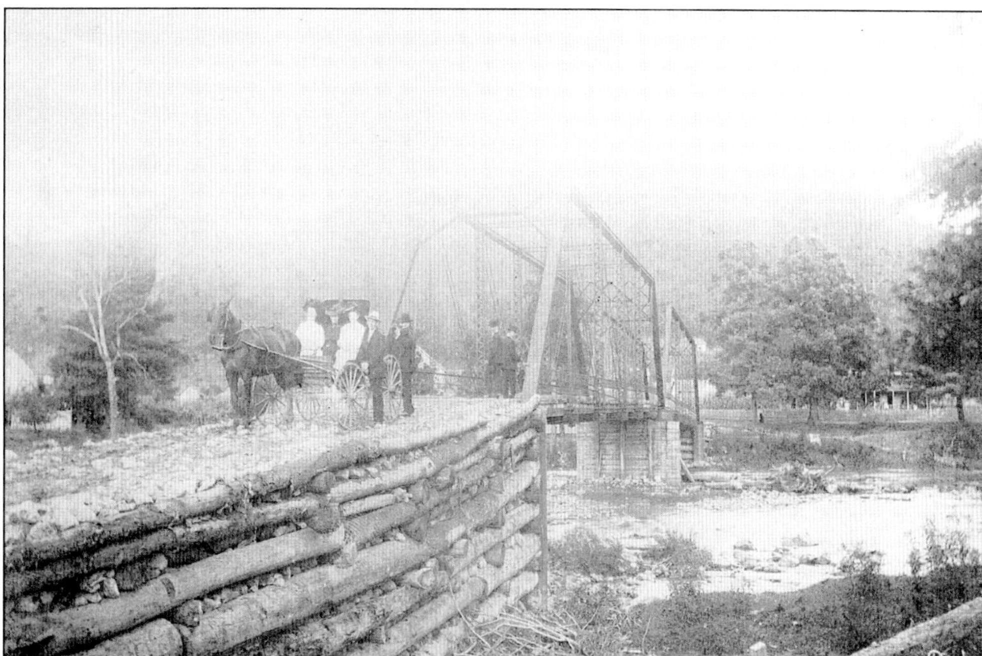

DAMASCUS BRIDGE, C. 1900. These folks are posed on a bridge that crossed either Laurel Creek or Beaverton Creek. The log and earthen supports of the bridge are visible under the lovely iron bridge. These men in bowler hats and ladies in fancy hats appear to be going to church or town. (Courtesy Virginia Cornett Smith.)

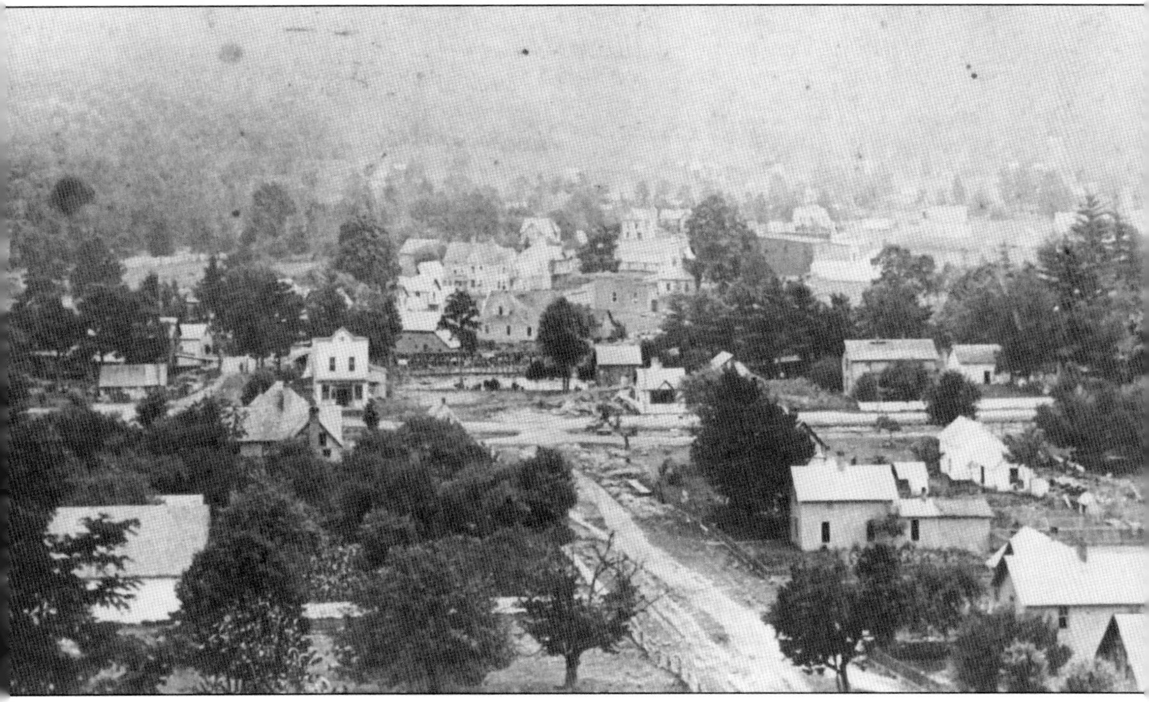

VIEW OF DAMASCUS, C. 1900. This view from a hill over Damascus from Mock Hill above Clifton Street shows the railroad running along Laurel Creek, as well as several small stores along the rail. Downtown Damascus is in the background of this view. On the left side of Laurel Avenue are the Fortune house, the funeral home, and the Saul house, while on the right side of Laurel are the A. A. Mock house, the Duncan Smith house on the corner, the Mongle house, Wilson house, and the Lutheran Mock's Chapel parsonage on the corner. On the road parallel to the railroad is a store, the Lowers house, and the Keys house. With a unique location at the confluence of Beaverton Creek and the Laurel Fork of the Holston River, Damascus experienced major growth from the late 1700s and especially after the railroad. The settlement was a critical halfway point between Abingdon and Mountain City, with its location on the Washington-Russell Turnpike (from Russell County, Virginia, to Mountain City, Tennessee). Serving as a convenient stop in the 19th century commercial goods transportation between Ashe County, North Carolina, and Lebanon, Virginia, this humble town often was the scene of travelers wagons and horses taking a break. (Courtesy Virginia Cornett Smith.)

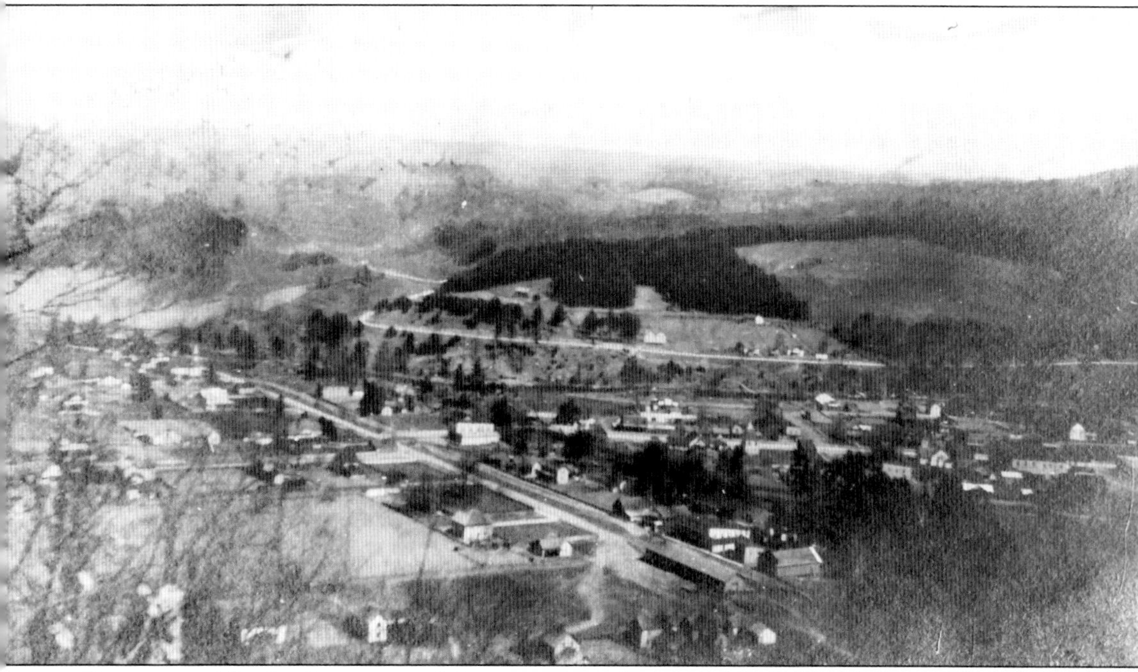

DAMASCUS. This bird's-eye view of Damascus was taken from Mock Hill. The railroad tracks are visible running straight down the center of the photograph, along with the depot building and stores, which are now gone. The former railroad bed has been converted to the Virginia Creeper Trail, a popular hiking and biking path. Note that much of the landscape had already been logged. Railroads were key to industry development in the region, especially in Damascus. In 1900, the Virginia-Carolina Railway completed a connecting line between Abingdon and Damascus. Later bought by the Norfolk and Western Railway, the rail lines were extended to Elkland, North Carolina, thus creating the perfect location for a logging center in the early 1900s. The abundant water resources provided power for sawmills to saw the plentiful trees surrounding Damascus. Branch railroad lines and smaller private lines were built to lumber the hidden coves and steep hillsides. Woodworking plants, extract factories, and other industries located in the area and employed many residents. However, as the lumber companies used up the trees, the railroads lost their major exports. The industries soon left, too. In 1972, the Norfolk and Western abandoned the trades and in 1982, Abingdon acquired the right-of-way and established the Virginia Creeper Trail, one of the first rails-to-trails projects in the Southeast. (Courtesy Virginia Cornett Smith.)

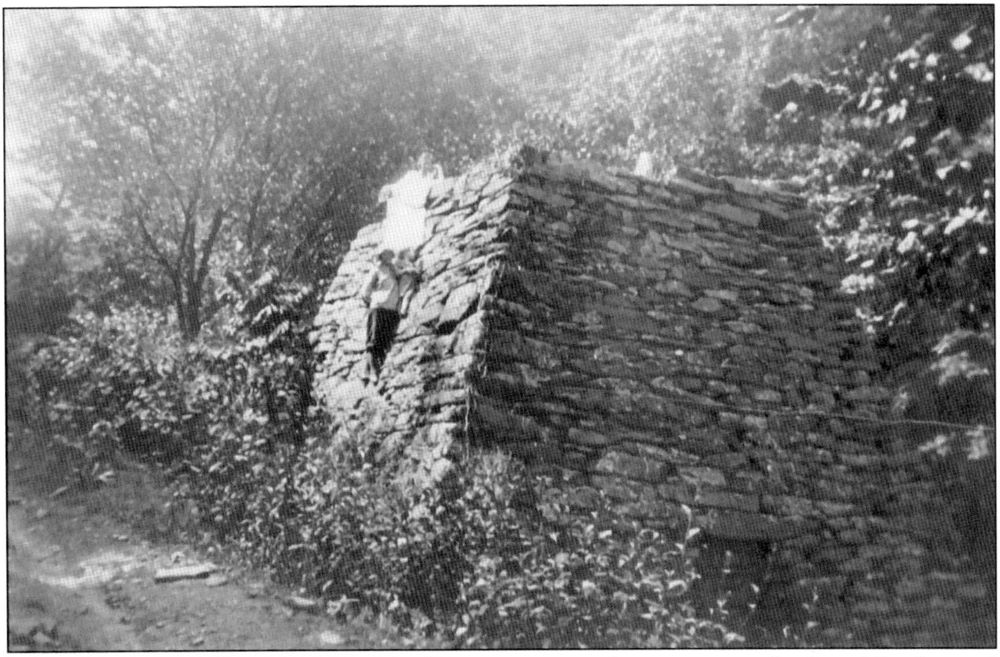

LIME KILN. Few folks may recognize this structure as the remnants of a lime kiln, located near Avens. Kilns were used to break down the abundant limestone in the area into powder in order to fertilize local soils. Very few lime kilns still remain in the region. (Courtesy Walter B. "Blair" Keller.)

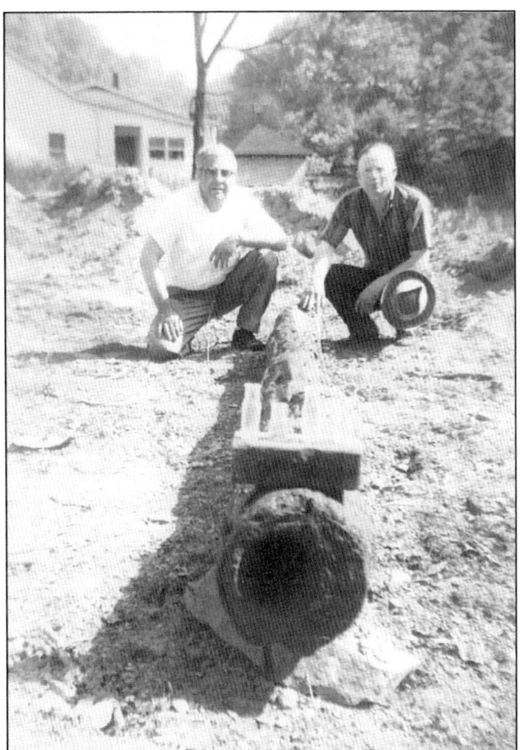

SEVEN SPRINGS LOG PIPES. Guy Testerman and Roy Rector stand behind log pipes with several bottles found at the previous location of Seven Springs on Old Mill Road. The nationally known Seven Springs resort was located just outside Glade Spring and provided springwater choices of sulfur, iron, chalybeate, alum, limestone, and freestone. The waters were bottled at the distillery in Abingdon and were quite famous in their heyday. (Courtesy Roy Rector.)

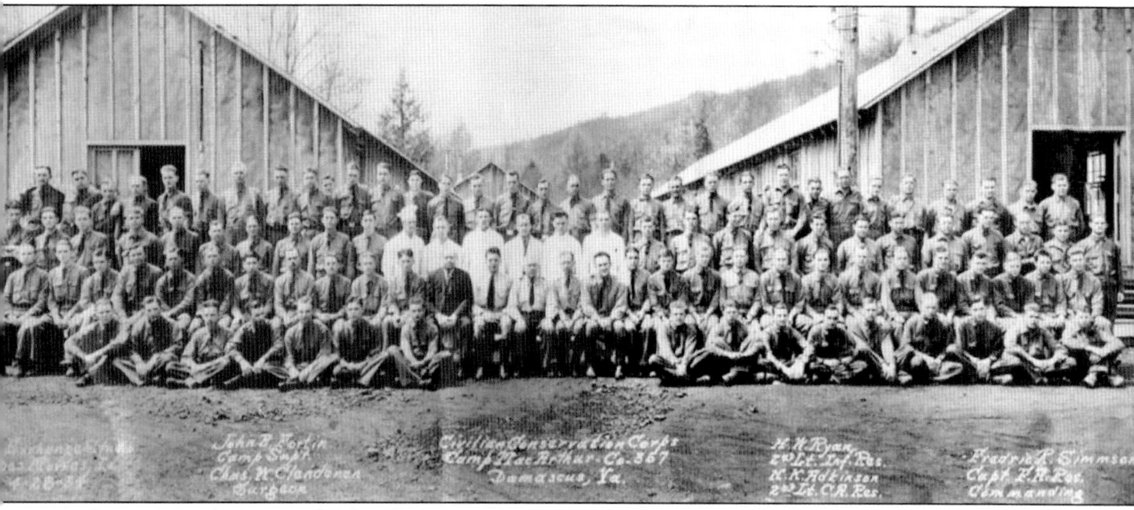

CAMP MACARTHUR CCC. Shown in this 1934 photograph is the Camp MacArthur Civilian Conservation Corps Company (CCC) No. 357, which was stationed in Damascus. These hardworking men from all over the United States built a telephone line from Damascus to Konnarock and to Carroll County. The barracks are visible in the background. Local ladies enjoyed the company of these CCC workers, and subsequent marriages resulted in several of the men remaining in Washington County. Information on the bottom of the photograph lists the following: John B. Fortin as camp superintendent, Charles Clendenon as surgeon, H. W. Ryan as 2nd Lt. Inf. Res., N. K. Adkinson as 2nd Lt. C. R. Res., Fredric R. Simmson Capt. F. A. as Res. Commanding. (Courtesy Jeffrey Weaver.)

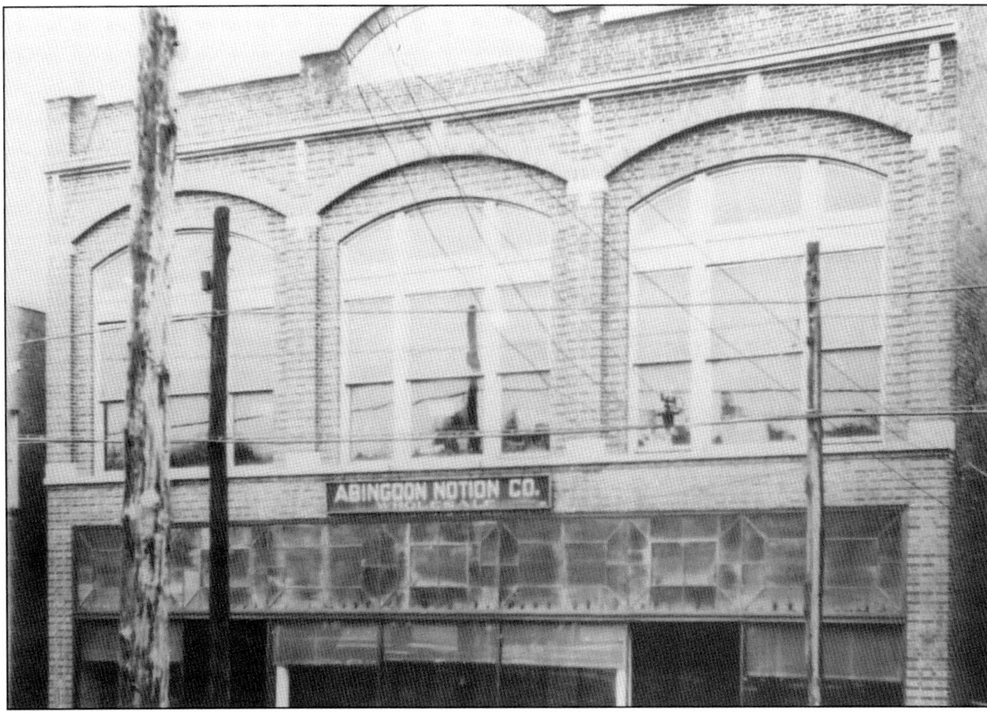

ABINGDON NOTION COMPANY. The Abingdon Notion Company, owned by Oscar L. James, was located along Abingdon's Main Street in this brick building until it was destroyed in the 1914 downtown fire. In 1918, C. A. Lester and A. A. McConnell built a brick store on the lot, and after 1940, the building was used by Parks Belk department store. Sadly the ornate facade has been covered over with a plain 1970s-type brick front, but perhaps this fancy storefront survives underneath and could be restored. (Courtesy Lowry Bowman.)

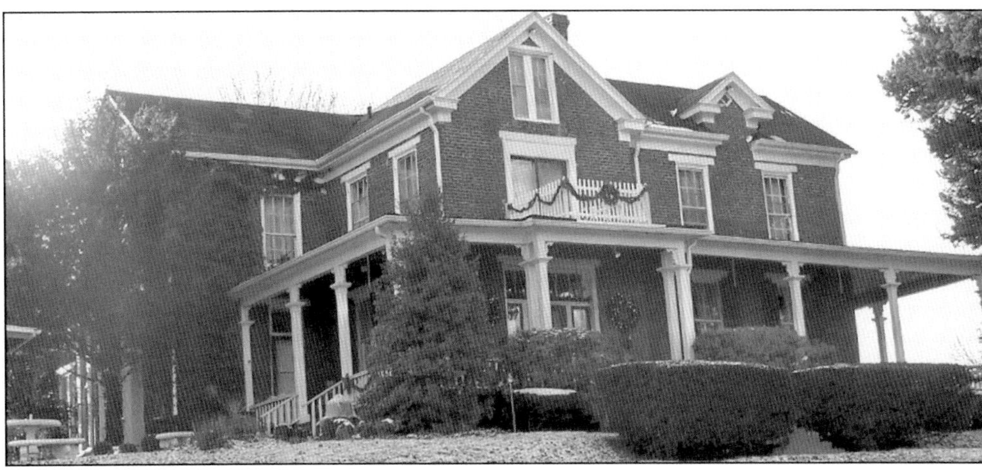

GREENWAY PARTY HOUSE. Built in 1874 by John G. White, this stately brick building stands on a hill on S.R. 700/White's Mill Road. Since 1954, the house has been operated as the Greenway Haven Party House, begun by Mr. and Mrs. Robert H. Smith and still owned and operated by family members Mary Ann Janson and Robert Janson. The house is a unique historic location for receptions, meetings, teas, and group dining. (Courtesy DeAnna Akers Greene.)

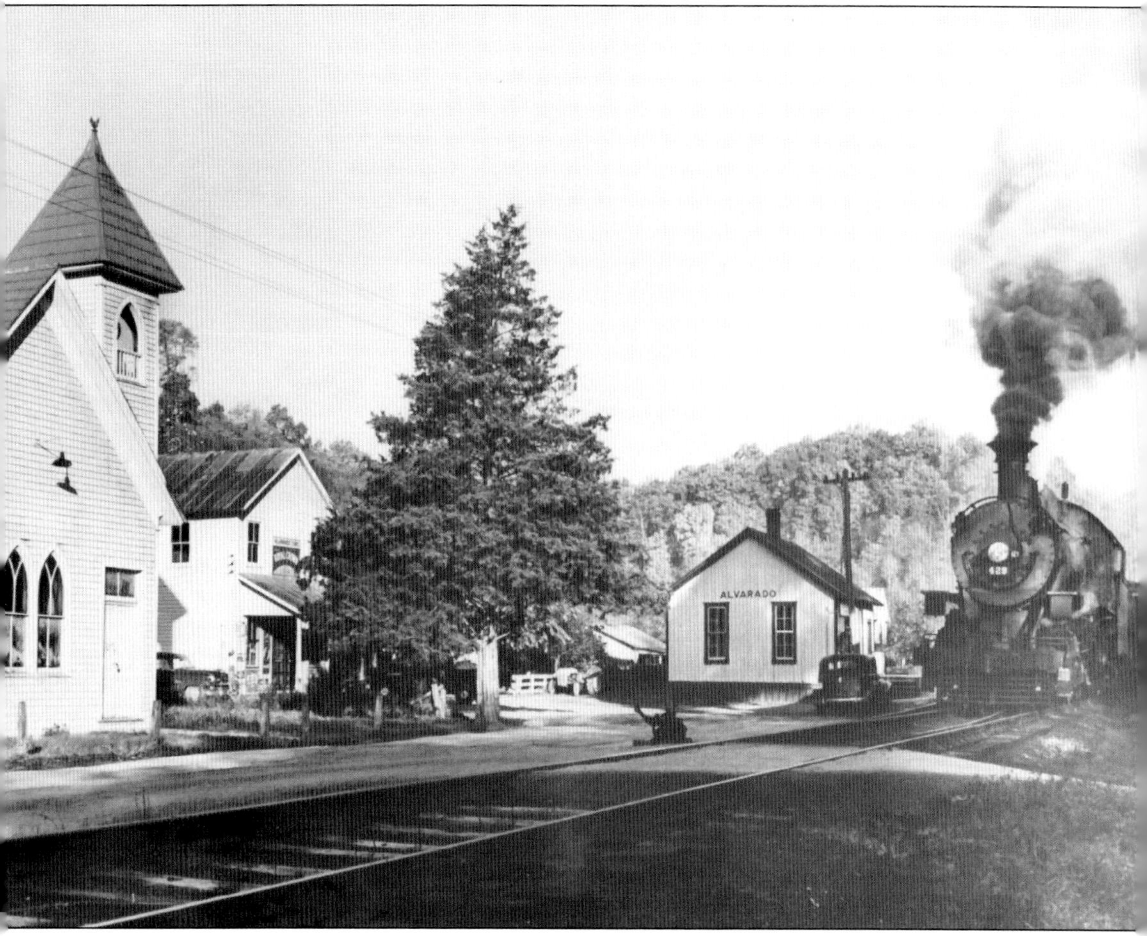

ALVARADO STATION. This photograph of the Alvarado Depot was taken around 1940 and shows the busy train stop. The church stands on the left next to the Alvarado Store and the station. Sadly, the station is no longer standing. Note the similar architecture for the railroad stations and depot buildings (see Meadowview, Emory, and Abingdon photographs). Although closed for a time, the store is now doing a good business as a pleasant stop on the Virginia Creeper Trail, serving food, drinks, and sundries to biker and hikers along the converted railway. Originally called Barron, this community somehow adopted the imported name of Alvarado. A post office operated here until 1962. Just a mile west, where the South Fork and Middle Fork of the Holston River meet, was the 1801 site for a planned town called Carrickfergus. Anticipated by Hugh Neely to develop into a port for boats and barges, the land never was developed. Today the Virginia Creeper Trail bridge provides lovely views of the confluence of two forks of the mighty Holston River. (Courtesy Virginia Cornett Smith.)

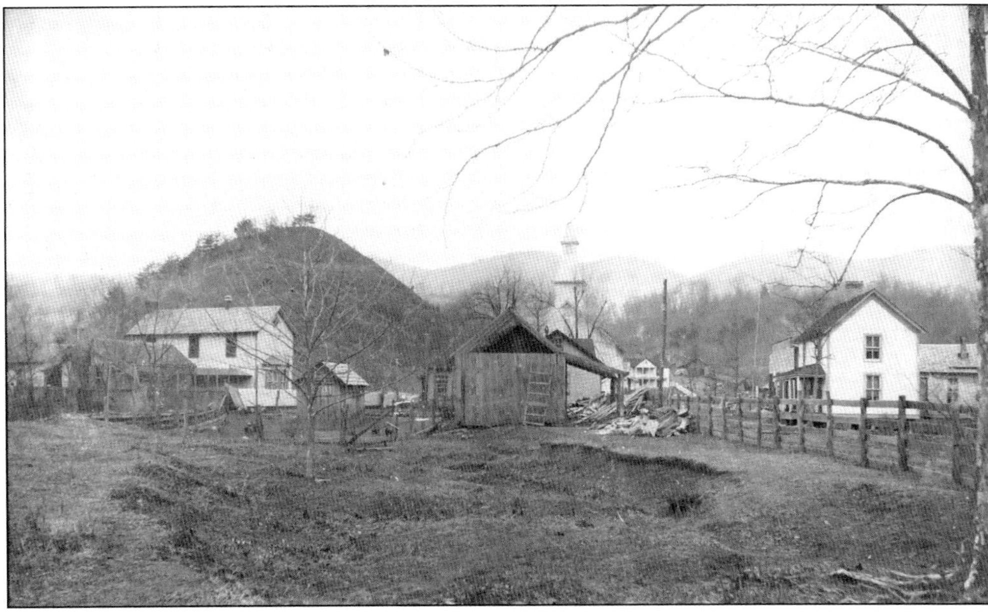

HAYTER'S GAP CROSSROADS. Once a bustling crossroads community of stores, churches, schools, gristmills, sawmills, and blacksmith shops, today's Hayter's Gap is a quiet residential community. An older store is visible in the center of the photograph, and the white steeple of the Hayter's Gap church towers in the background. The steep Clinch Mountains rise above the community. (Courtesy Hayter's Gap Branch Library and Jack Kestner family.)

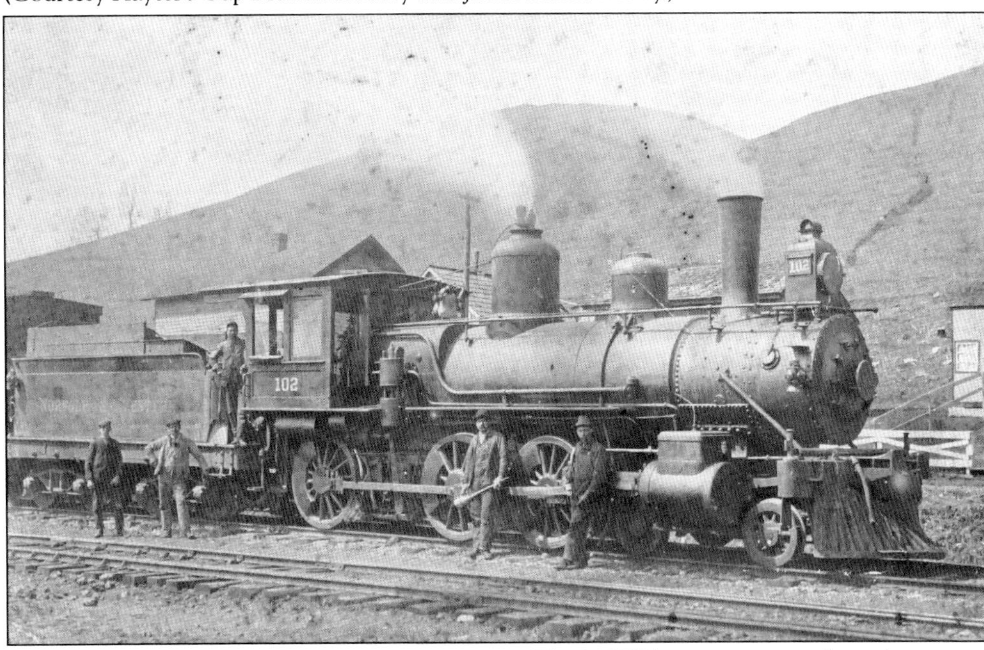

NORFOLK AND WESTERN LOCOMOTIVE NO. 102. This N&W locomotive stands ready to steam by rail out of Saltville. The only identified person is G. W. Francisco, at far right. With several industries in the area, Saltville was a major stop for the railroad. The section connecting to Glade Spring was called the Salt Line. Plans are under way to convert that section to a bike/pedestrian trail similar to the Virginia Creeper Trail. (Courtesy Dorothy Johnson Kelly.)

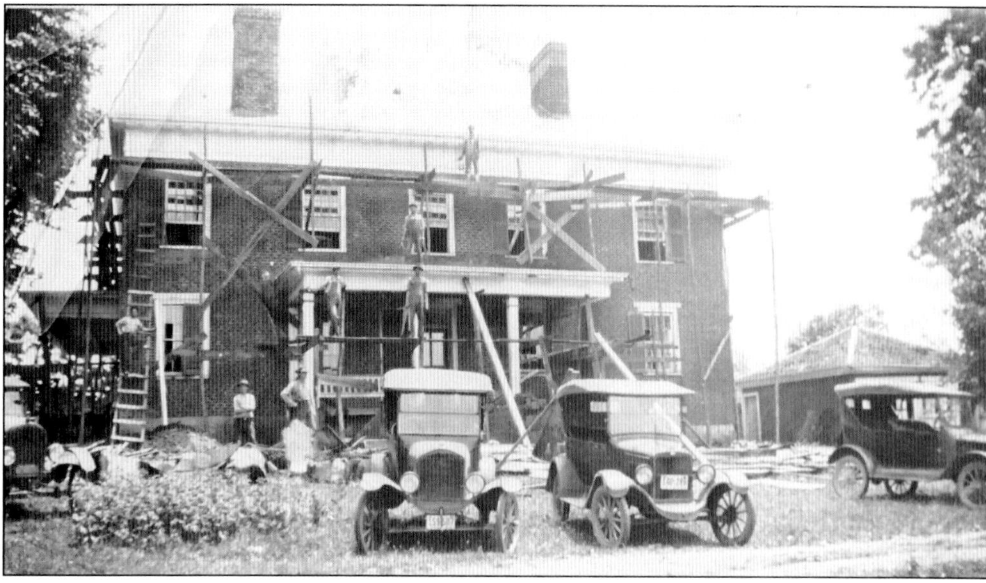

EMORY AND HENRY BUILDING. L. R. Johnson, a local builder, and his crew built many local structures, including this one, perhaps today's financial aid office on the Emory and Henry campus, about 1930. The simple scaffolding and handmade ladders show the challenges of building in the early days. (Courtesy Irene Johnson Meade.)

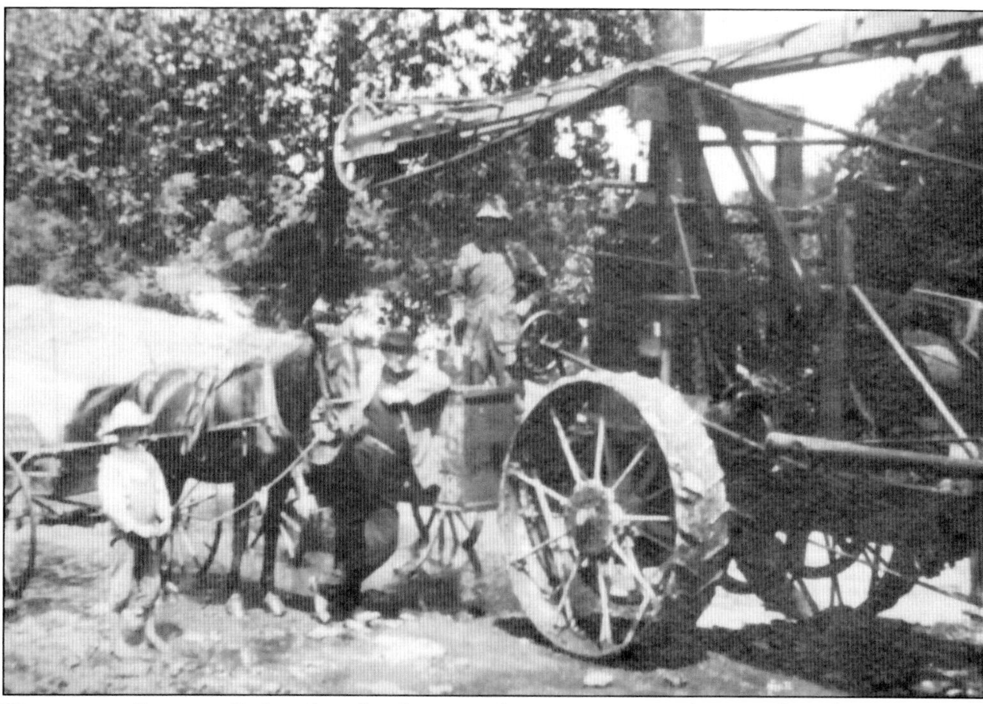

THRESHING ENGINE. Only a few threshing machines were privately owned in the community, and the owners would travel to farms to thresh the grains, or separate the grains from the straw, for a toll or cash payment. This machine replaced the hand flail to thresh oats, wheat, and other grains. The entire community would work together and help on one another's farms when the threshing machine arrived. (Courtesy Dorothy Johnson Kelly.)

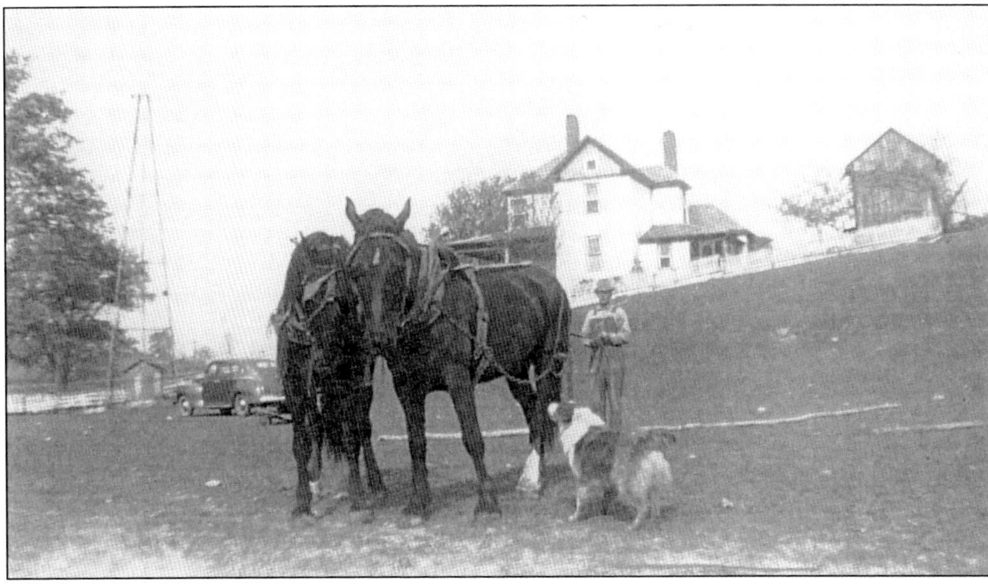

HORSE TEAM. Steward B. Copenhaver is holding the reins of two draft horses. Such horses were critical to farming before automated machines. The house of Steward and Goldie Neese Copenhaver, located on Rockspring Road in Lodi, is standing in the background. (Courtesy Susie Copenhaver Lang.)

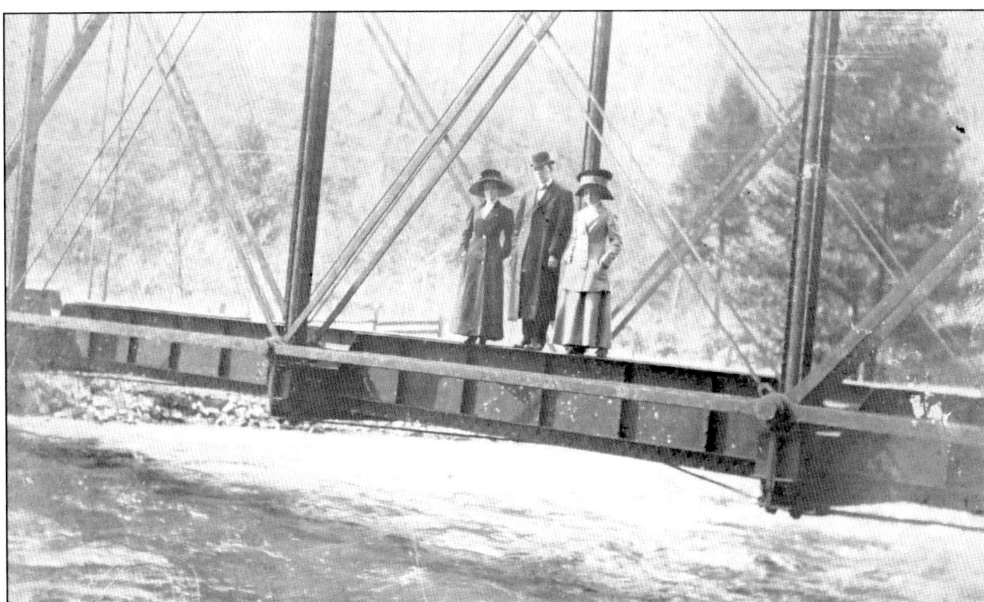

DAMASCUS BRIDGE. This dapper gentleman is posed with two ladies in fine hats on the heavy iron bridge in Damascus. Their dress indicates it is fall or winter here. These early bridges were attractive and functional, unlike the ones built today. (Courtesy Virginia Cornett Smith.)

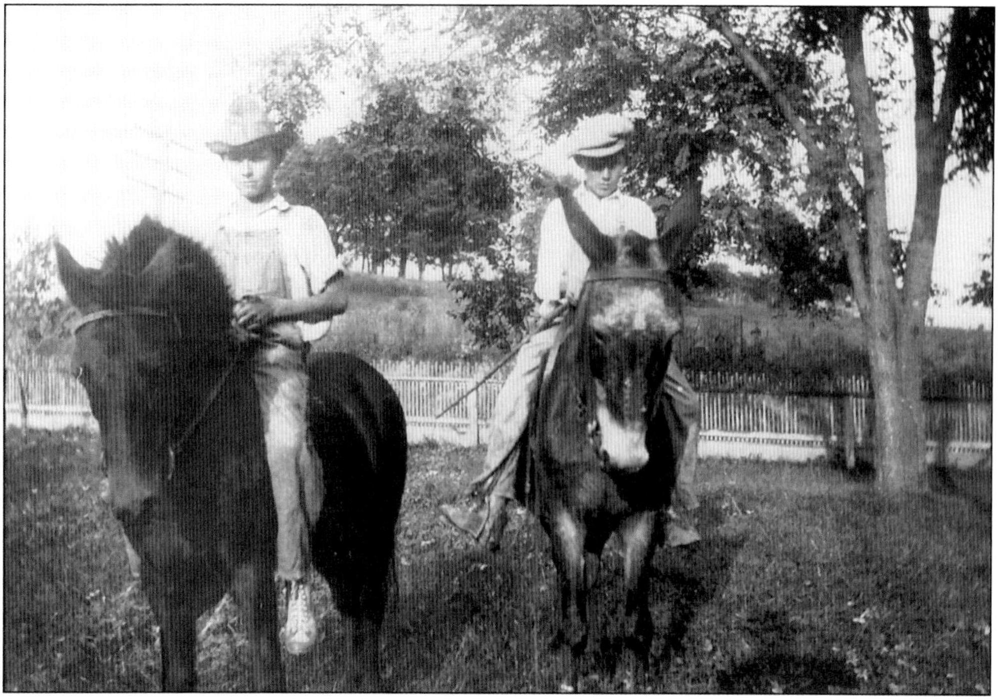

HORSING AROUND. Billy Megginson (left) and Eugene Gregory are riding a horse and mule, respectively, in the front yard of lovely historic Edmundson Hall outside Meadowview. The main road is behind the decorative fence. Megginson worked at the Abingdon Motor Company, and Gregory died when thrown from a horse. (Courtesy Judy Owens.)

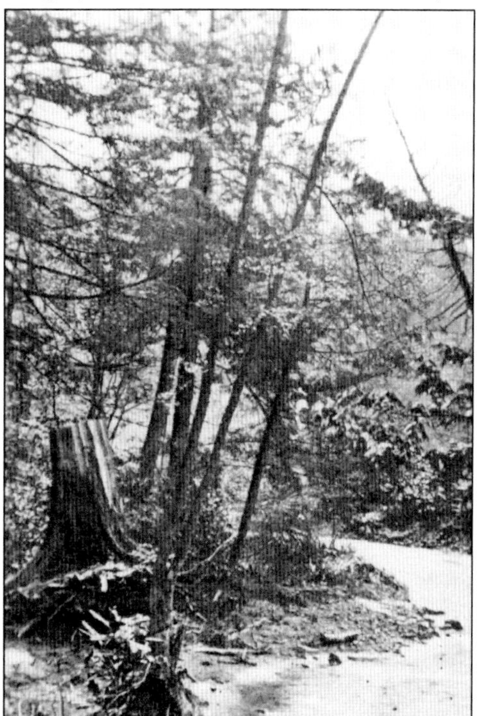

WHITETOP LAUREL. This scenic view of Whitetop Laurel in Konnarock was printed on an early postcard. The message on the back was written to Rebecca Ramsey in Damascus and reads, "Dear Sis, tell Mama that we shipped her chestnuts yesterday from Green Cove." Sadly the days of the chestnuts are gone. (Courtesy Virginia Cornett Smith.)

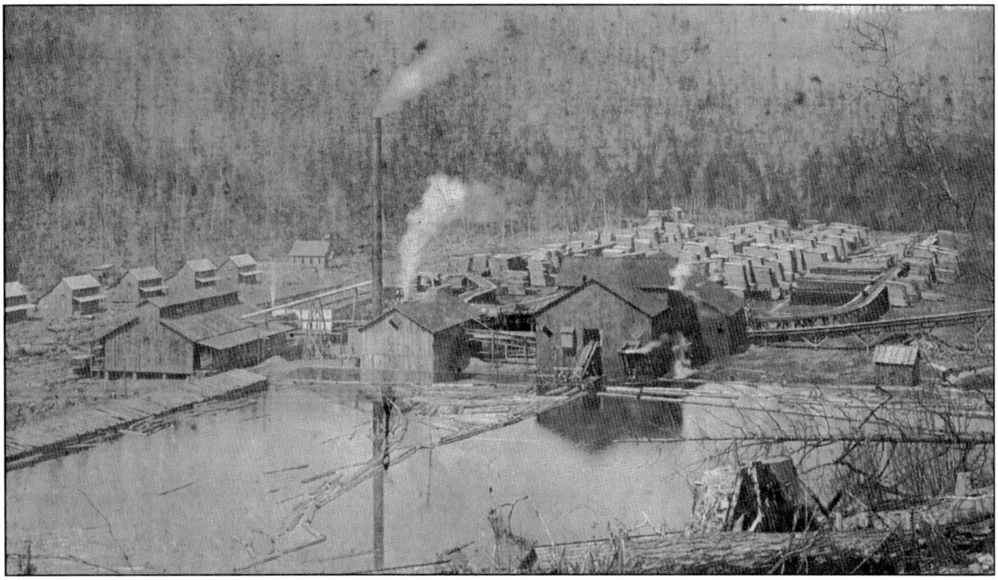

DOUGLAS LUMBER COMPANY. The Douglas Lumber Company of Damascus was the earliest one in the area. Douglas Robinson established the company in 1900 and built a sawmill on the Laurel River. Robinson lived in New York City, visited Damascus via private train cars, and brought his own servants. In 1901, the timber boom was in full swing, facilitated by the railroad connections. The boom lasted about 25 years, and at least 3.5 billion feet of lumber were shipped out of Washington County. (Courtesy Virginia Cornett Smith.)

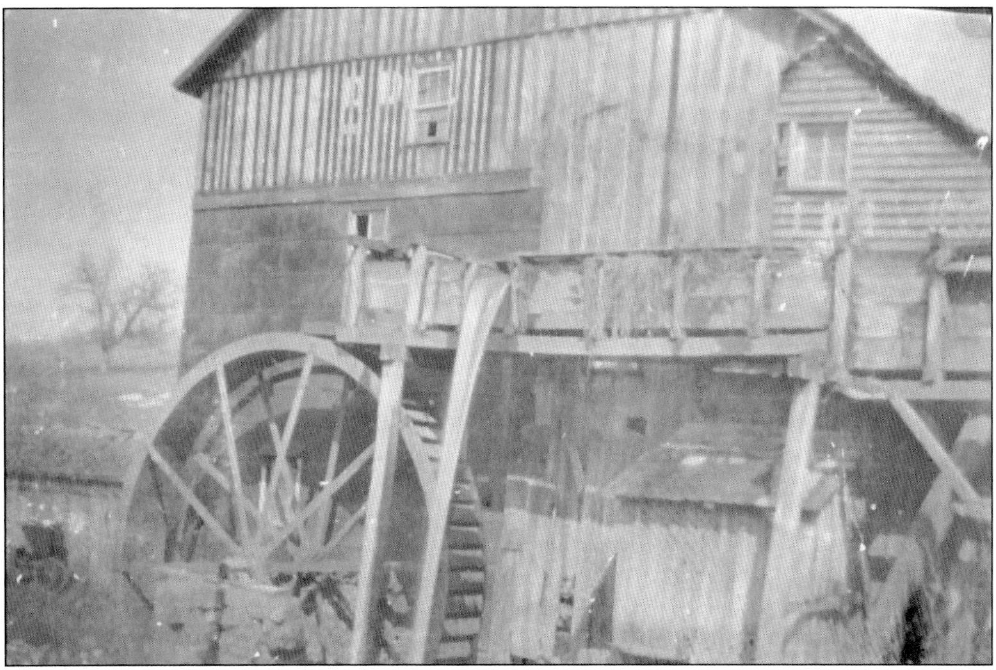

HASSINGER LUMBER COMPANY MILL. This lumber company mill was located in Konnarock, a company town founded in 1906. Konnarock included a hotel, the mill, a company store, and about 2,000 residents. After the trees were harvested, it became a peaceful residential community. (Courtesy Virginia Cornett Smith.)

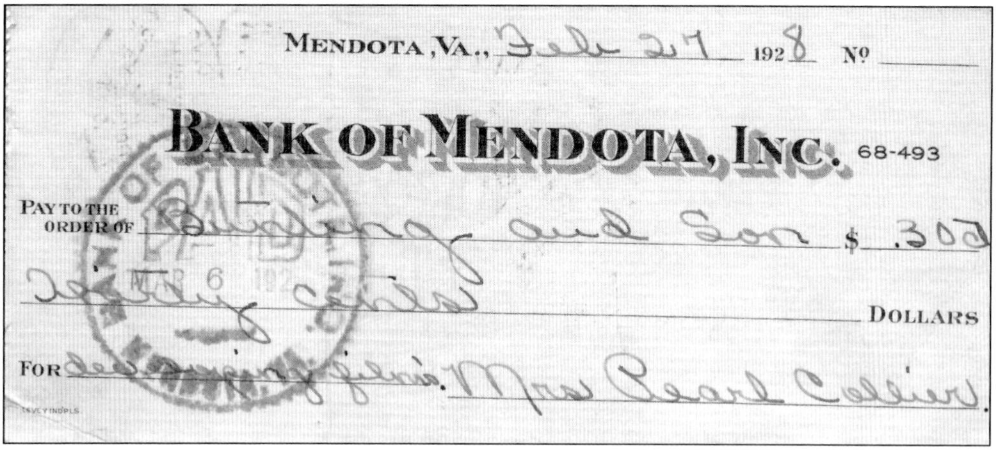
MENDOTA, VA., Feb 27 1928 No ______

BANK OF MENDOTA, INC. 68-493

PAY TO THE ORDER OF Bunting and Son $ .30

Thirty cents DOLLARS

FOR developing film. Mrs Pearl Collier

MENDOTA BANK. This check for 30¢ for film processing was written in 1928 by Pearl Collier from her account at Mendota Bank to Buntings Drug Store, a popular soda fountain and drugstore in Bristol. The brick Mendota bank building was located near S.R. 614 and S.R. 802, and it was also home to a post office and a doctor's office. In 1930, the bank went bankrupt. (Courtesy Terri Collier McCroskey.)

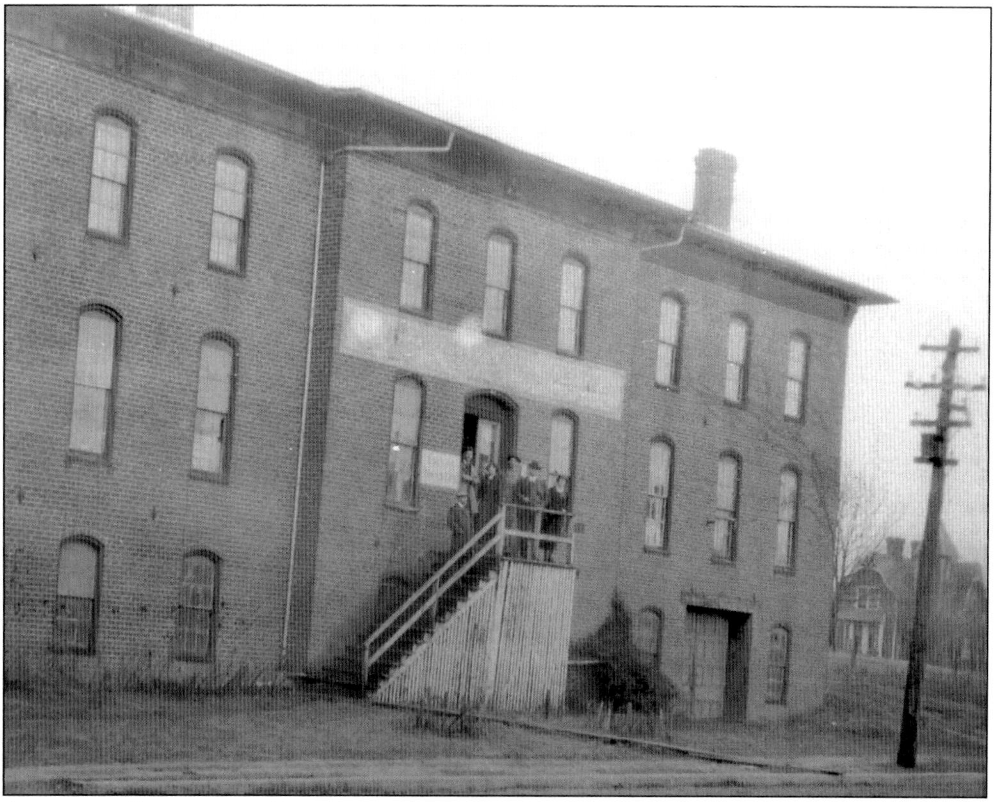

ABINGDON COMMERCIAL BUILDING. This early-1900s photograph shows a two-and-a-half-story brick commercial building in downtown Abingdon, possibly a building that was previously located at the corner of Russell Road and Valley Street. At the time of this picture, electric lines had been installed along the street, but a boardwalk, rather than a sidewalk, ran along the road. (Courtesy Lowry Bowman and Doug Patterson.)

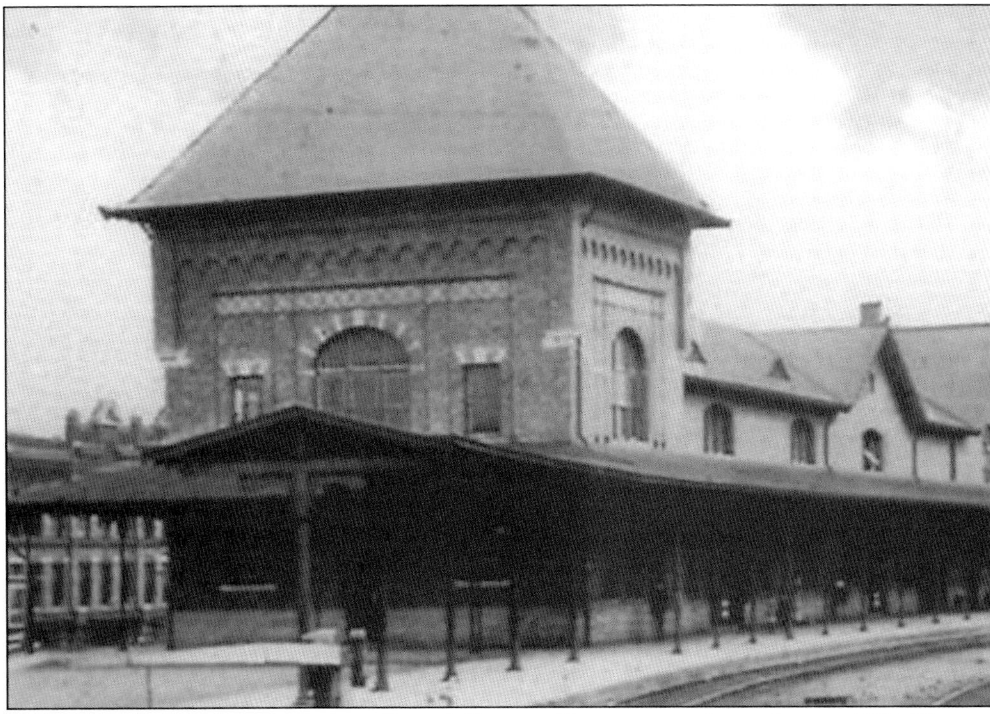

UNION STATION. Union Station in Bristol, Virginia/Tennessee, is shown here *c.* 1902. The city was a major stop for the railroad after it was connected in 1856, thus Bristol received a more ornate train station. Downtown used to be filled with shoppers and travelers to the hotels, stores, and restaurants in this major commercial center that spans two states. The 60-foot-wide sign reading "Bristol Va-Tenn: A Good Place to Live" still spans the state line as it has since 1915. The Train Station Foundation is working to restore this lovely landmark. The Bristol Main Street program has accomplished much to add new life to State Street. (Courtesy Jeffrey Weaver.)

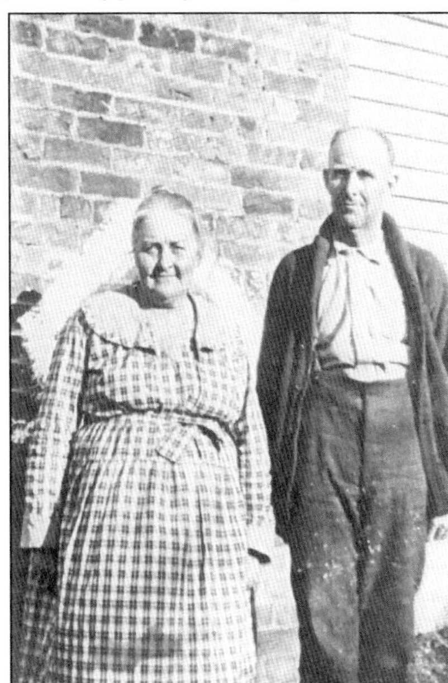

HELTON FAMILY. Lilburn and Mary Scott Helton from the Blackwell Chapel community are pictured here around the 1920s. Both the Heltons and the Scotts were early settlers in the region. The Helton name is derived from the Hylton name that is traced back to the early 1700s in eastern Virginia. (Courtesy Tammy Martin.)

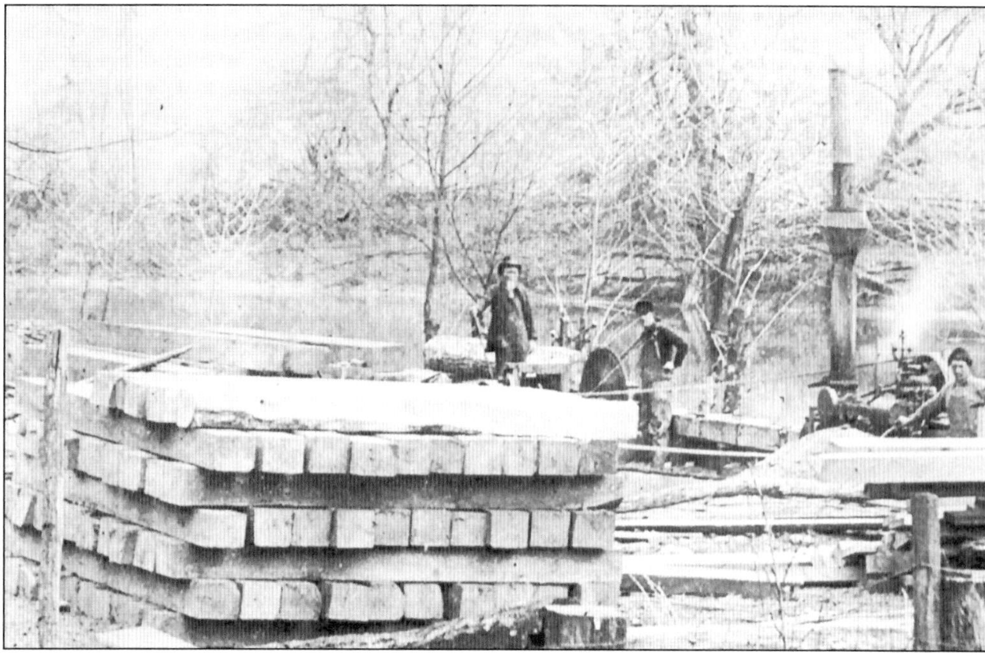

Snodgrass Sawmill. Pictured is the Snodgrass sawmill, which was located close to the North Fork of the Holston River beside Riverbend School in scenic Hayter's Gap. C. W. Snodgrass first operated the mill, and then his son Jack ran the sawmill. Many small communities operated their own sawmills, often associated with a gristmill. (Courtesy Lois Snodgrass Shupe.)

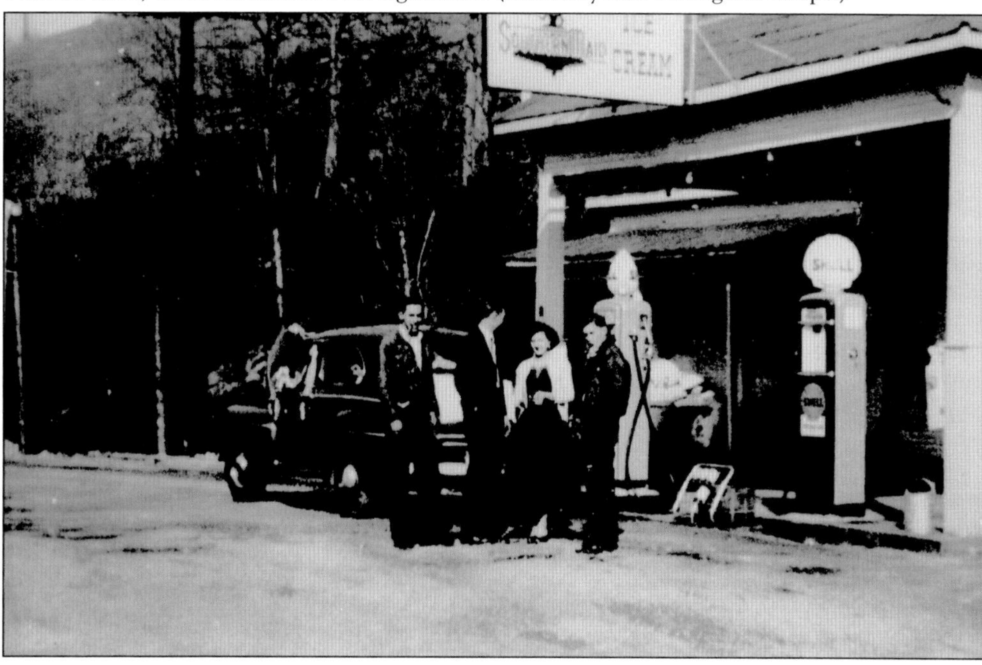

Greendale Shell Station, c. 1940. Pictured are two unidentified men flanking the couple in the middle, Dave Robinette and Kate Colston Robinette. They are posed in front of a 1937 Ford. At that time, five gallons of gasoline might cost $1. Neighborhood service stations were favorite community gathering places. (Courtesy Roger Brannon.)

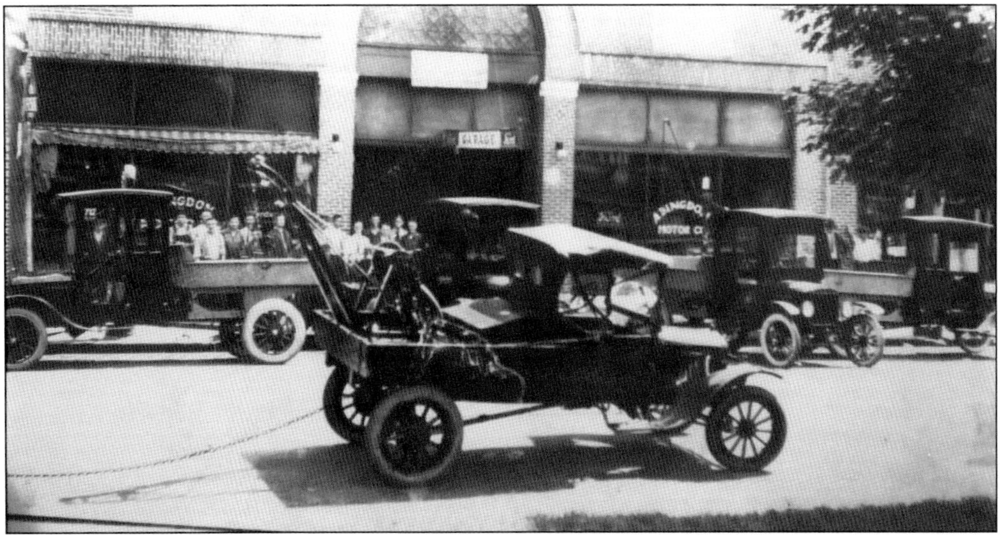

ABINGDON MOTOR COMPANY, C. 1920. The Abingdon Motor Company and garage was a popular location on the west end of downtown Abingdon's Main Street. William M. and J. T. McConnell were the owners and operators. An early tow truck is pictured in front of the building. (Courtesy Lowry Bowman.)

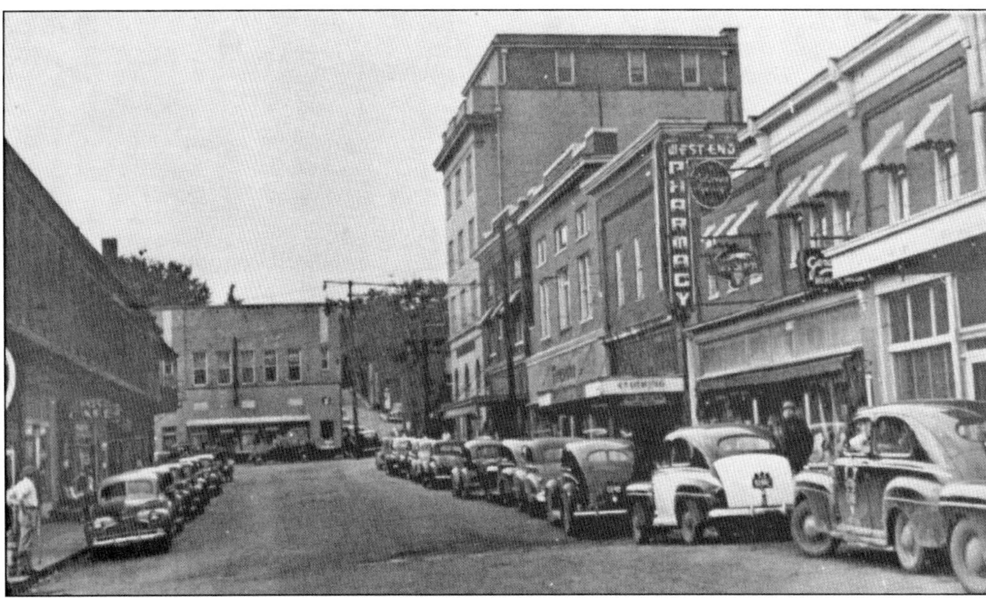

WALL STREET. This 1939 Wall Street scene of downtown Abingdon is typically crowded. A clothing store, the West End Pharmacy, and a beauty salon can be seen on the signs. A restaurant, the Belmont Hotel, pool halls, and the train station added to the busy commercial and entertainment street. Residents say Wall Street was once like the Wild West, with gambling, bars, and even gunfights. (Courtesy Walter B. "Blair" Keller Jr.)

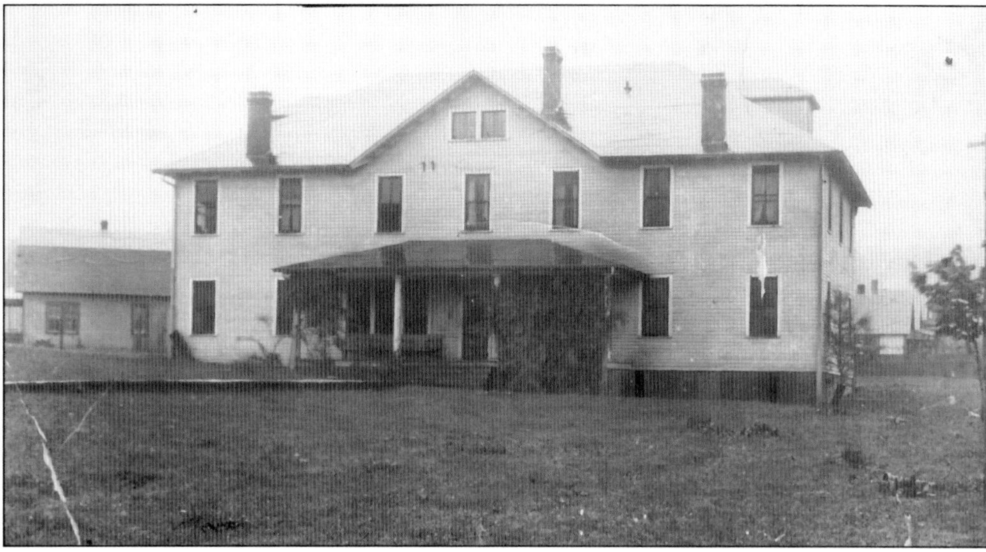

HOLSTON LUMBER COMPANY HOTEL. The Holston River Lumber Company hotel, located in Clinchburg, is shown in this photograph from about 1920. The lumber company provided income for area residents but left when the timber supply was exhausted. (Courtesy Roy Rector.)

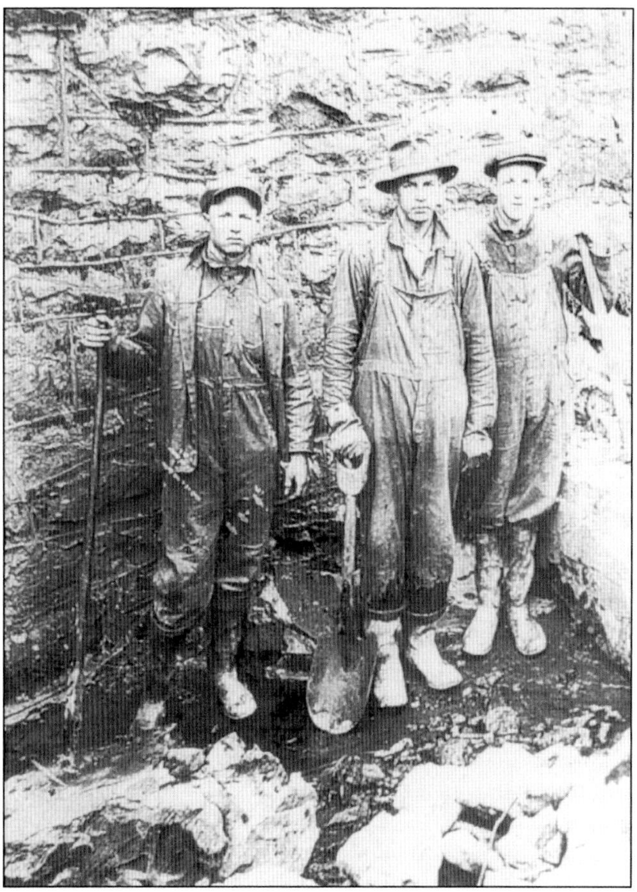

COAL MINERS. Even as early as the 1900s, many men from the region traveled to West Virginia to earn a living in the coal mines and send the money back home. On the left is James Newton Stovall, a Washington County native, standing with two unidentified men in a mine in Baileywood, West Virginia. (Courtesy Ruby Stovall Clark.)

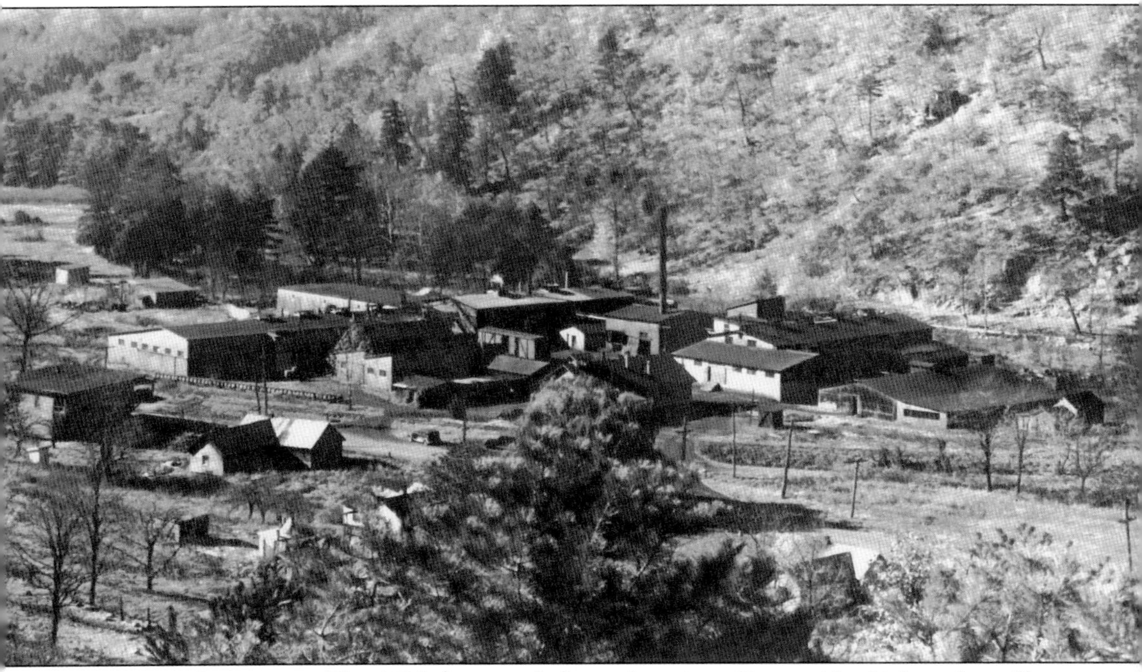

AMERICAN CYANAMID. This 1936 photograph shows American Cyanamid, which made artillery shells in the 1930s, just outside Damascus. First formed in 1902, the Acme Bark-Extract Company processed chestnut bark into tannin extract. In 1905, the Smethport Extract Company was founded by Clarence A. Backer and bought out Acme. Backer expanded it into a large manufacturing enterprise, selling bark extracts. The Backers were major supporters in Damascus and were instrumental in the planning and building of the Damascus School. For many years, the Backers provided a college scholarship to a high-achieving high school senior. Chestnut trees were gone by the mid-1920s, and Smethport was purchased by the Meade Corporation, John H. Heald Division, and later by the American Cyanamid Company. Even today, that section of Damascus is known as "the Extract." (Courtesy Roger Brannon.)

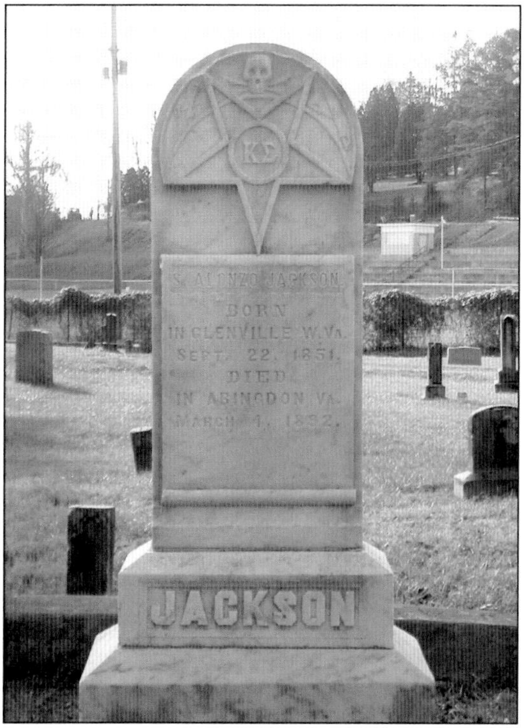

STEPHEN ALONZO JACKSON (1851–1892). Jackson, a local merchant who attended Emory and Henry College in 1868 before transferring to the University of Virginia, is credited as the national leader for restructuring and expanding Kappa Sigma Fraternity. Jackson married Mary Cloyd Ernest at Brook Hall near Glade Spring and they lived at 102 East Main Street, formerly the Silversmith Inn, until his untimely death in 1892. He is buried at historic Sinking Spring Cemetery in Abingdon. (Courtesy Garrett Jackson.)

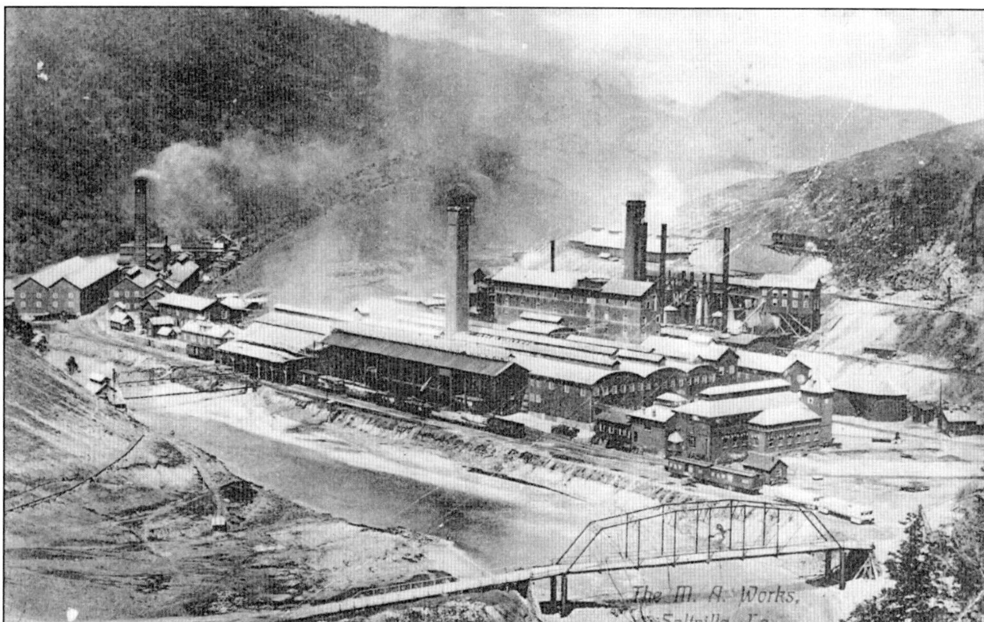

M. A. WORKS. The Mathieson Alkali Works salt and plaster company bought out the Holston Salt and Plaster Company in 1892. The saltworks of Saltville have been in business since the Civil War and were owned by George Palmer, Benjamin Buchanan, William A. Stuart, and others. The company merged with Olin Corporation in the 1950s and was later called Olin-Mathieson. The factory provided many jobs, and its closing in 1970 hurt the local economy. (Courtesy Virginia Cornett Smith.)

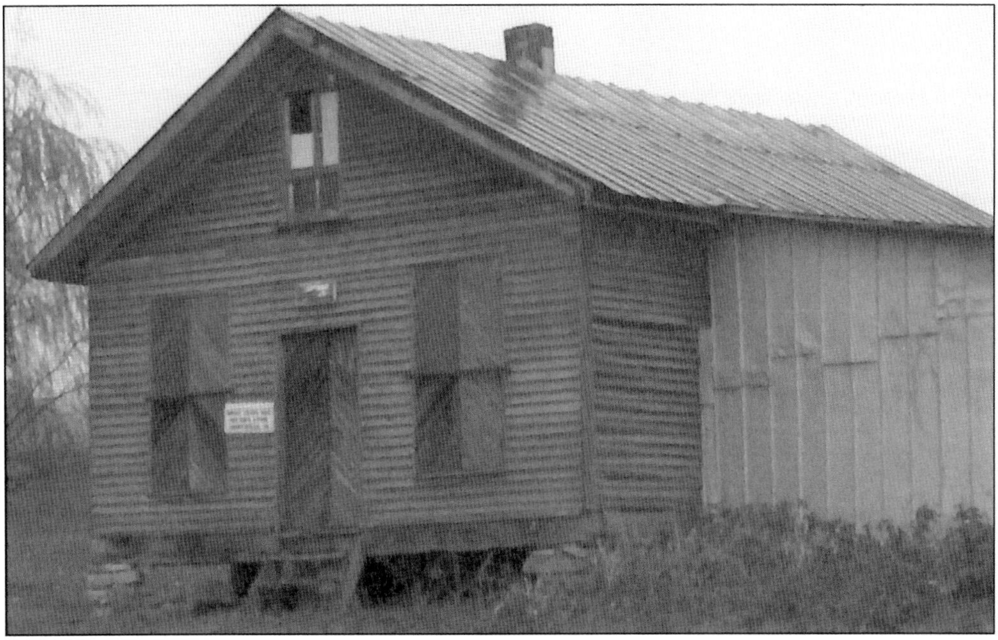

HAYTER'S STORE. This building was once the busy Hayter's Store, built at Shortsville on the busy intersection of S.R. 741/Maiden Creek Road and S.R. 703/Shortsville Road. Shortsville was named for Americus D. Lafayette Shortt, a local butcher, tanner, and postmaster here in 1886. (Courtesy Owen August Warmuth.)

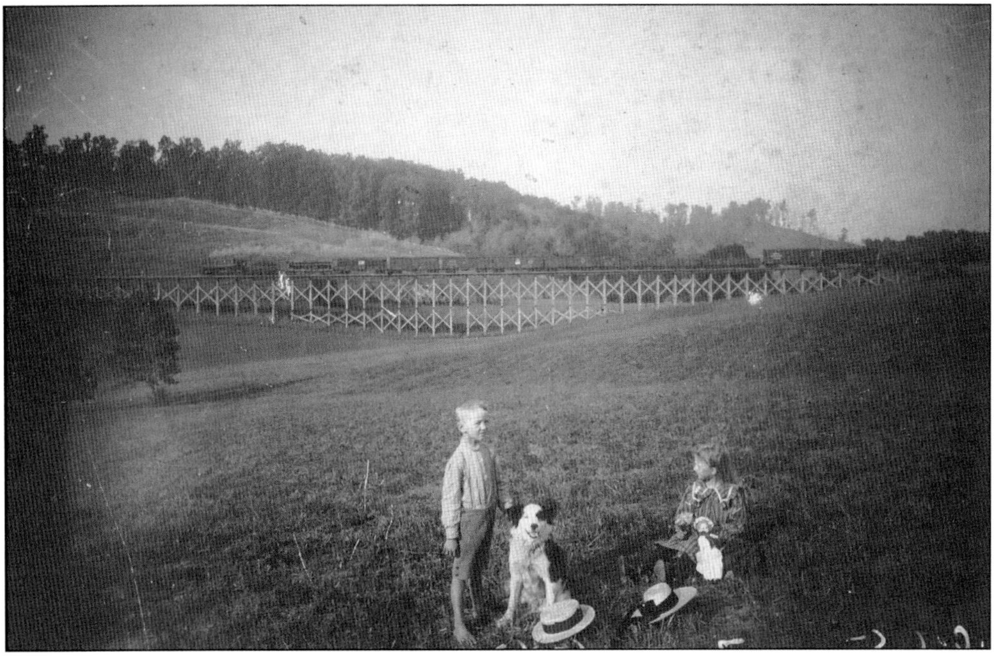

WATCHING THE TRAIN. Walter Blair Keller Sr. and Naomi Keller are sitting with hats off to watch the Norfolk and Western train steam by their family farm. The railroad line is now the Virginia Creeper Trail, offering a pedestrian and bike path for many folks to enjoy. The trestle looks much the same today as it does in this photograph. (Courtesy Walter B. "Blair" Keller Jr.)

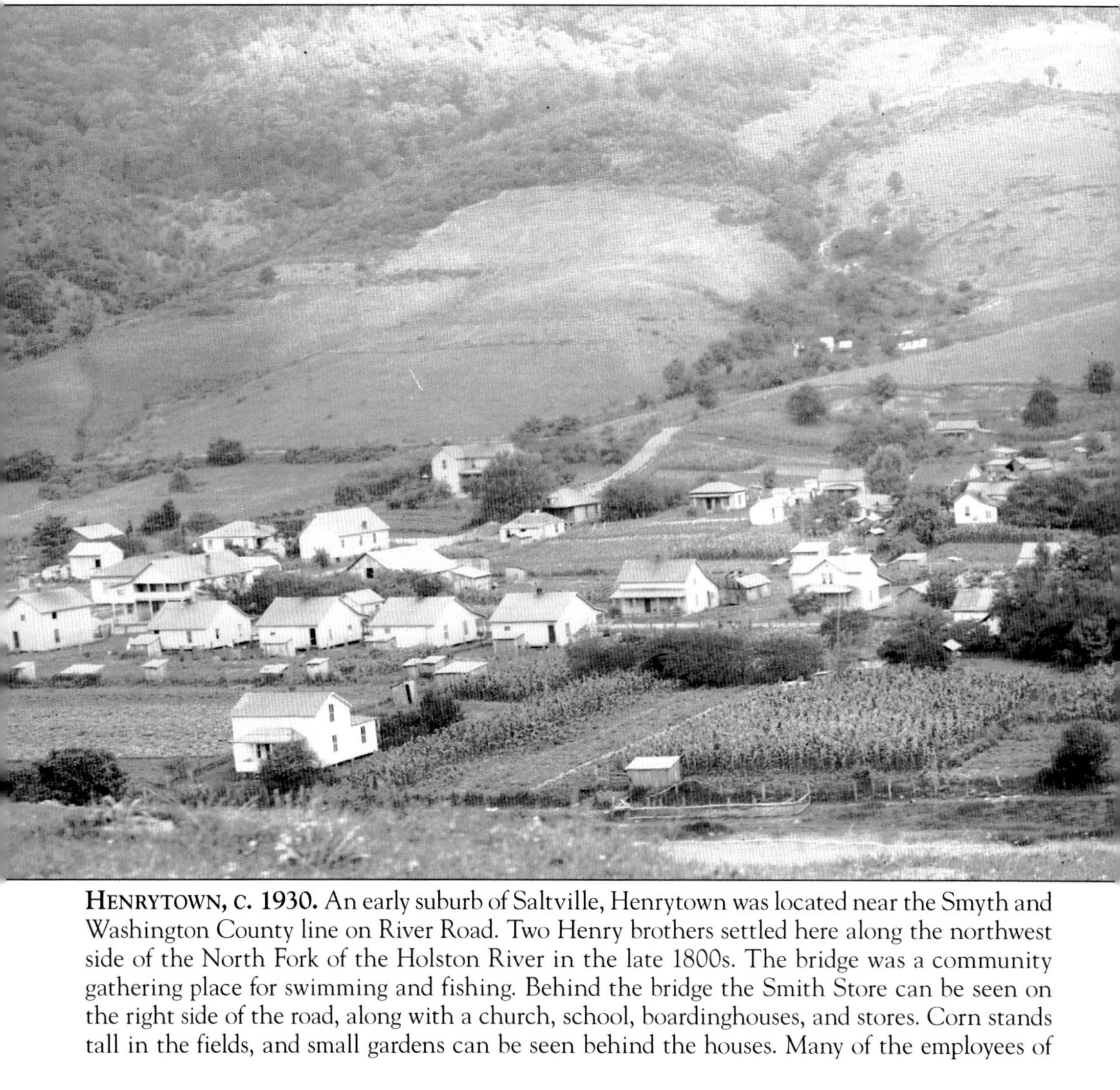

HENRYTOWN, C. 1930. An early suburb of Saltville, Henrytown was located near the Smyth and Washington County line on River Road. Two Henry brothers settled here along the northwest side of the North Fork of the Holston River in the late 1800s. The bridge was a community gathering place for swimming and fishing. Behind the bridge the Smith Store can be seen on the right side of the road, along with a church, school, boardinghouses, and stores. Corn stands tall in the fields, and small gardens can be seen behind the houses. Many of the employees of

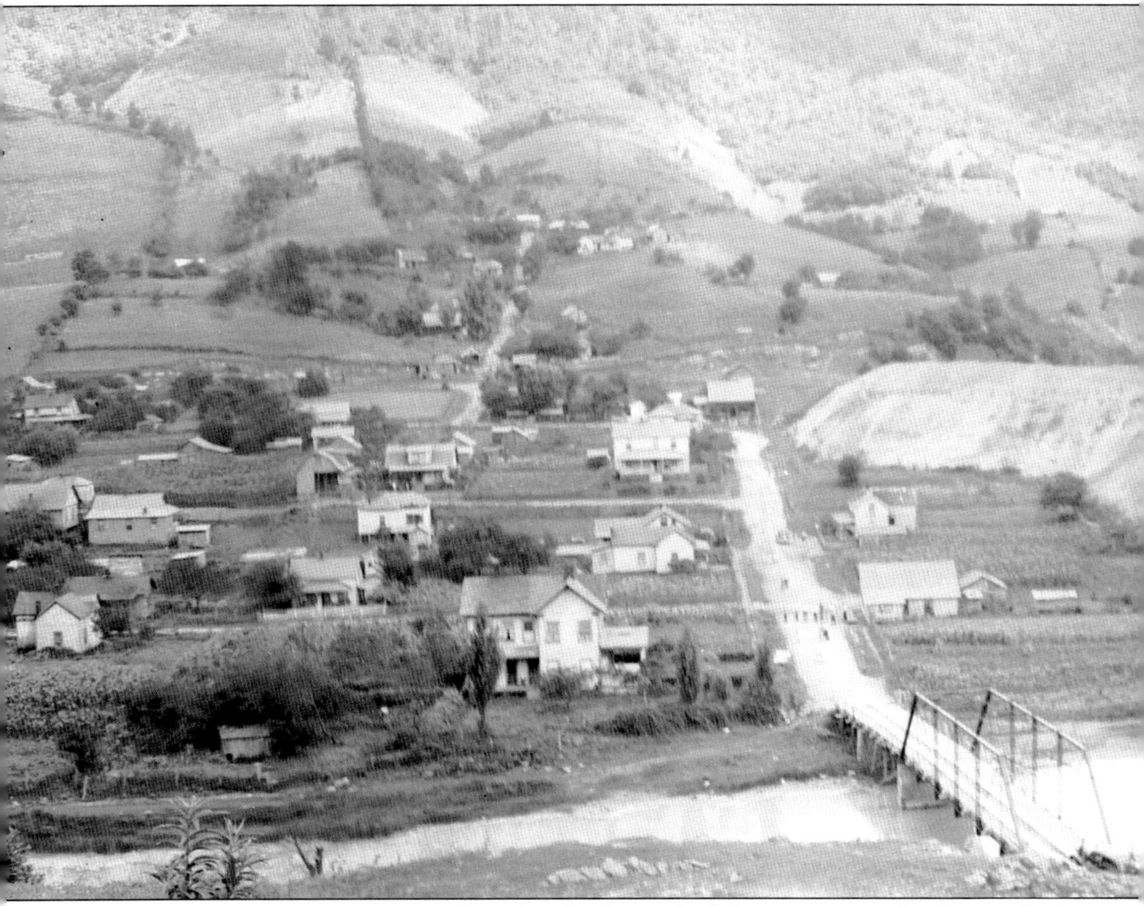

Mathieson Alkali lived here, and without local police, it had the reputation of a place to find trouble. By 1963, Henrytown lay buried beneath a sludge holding pond, a "muck dam" (right), that was expanded by Mathieson (later Olin-Mathieson). The re-established Henrytown now is located southeast of the river. Many small communities like Henrytown have grown and died in this area because of the industry, logging, and railroads that have since disappeared from the landscape. (Courtesy MOMA.)

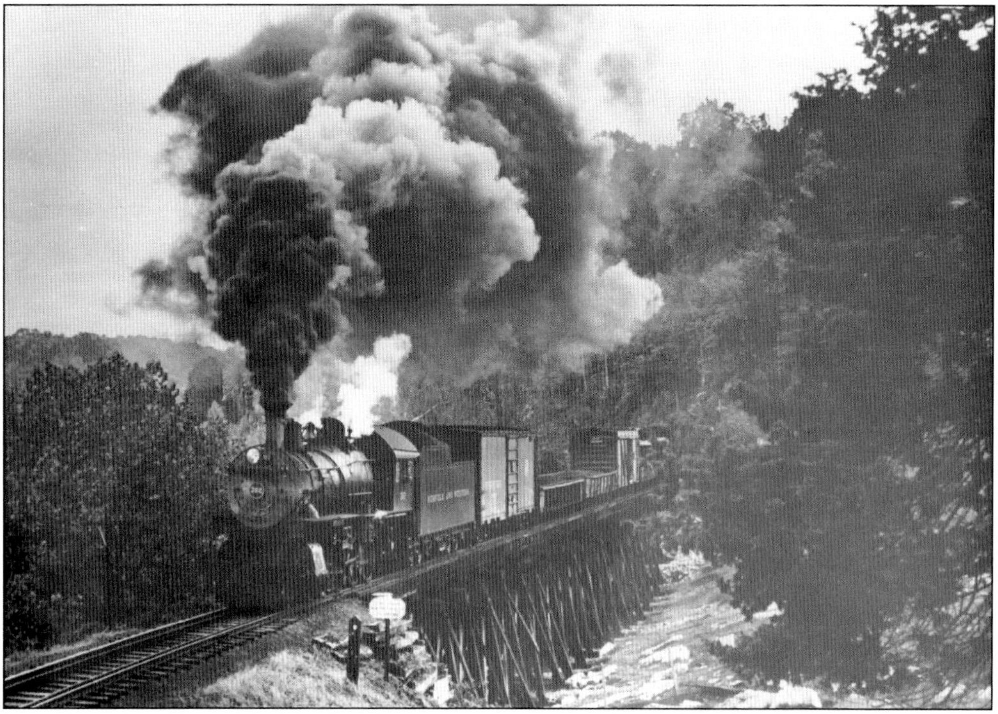

CROSSING A TRESTLE. Engine No. 382 with the Norfolk and Western Railway is steaming across a trestle in the area. Once a common sight and sound along the railroad, these iron horses were brief visitors on the landscape. The end of the logging industry in Washington County caused the end of the rail as a major transportation mode in the area. (Courtesy Virginia Cornett Smith.)

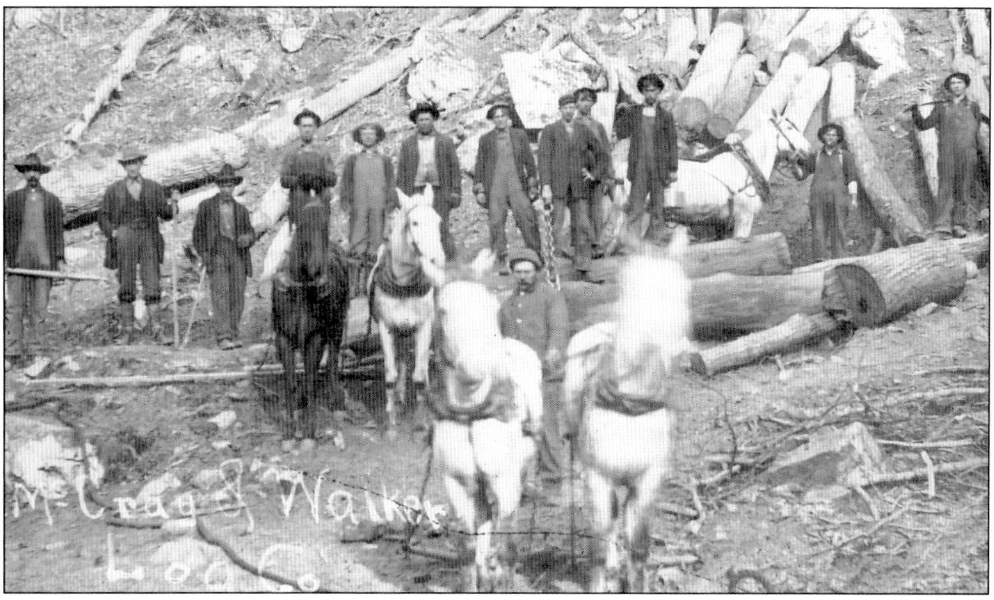

MCCRAY AND WALKER LOGGING COMPANY. The logging company of McCray and Walker was located in the Tumbling Cove area. This c. 1930 photograph shows the workers. The only people identified are Rufus McCray (1851–1926), third from left, and Jasper McCray (1891–1974), seventh from left. (Courtesy Troy Taylor.)

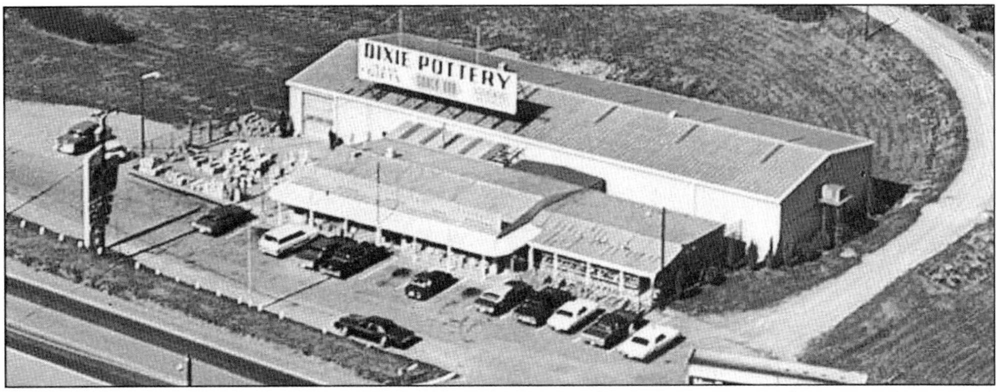

Dixie Pottery. This *c.* 1960 postcard of Dixie Pottery shows a major retail store of the region. The company was an early importer of goods and a major shopping destination when imported items were difficult to find. The store remains a popular commercial destination in the region. (Courtesy Jeff Weaver.)

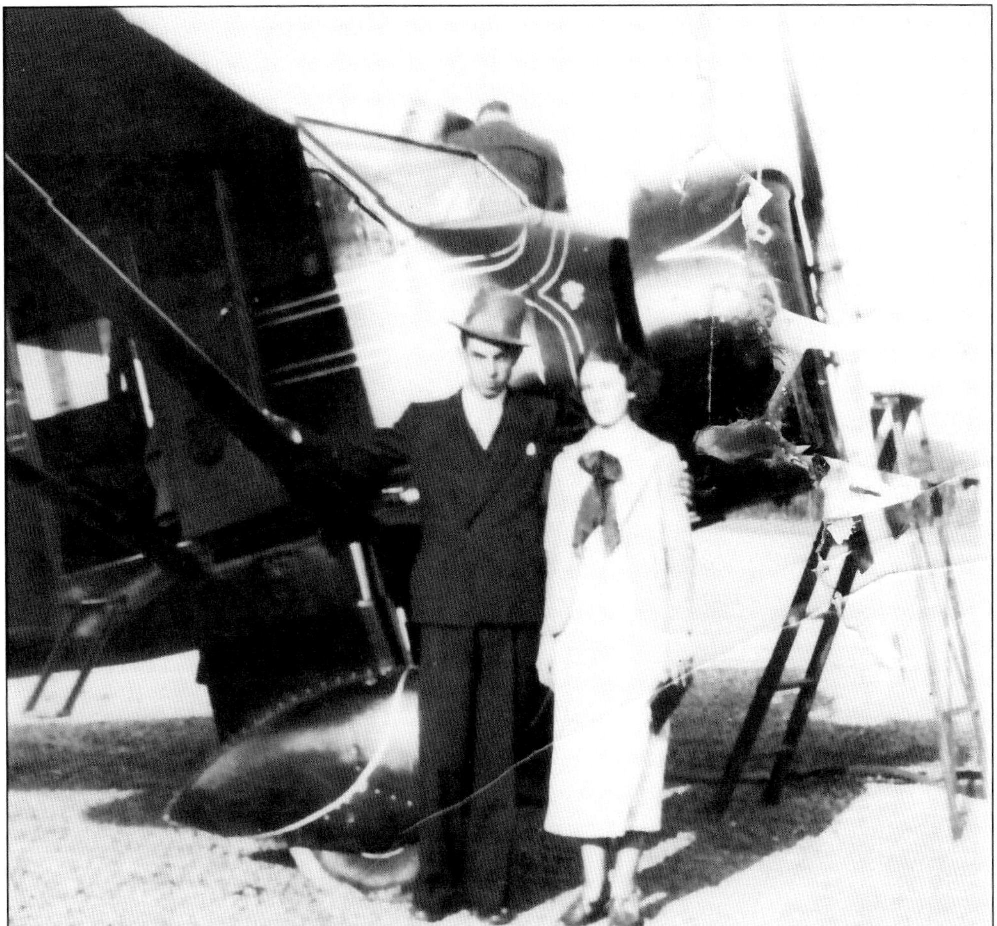

Flying Taylors. Stuart Taylor (1915–2006), of the River Hills area near Lindell, is posed with his cousin Mattie Ann Taylor alongside an airplane in 1937. Planes were a rare sight in the area at that time. (Courtesy Troy Taylor.)

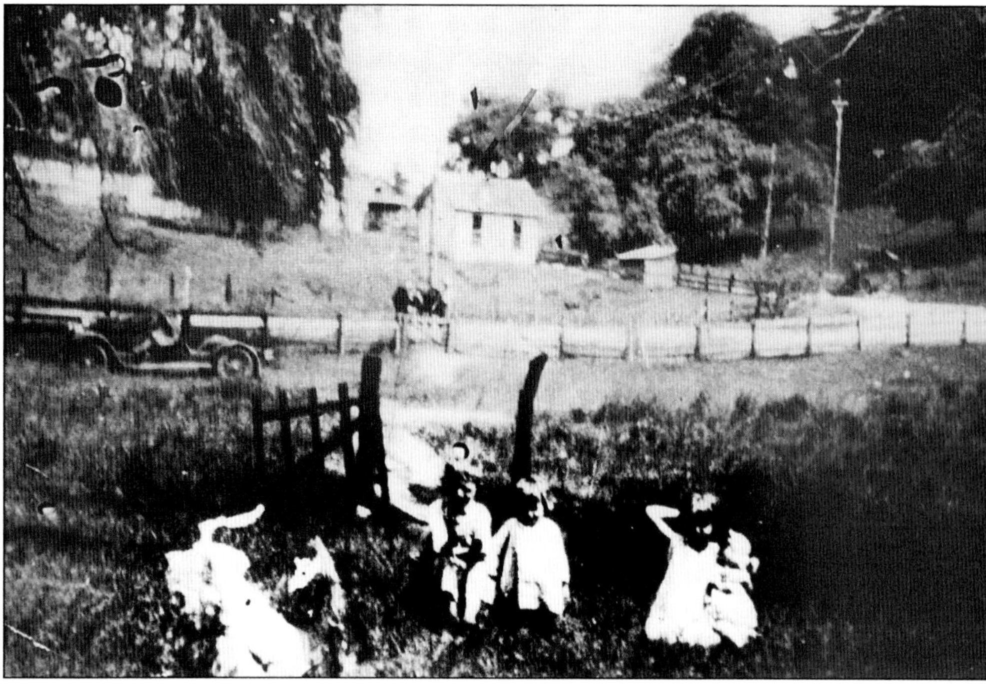

Lodi Post Office. The Lodi Post Office building is marked on this photograph. It was established in 1877 just west of Rock Springs Church on the Blue Springs Road. Alfred W. Speer was the first postmaster. About 1900, it was moved to the home of Speer. The children, the horse, and the old car recall the bygone days. (Courtesy Evelyn McThenia Hale.)

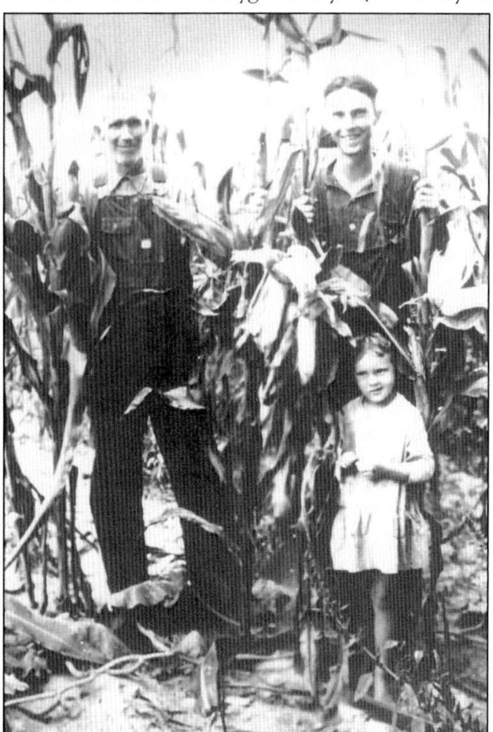

Cornfield. Isaac Newton McCall, his son John Andrew McCall, and daughter Margaret McCall are standing among a tall corn crop in this c. 1930 photograph. Corn was a staple of residents' diets and was also livestock food. (Courtesy Susie Copenhaver Lang.)

Five

Friends, Families, and Home

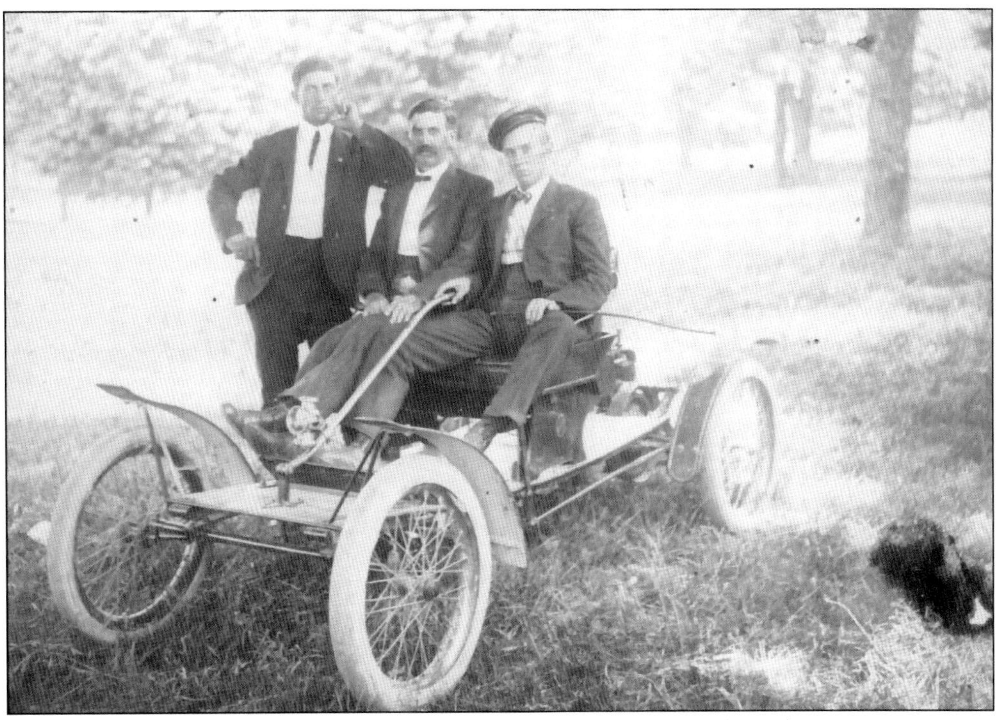

Runabout in Hayter's Gap. Pictured riding in this early runabout from the Hayter's Gap area are, from left to right, Arvil Crabtree, Sam Helton, and possibly Coy M. Helton at the wheel. Sam's driving cap adds a note of seriousness to this friendly outing. (Courtesy Troy Taylor.)

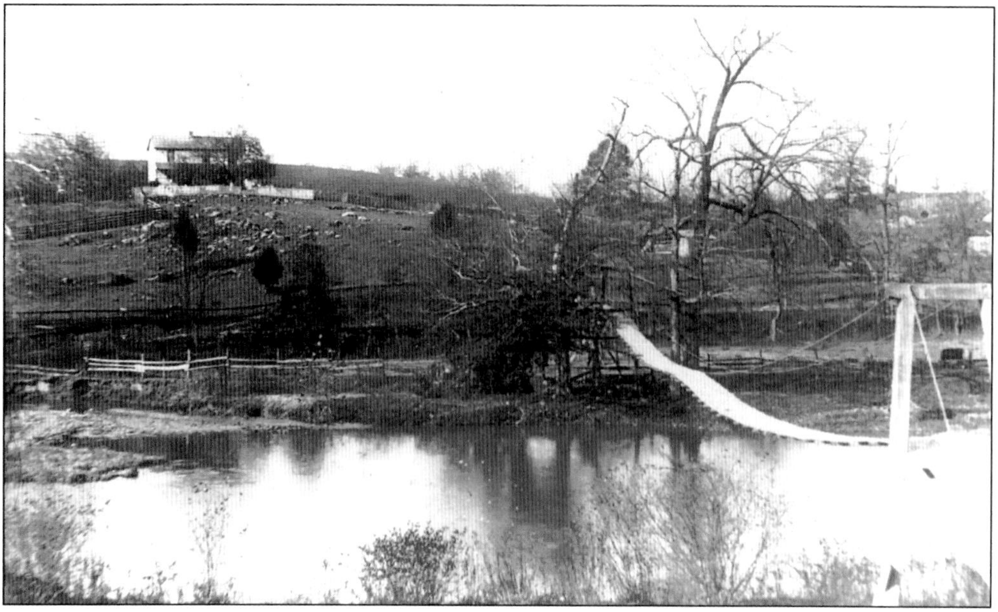

BUCHANAN HOME PLACE. A bridge swung for many years across the South Fork of the Holston River just above Rush Creek to connect the Buchanan family to the South Fork River Road. William Russell Buchanan and his wife, Martha Ann Snodgrass Buchanan, had the house built about 1873. Buchanan was a Civil War veteran and a mail carrier. In the bottom photograph, members of the Buchanan family are posed outside the home place. The house was a simple I-house vernacular style and served the family for many years. (Courtesy Susie Copenhaver Lang.)

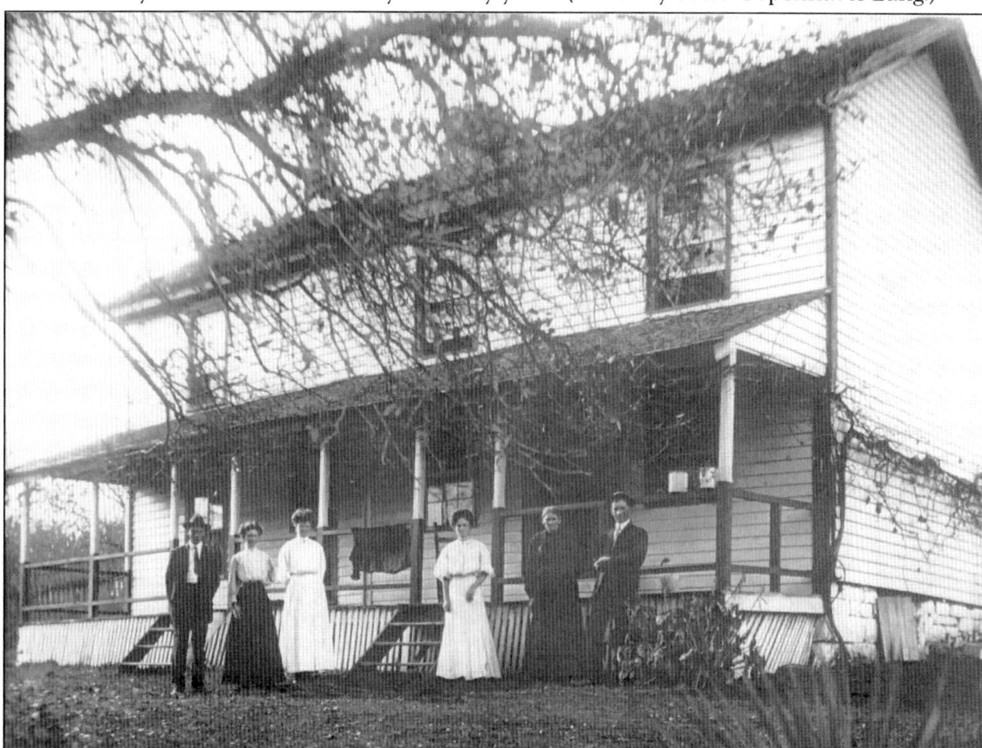

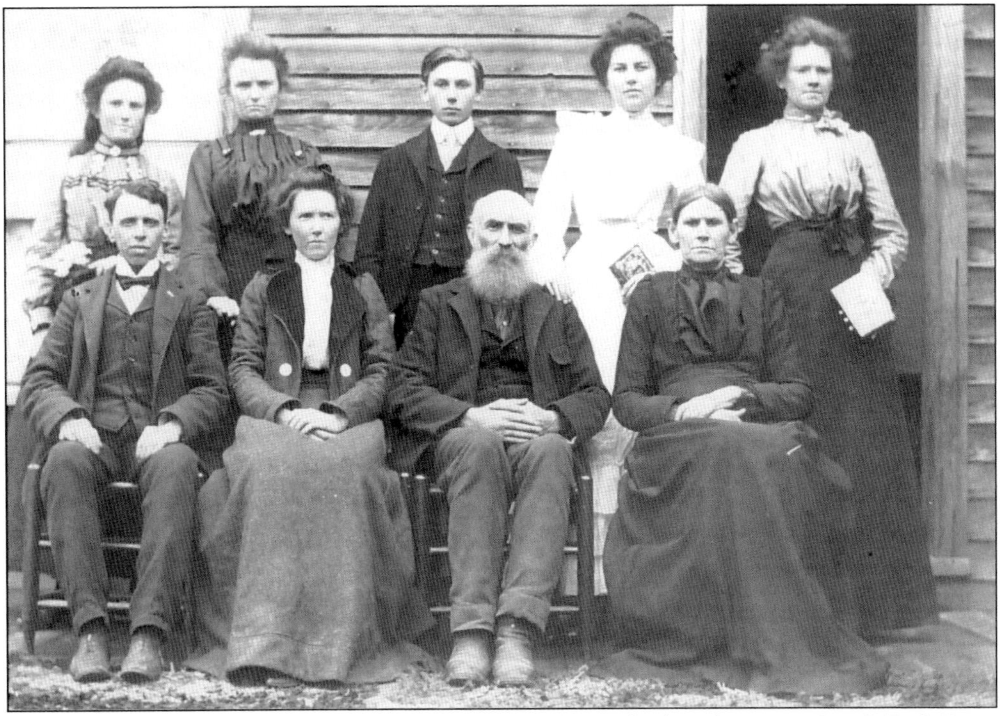

BUCHANAN FAMILY. The Buchanan family is seated outside their home on South Fork River Road. From left to right are (seated) Jim Parker, Annie Buchanan Parker, William R. Buchanan, and Martha Ann Snodgrass Buchanan; (standing) children Rhea, Edna, Grover, Kate, and Laura Buchanan. Note that several of the ladies are holding Bibles. William Buchanan was a Civil War veteran and local mail carrier. (Courtesy Susie Copenhaver Lang.)

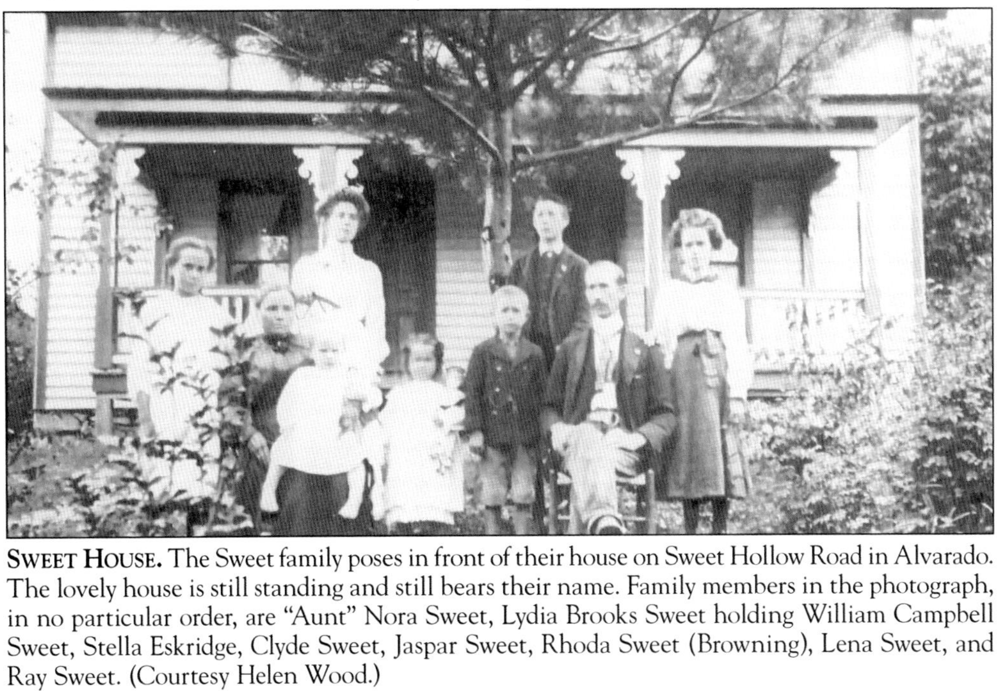

SWEET HOUSE. The Sweet family poses in front of their house on Sweet Hollow Road in Alvarado. The lovely house is still standing and still bears their name. Family members in the photograph, in no particular order, are "Aunt" Nora Sweet, Lydia Brooks Sweet holding William Campbell Sweet, Stella Eskridge, Clyde Sweet, Jaspar Sweet, Rhoda Sweet (Browning), Lena Sweet, and Ray Sweet. (Courtesy Helen Wood.)

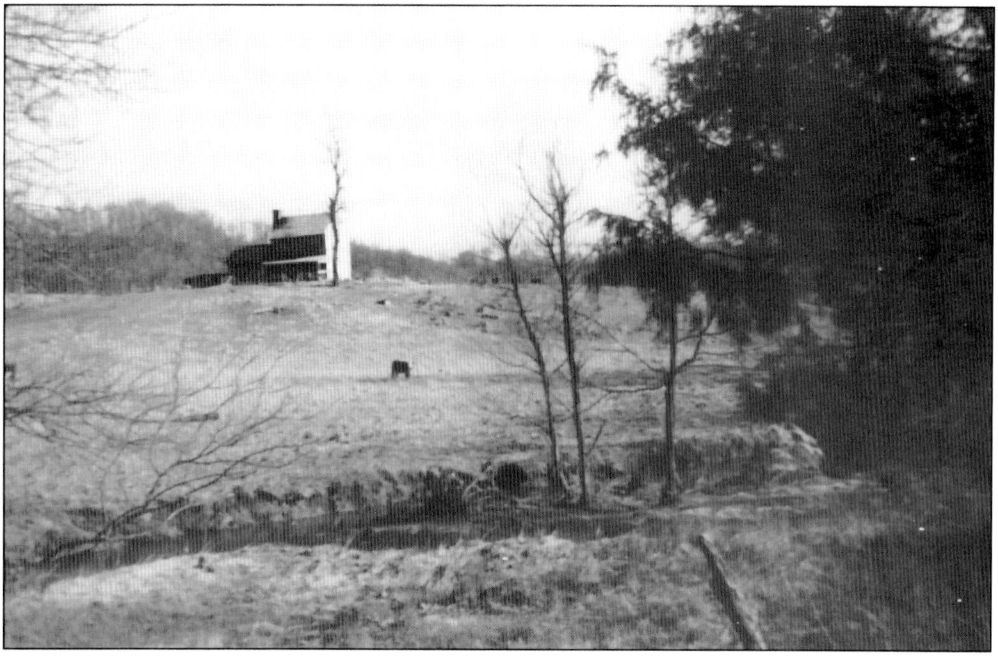

Snodgrass Cabin and Fort. This pre–Revolutionary War log cabin was built by David Snodgrass in 1774. Located off S.R. 736, the house reportedly served as a fort for protection against Native Americans in the late 1700s and then later became a residence. This unique house is one of the last remaining of the nine forts in Washington and Smyth Counties along the Holston River. In the recent photograph below, an addition can be seen constructed on the left of the cabin. Fortunately the owners tried to match the architectural style of the building, and much of the original integrity of this rare cabin/fort remains. Although outfitted with modern conveniences, the interior of the house, with its large fireplace, still seems from the past. (Above courtesy Linda Orfield Crane; below courtesy the author.)

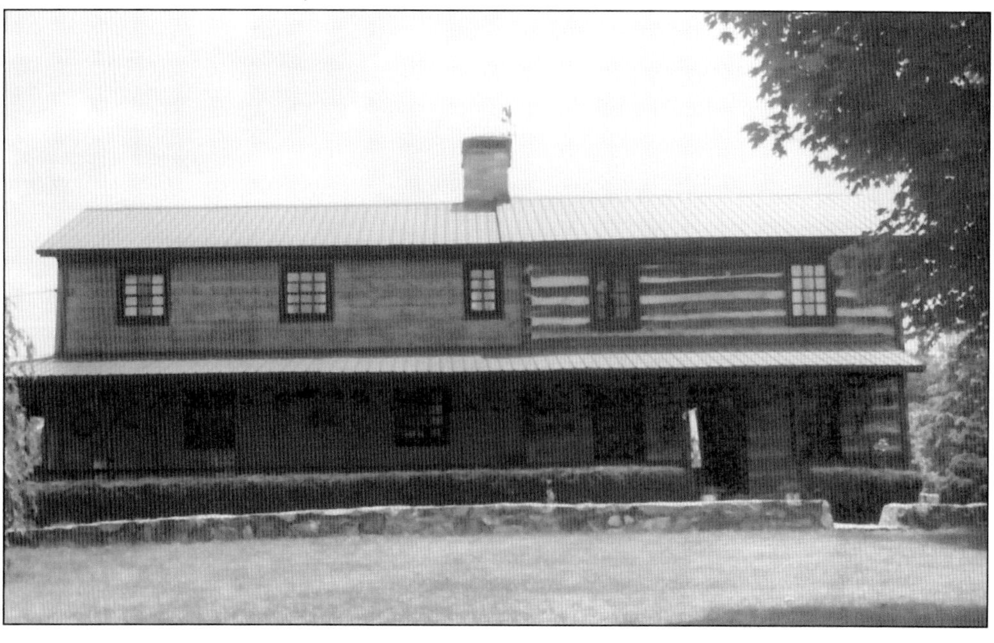

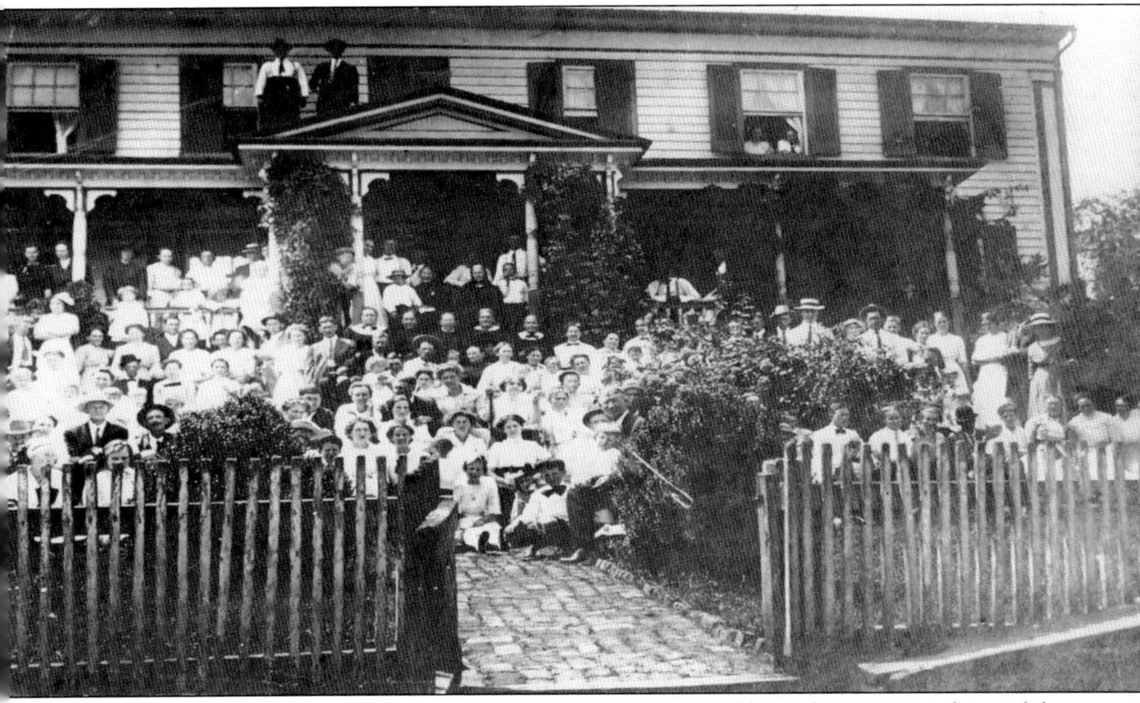

DUFF REUNION. The Duff family and descendants are gathered here about 1910 in front of the well-known Duff House in Alvarado. The Duff family can be traced back to the earliest settlers in the county. This residence was built for Capt. William Duff, who owned 400 acres along the Holston River as early as 1785. A town named Carrickfurgus was planned for this location with a plat showing lots, churches, and a school, but it was never developed. Locals call the house the Alvarado Hotel, since loggers employed by Hassinger Lumber Company were boarders there in the early 1900s. This historic house is still standing, and its historic character has been well preserved by caring owners through the years. (Courtesy Virginia Cornett Smith.)

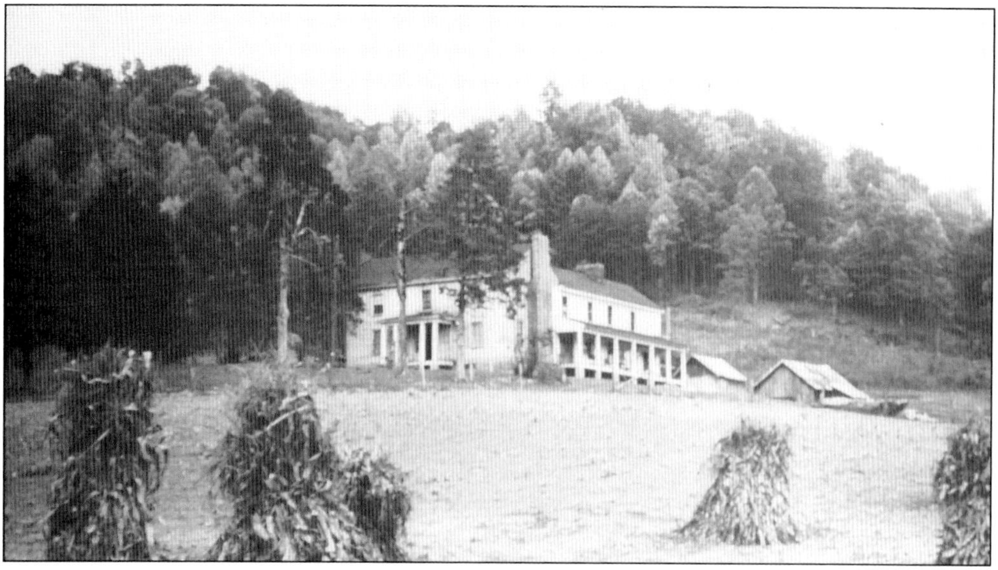

JAMESON-HAYTER HOUSE. This lovely frame house still stands on S.R. 700 near Toole's Creek Road. The original section likely dates to the late 1700s, and it was renovated and restored about 1950 by the Price family. It was originally owned by the Thomas Jameson family, whose farm included many acres in Rich Valley as well as White's Mill. Connie and Mark Simcox live in this house and farm the surrounding land. (Courtesy Mark and Connie Simcox.)

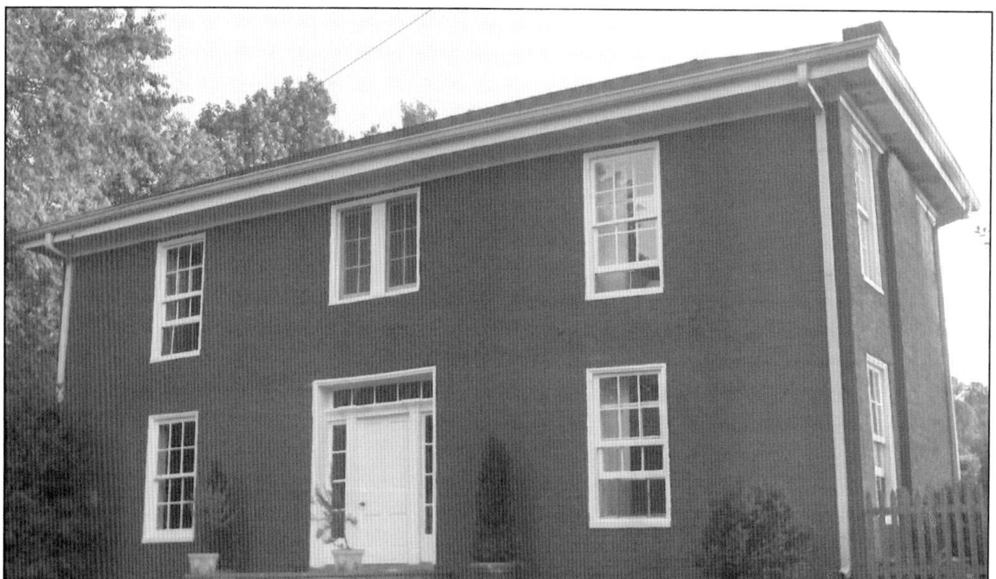

GRUBB HOME. First built as a log cabin *c.* 1803 for the Grubb family, a brick addition was built onto this Rich Valley cabin about 1862. The logs can be seen on the interior of the house, which has been carefully preserved by Dr. John Johnston and his wife, Jo. This house is an excellent example of the settlers' improving socioeconomic status, as they prospered and could afford to build brick and frame additions onto their cabins and add decorative elements to the interior and exterior. (Courtesy the author.)

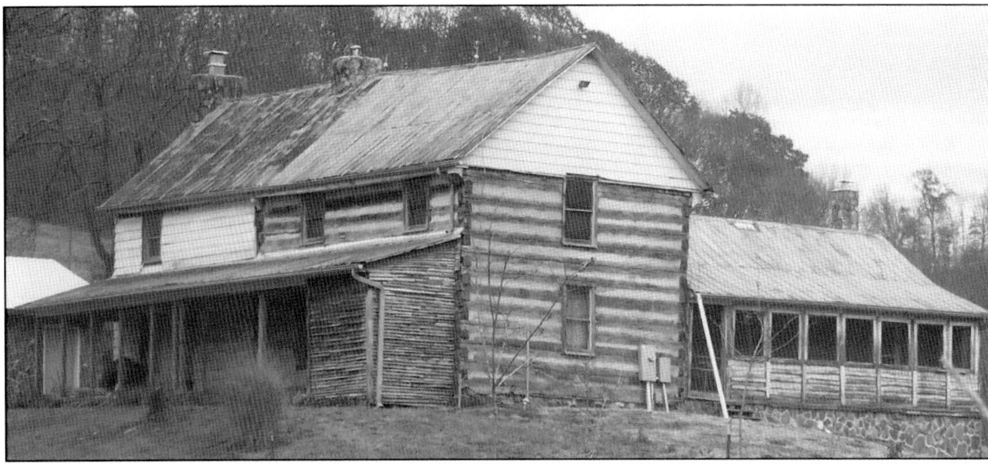

Rich Valley Cabin. The Tedder cabin, located on S.R. 700/Rich Valley Road, was built in the late 1700s or early 1800s and is being carefully restored by the current owners. It represents a typical cabin plan with an earlier single pen expanded with a dogtrot to a double-pen structure, and a later rear addition. Some local residents believe it was used as a Civil War hospital during the war and that the nearby graves in a field are the final resting place for some soldiers. (Courtesy DeAnna Akers Greene.)

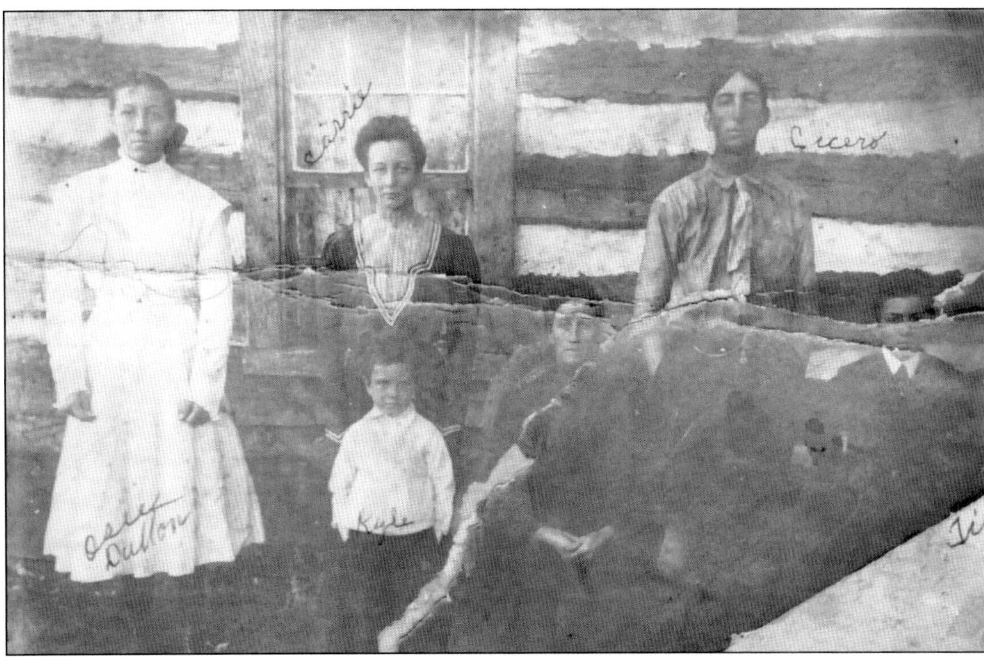

Jones Family. Posed in front of their log cabin are the Jones family: from left to right, Ocie Jones, Carrie Jones, Kyle Jones (in front of Carrie), Rebecca Thomas Jones (seated), Cicero Jones (standing), and Tivus Jones. Cicero was a farmer who originally came from Russell County but moved to Washington County and settled in the Frog Hollow community along Branch Street. (Courtesy Mary "Meemaw" Jones Hardwick.)

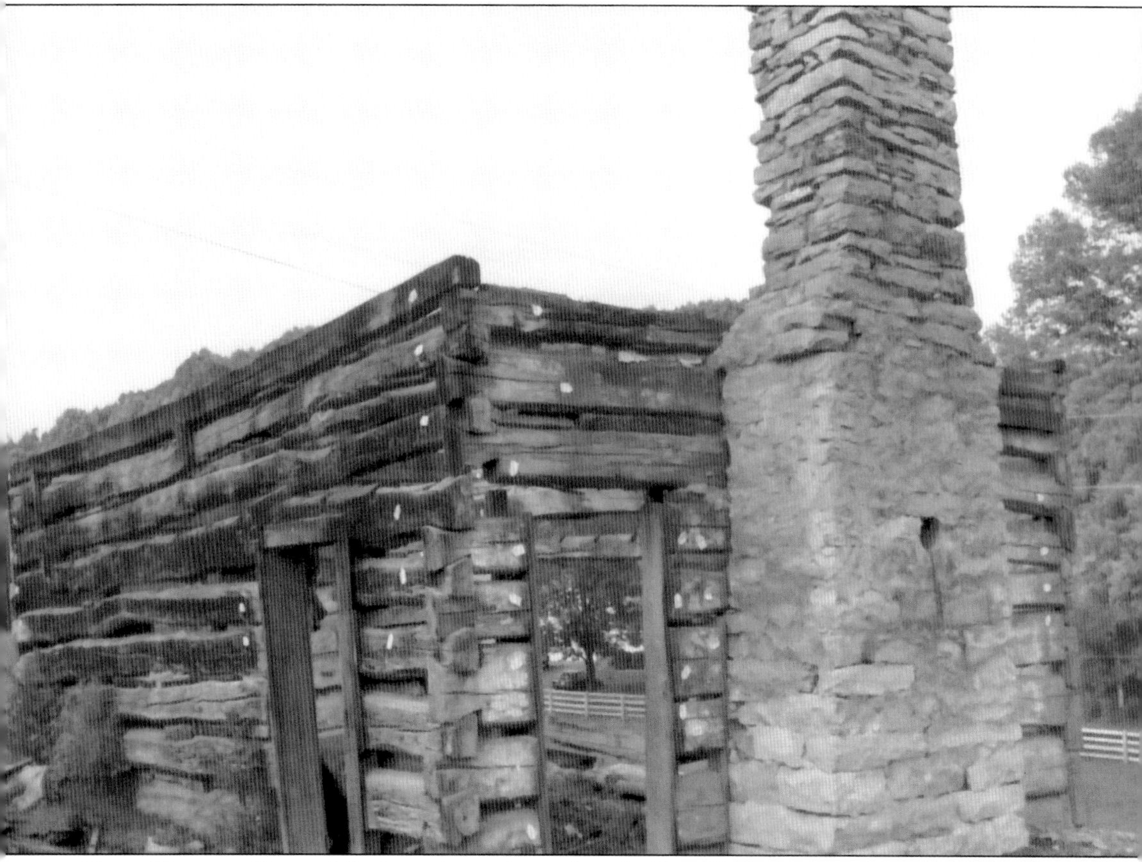

FROG HOLLOW CABIN. The log cabin is located in the Frog Hollow community, just off Branch Road. This hollow once was home to four log cabins, originally housing early settlers and later used for sharecroppers and renters. Families including the Haydens, Joneses, and Kestners have lived in the cabin, which dates to the early 1800s. As pictured, the historic building is in the process of being dismantled and moved to Fairview, a historic agricultural museum with the original Hagy family log cabin being developed by the Town of Abingdon at a site along the Hillman Highway. (Courtesy Mary "Meemaw" Jones Hardwick and the author.)

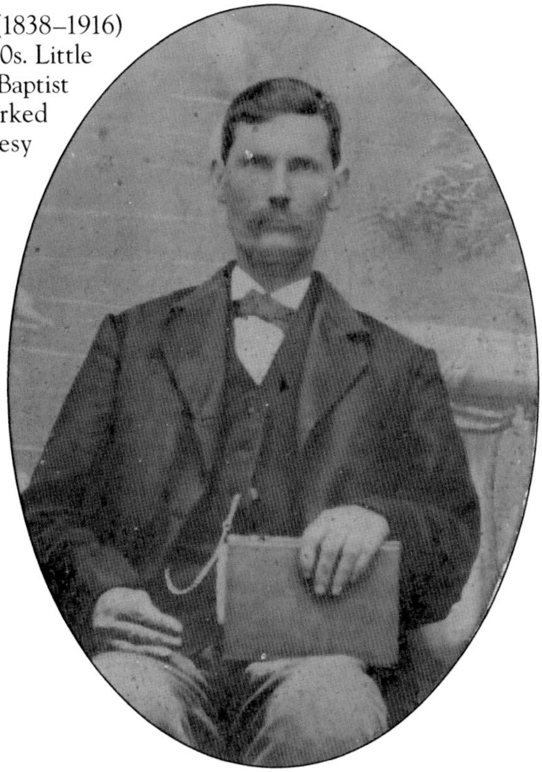

Rev. Branson Little. Reverend Little (1838–1916) is pictured in this tintype from the late 1800s. Little was a Confederate veteran and a Missionary Baptist circuit-riding preacher who lived and worked in the Hayter's Gap community. (Courtesy Troy Taylor.)

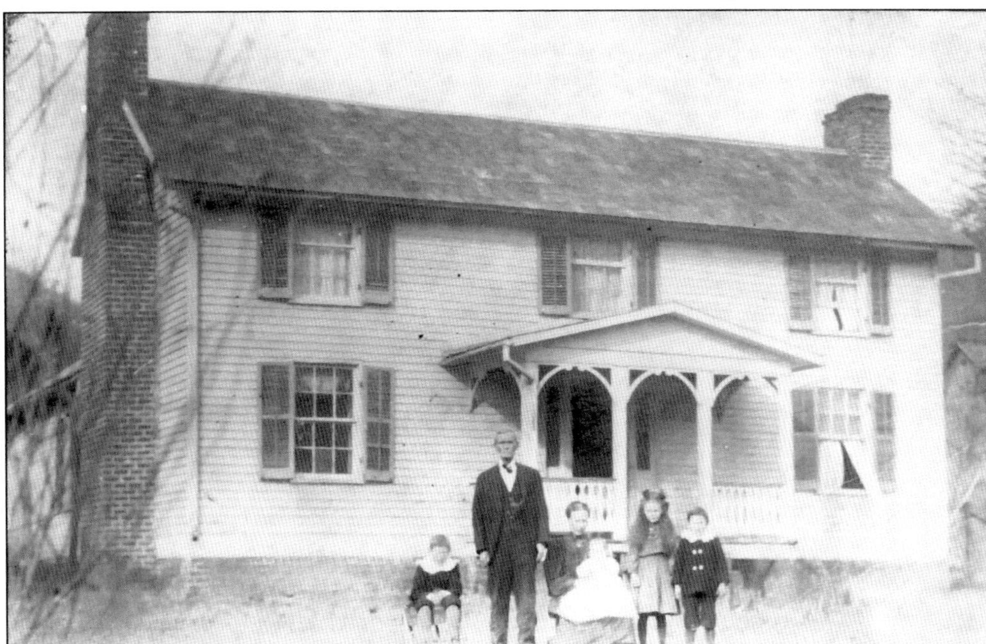

Little Home Place. Pictured in front of their house in the Hayter's Gap community are, from left to right, Earnest Little (1903–1942); Reverend Branson Little (1838–1916); Branson's wife, Theodosia Little; Bascom Little (1910–1995); Venner Little (1904–1995); and Howard Little (1906–1998). (Courtesy Troy Taylor.)

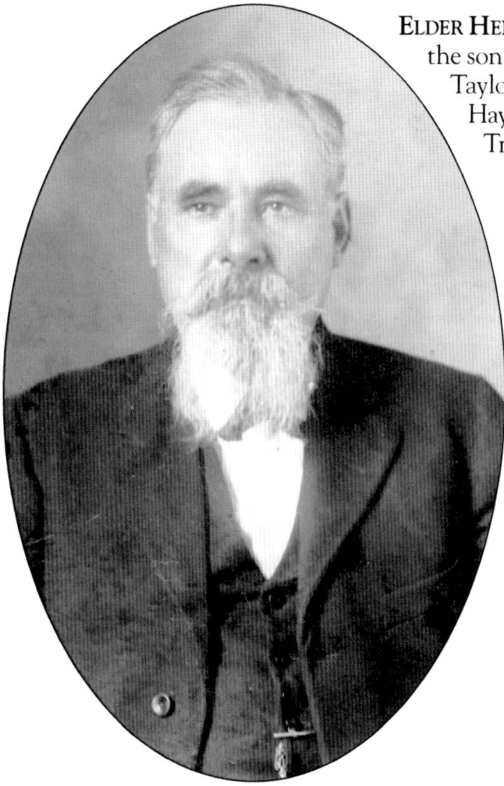

ELDER HENRY TAYLOR. Elder Henry Taylor (1857–1928) was the son of Andrew Jackson Taylor and Nancy Eastridge Taylor. He was a Primitive Baptist minister in the Hayter's Gap area and a community leader. (Courtesy Troy Taylor.)

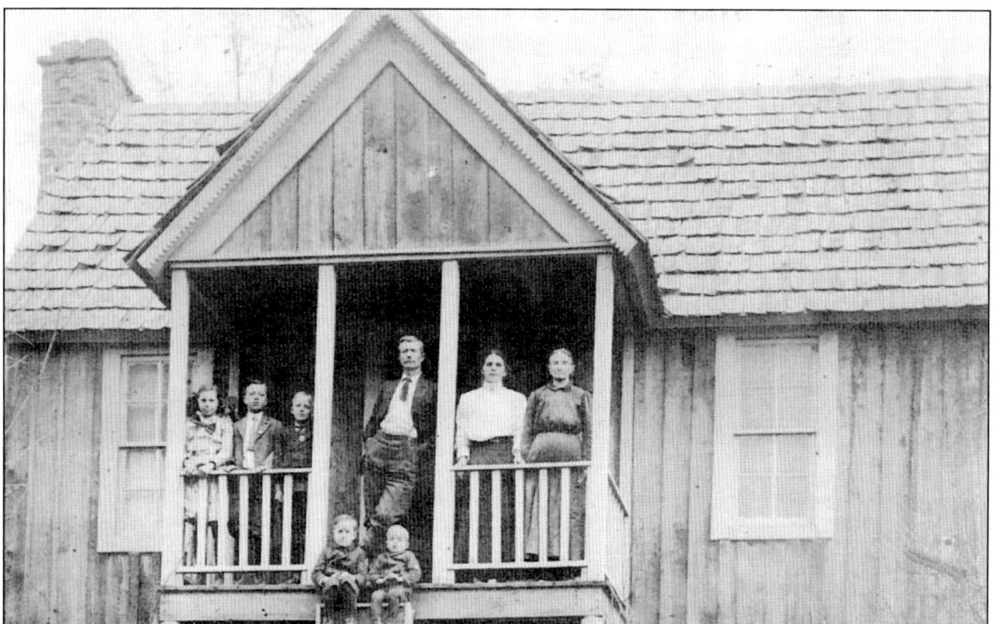

CHARLES MCCRAY FAMILY. Posed in front of their house are Charles McCray and Cara Alice (Boardwine) McCray. Susan Johnson McCray (1851–1941) is standing on the far right. The children are unidentified. The house is still standing on Poor Valley Road/S.R. 613. (Courtesy Troy Taylor.)

McCray Men. These men lived in the Tumbling Cove area. From left to right are William R. McCray (1879–1968), Rufus F. McCray (1851–1926), and Arthur L. McCray (1893–1981). William later became a coal miner, and Rufus was a farmer and co-owner of a logging and sawmill operation in Tumbling Cove. Arthur worked for the Pocahontas Fuel Company. (Courtesy Troy Taylor.)

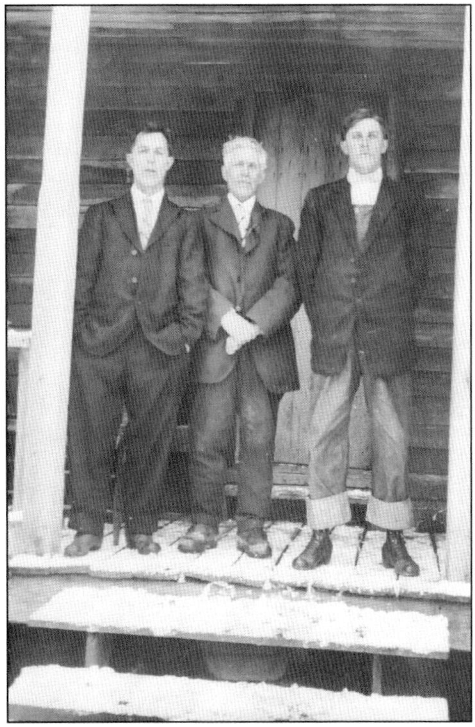

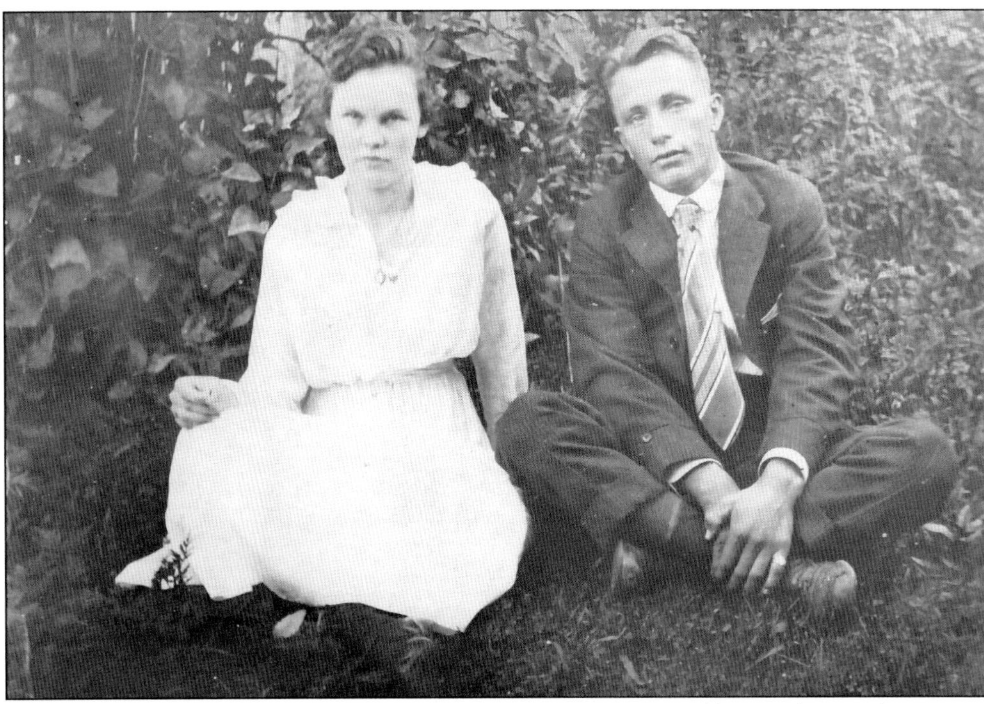

Sweethearts. These two Tumbling Cove sweethearts are pictured here in love in the summer of 1919. Carl McCray (1899–1981) and Venner Lou Little (1904–1995) would later be married. Carl was a farmer, builder, mail carrier, and carpenter for Olin-Mathieson, and Venner was the daughter of Reverend Branson and Theodosia Little of Hayter's Gap. (Courtesy Troy Taylor.)

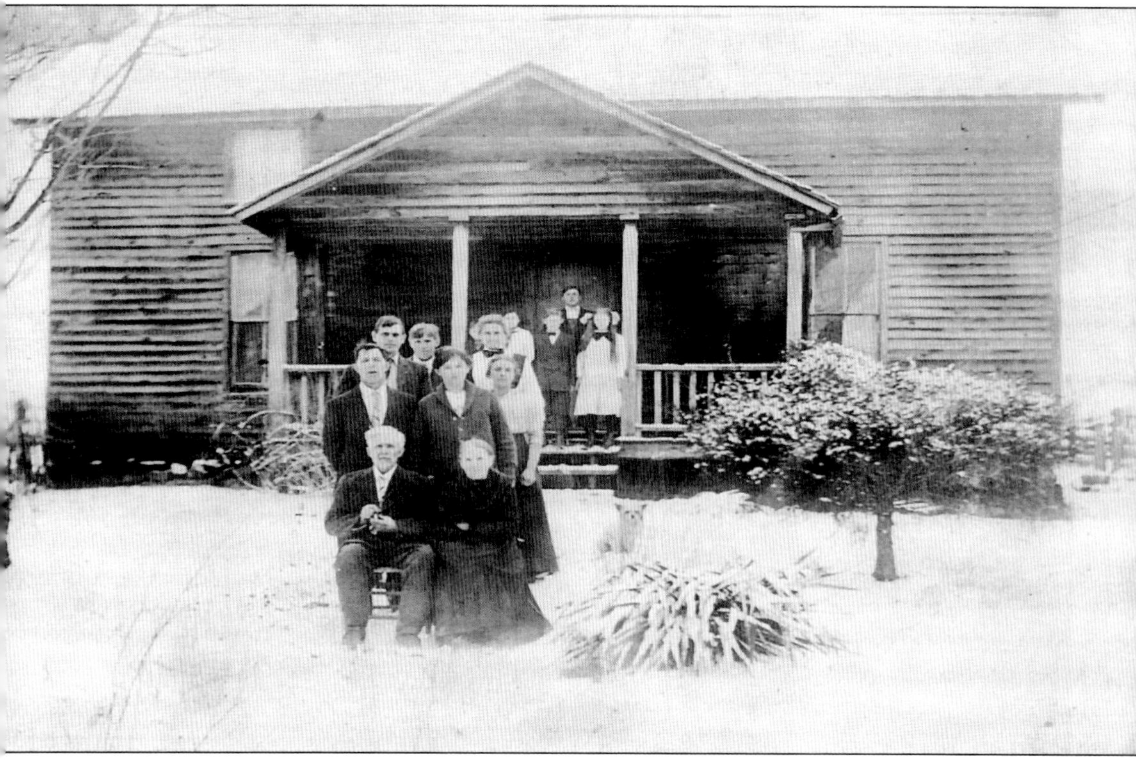

RUFUS FOWLER MCCRAY HOMEPLACE. Pictured in the snowy front yard of the McCray house are (first row) Rufus F. McCray (1851–1926) and his wife, Susan Johnson McCray (1851–1941); (second row) William McCray (1879–1968) and Viola Woodward (Snodgrass) McCray; and (third row, far left) Marion Abraham McCray. The tall man on the porch is Arthur McCray (1893–1981), and the others are unidentified. The house is still standing in a hollow near S.R. 613 and S.R. 80. (Courtesy Troy Taylor.)

DOUG COOK, C. 1900. This gent was a well-known local musician from the Widener's Valley area. Many talented musicians have hailed from this region thanks to the prominent role of traditional music in this Appalachian culture. (Courtesy Rick Rouse.)

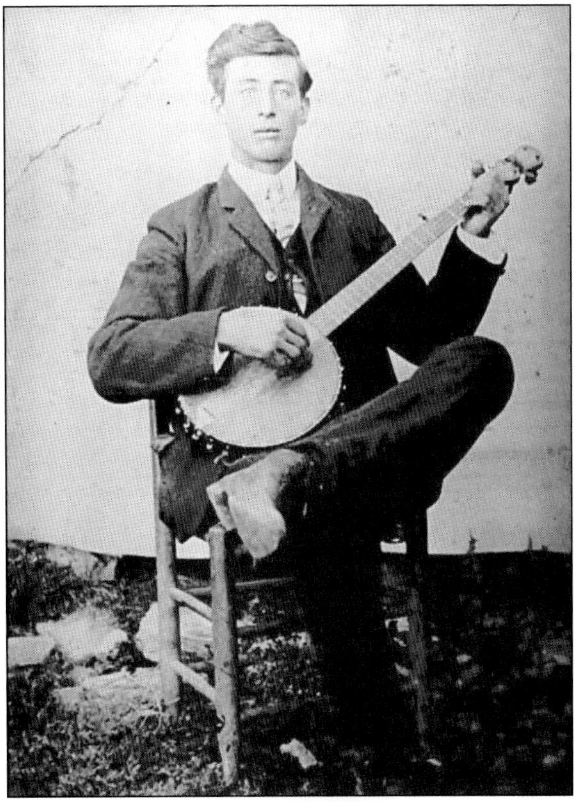

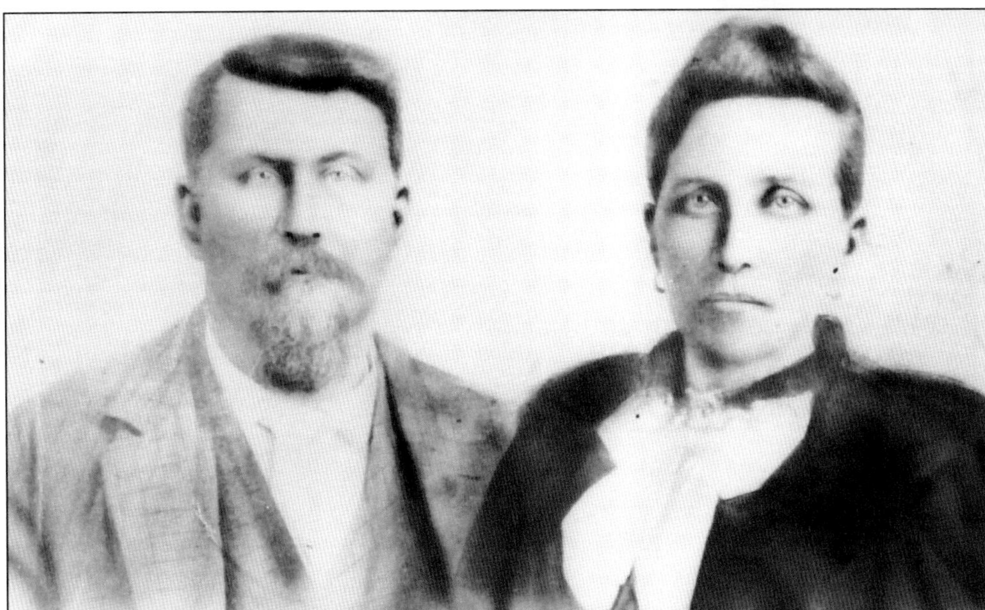

DR. JAMES T. MARTIN. Pictured here are Dr. James T. Martin (1846–1908) and his wife, Martha Livingston Martin (1858–1937), of the Mendota area. Dr. Martin was a schoolteacher, a doctor in Mendota for 31 years, and an officer at Hamilton Institute in Mendota. (Courtesy Terri Collier McCroskey.)

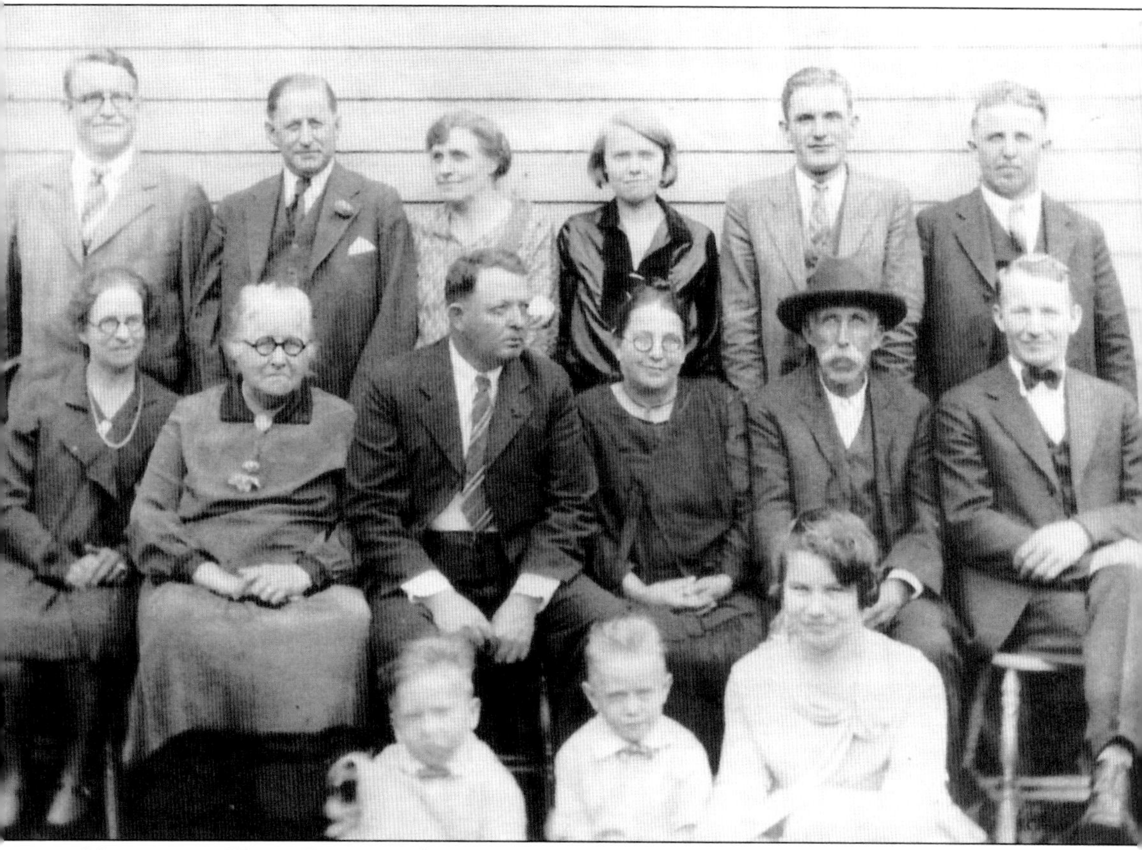

MARTIN AND HOBBS FAMILIES. The Martin and Hobbs families of the Mendota and Nordyke areas, respectively, are pictured here; from left to right are (first row, seated) ? Martin, ? Martin (both sons of James T. Martin Jr.), and Helen Martin; (seated) Ida Martin Wagoner, Martha Livingston Martin, William D. Wagoner, Martha A. Hobbs, Sheffy Hobbs, and James T. Martin Jr.; (standing) Robert S. Martin, Dr. William M. Martin, Margaret Groseclose Martin, ? Martin (wife of Cornet), Cornet Livingston Martin, and Garland Hobbs. (Courtesy Terri Collier McCroskey.)

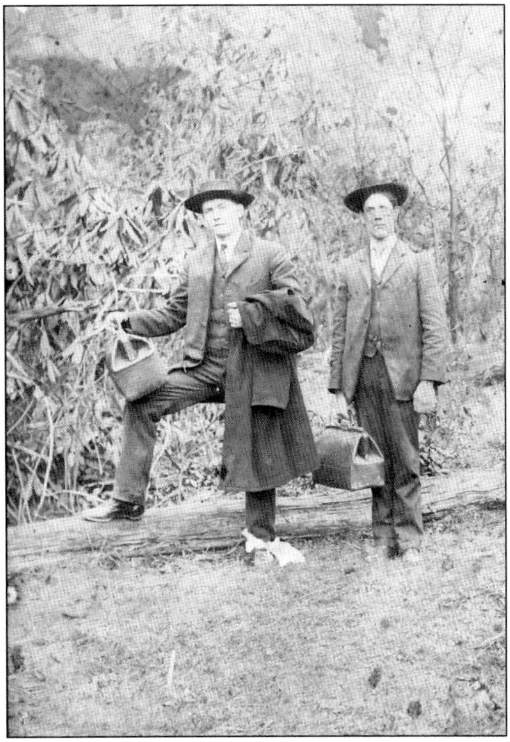

TRAVELING SALESMEN. On the right is Douglas M. Collier, a self-made success story who owned furniture stores in southwest Virginia and Kentucky. He married Pearl Dew Nickels of Mendota. Collier and the unidentified man on the left are carrying old-fashioned briefcases. (Courtesy Terri Collier McCroskey.)

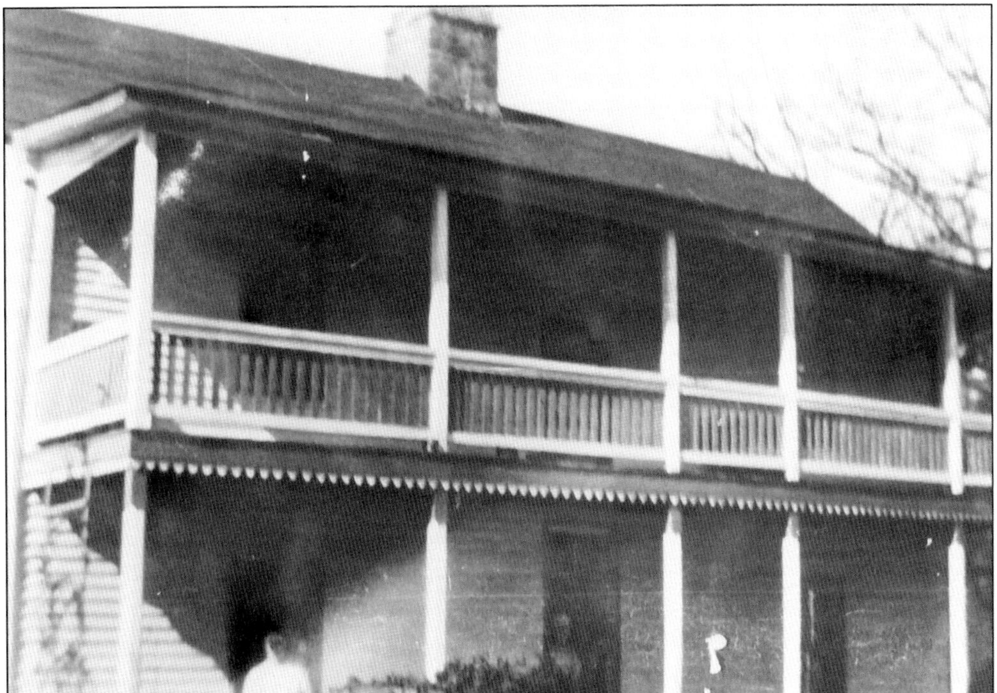

SNODGRASS HOUSE. The Snodgrass family house is located in Riverbend off North Fork River Road and has been in the family since the Civil War. Although it has been renovated, the house still maintains its historic character. (Courtesy Lois Snodgrass Shupe.)

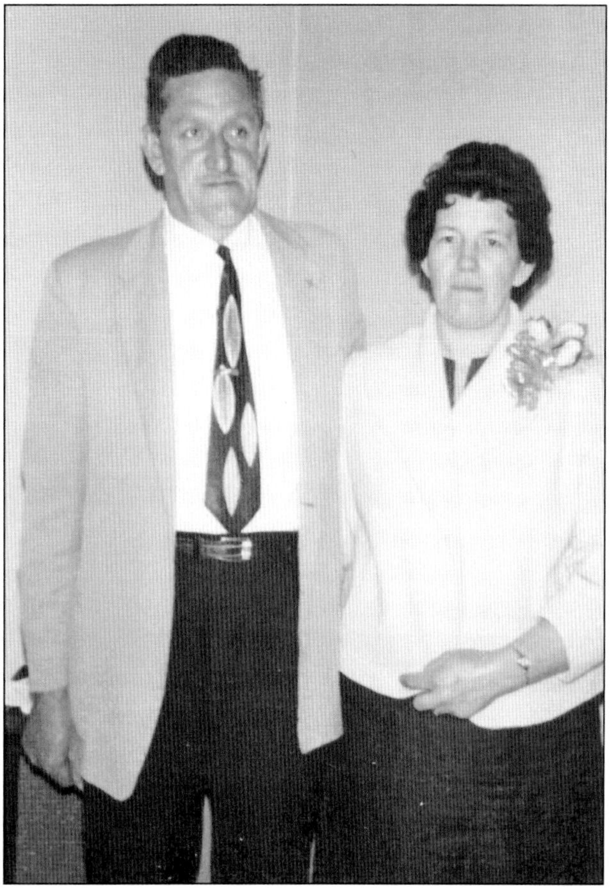

MELVIN AND VIRGIE SNODGRASS. Melvin Snodgrass and his wife, Virgie Nipper Snodgrass, were longtime residents of Riverbend. Melvin worked as a farmer, store operator, and mechanic and was the coordinator for the Hayter's Gap community center. Today the center provides space for a Head Start program, branch library, and senior citizens' center. (Courtesy Lois Snodgrass Shupe.)

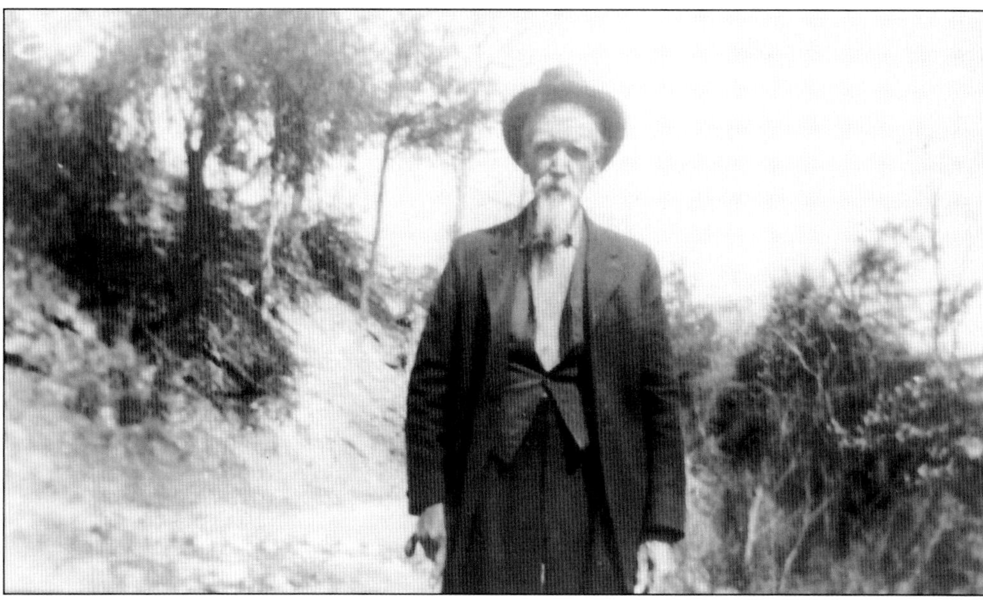

CHARLES SNODGRASS. Charles Snodgrass (1841–1929) was a Confederate veteran and a farmer in the Hayter's Gap community. He was a leader in the community. (Courtesy Troy Taylor.)

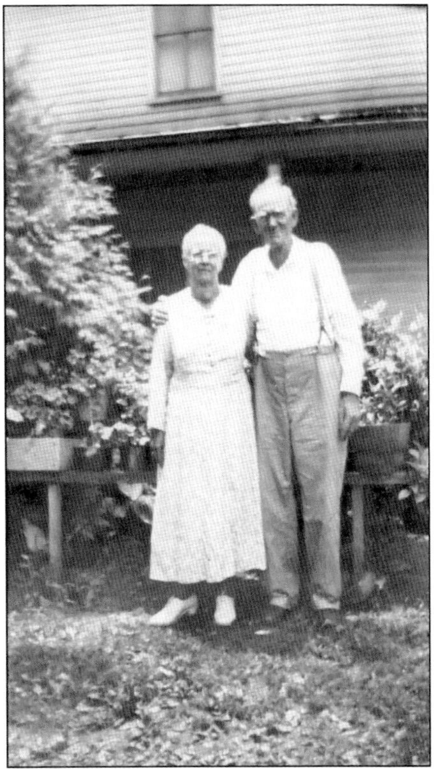

JACK AND IDA SNODGRASS. Jack Snodgrass was a farmer, sawmill owner, and carpenter in the Riverbend community near Hayter's Gap. His wife, Ida, was a well-known midwife and minister. (Courtesy Lois Snodgrass Shupe.)

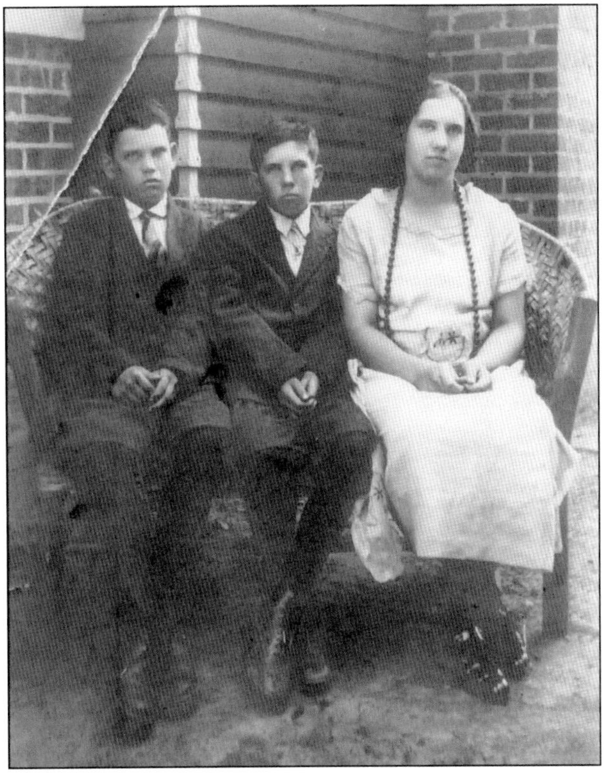

COLLIER SIBLINGS. These three siblings from Mendota are captured by the camera around 1920. From left to right are Ralph Collier (1912–1976), Rhea Collier, and Hazel Collier. (Courtesy Terri Collier McCroskey.)

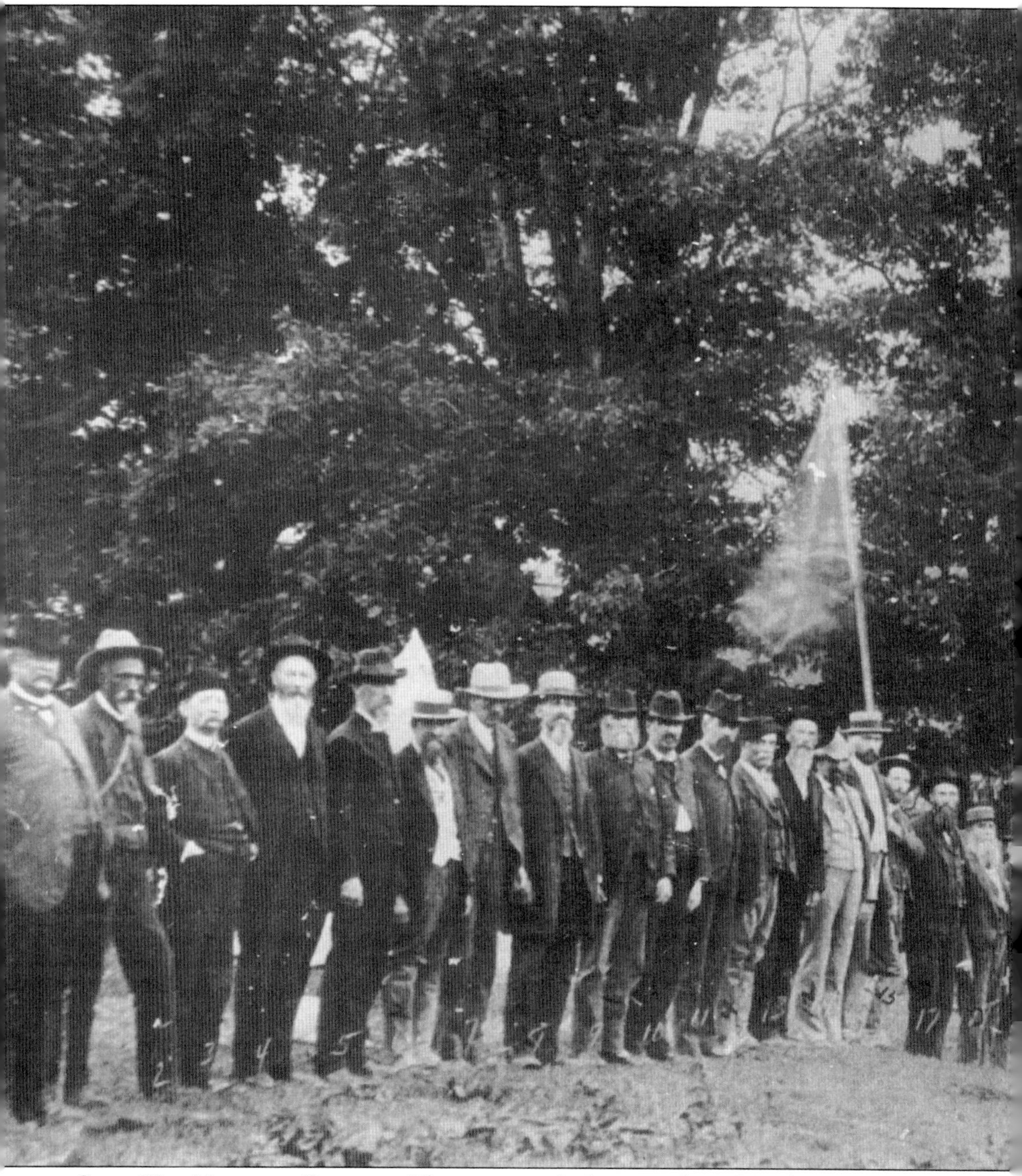

CIVIL WAR VETERANS REUNION. This reunion of a large number of Civil War veterans of Washington County took place at Keywood. At least 2,000 of Washington County's sons served in the Confederacy, and a few even joined the Union troops. Although all the men's images are hand-numbered for identification, only a few names are listed on the photograph. From left to right, the following men are identified: 2. Tom Colley, 6. Dr. William Logan Dunn, 25. ? Edmundson, 32. Dr. ? Farnsworth, 27. ? Berry, 28. ? Edmunds, and 31. Brock Clark. A brass band is standing on the far right of the photograph, and a house can be seen behind them. The two men standing in front may have been officers. Dr. Dunn (1838–1922), a graduate of Emory and

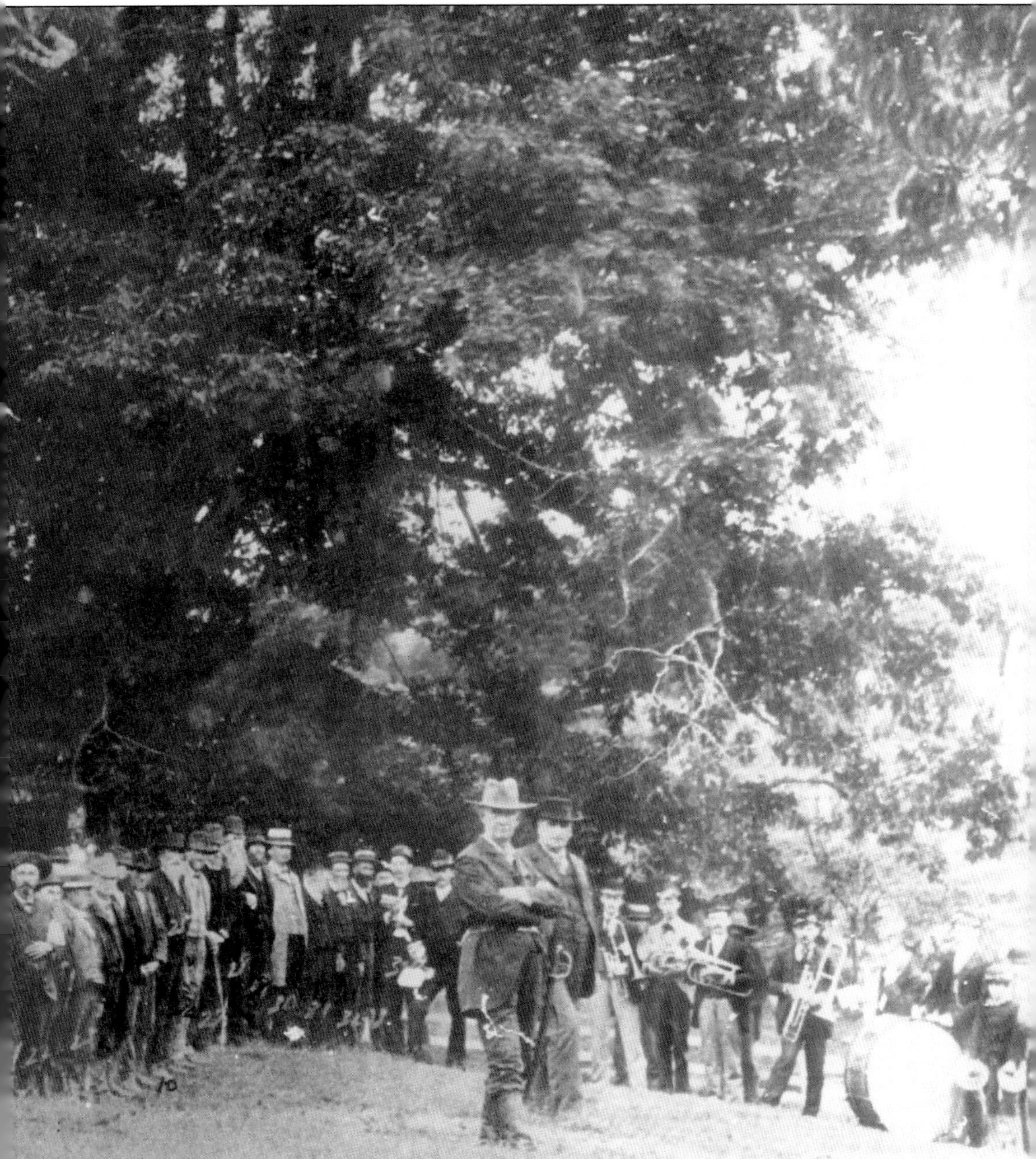

Henry College, served under Gen. William "Grumble" Jones, who had married Dunn's sister. This intrepid doctor also was a surgeon with Col. John S. Mosby's Rangers. After the war ended, he practiced medicine in Glade Spring until his death in 1922. Dunn's brick house, built *c.* 1878, still stands in Glade Spring between Main and Broadway Streets. With soldiers from both sides, bushwhackers, deserters, and regulators taking their food, money, supplies, horses, and livestock, the locals suffered terribly during the Civil War. Northern troops marched through Washington County at least two times to destroy the railroad lines and on their way to Saltville to cut off the salt supply for the Confederacy. (Courtesy Ruby Stovall Clark.)

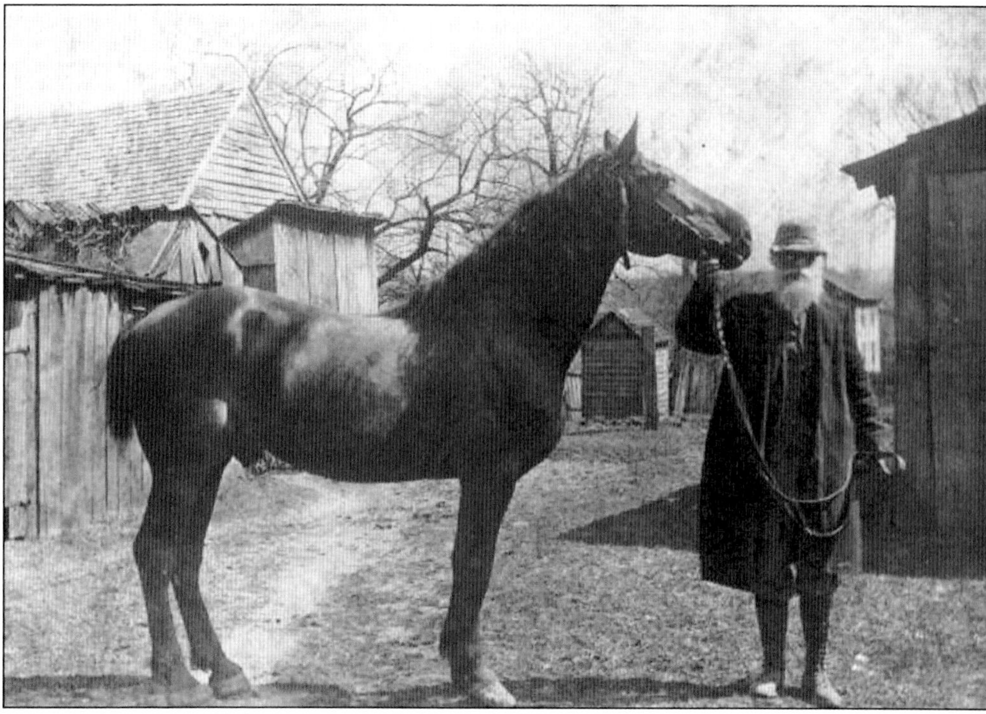

ROBERT CAMPBELL. Robert M. C. "Bob" Campbell (1843–1911) fought in the Civil War, serving as a private in the E Company, 63rd Regiment. He is buried in the Jamison-Davis Cemetery off S.R. 700. (Courtesy Doris Campbell Peters.)

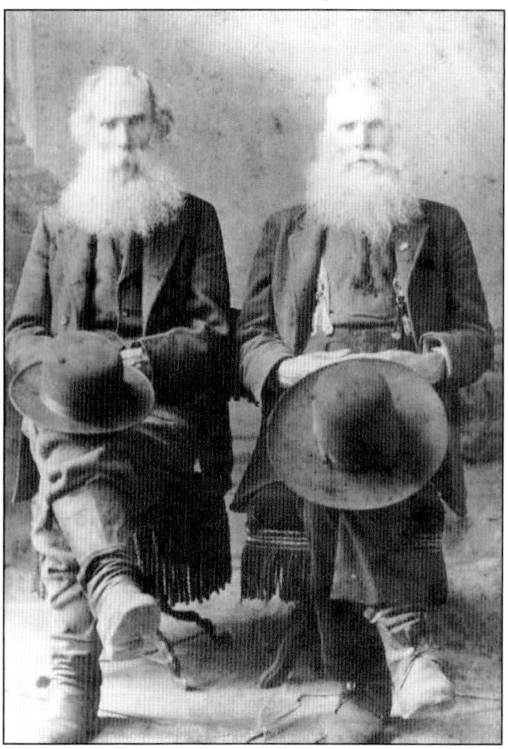

CAMPBELL TWINS. John C. Campbell is on the left and his twin brother Robert M. C. Campbell is on the right. Even their beards are identical. These men lived in the Rich Valley community near White's Mill. (Courtesy Doris Campbell Peters.)

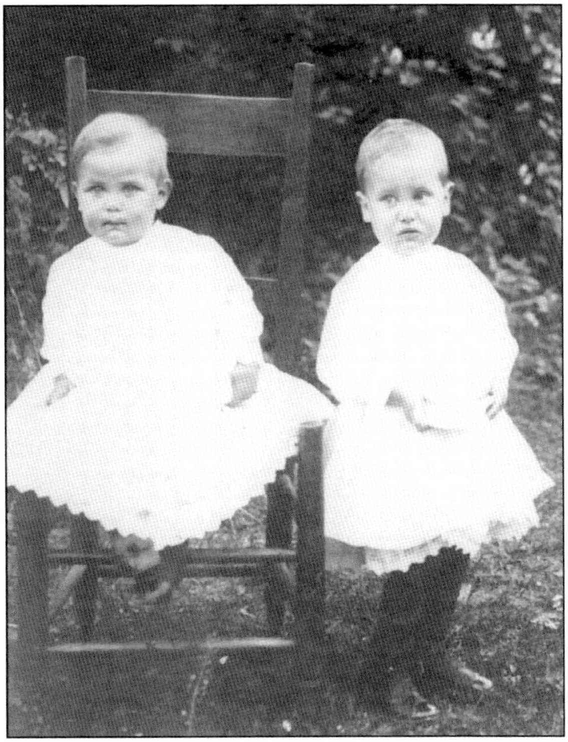

CAMPBELL BROTHERS. James L. and Robert Lee Campbell, brothers born just 11 months apart in the Rich Valley community, pose in the lacy white dresses commonly worn by children of both genders in the early 1900s. The men became farmers and community leaders, and worked at White's Mill. (Courtesy Lynda Campbell.)

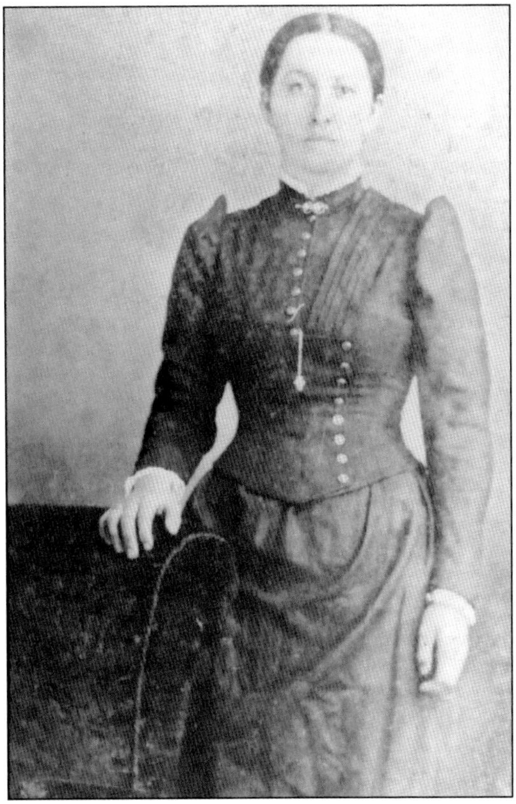

LAURA AMANDA DAVIS, C. 1890. Laura Amanda Davis (1871–1944) was a descendant of several generations of early settlers in Rich Valley, including the McCulloch, Jameson, and Davis lines. She married James Willie Akers (1856–1945) of Hayter's Gap, and they lived on her family farm in Rich Valley just past Toole's Creek Road. (Courtesy Ken and Nellie Akers.)

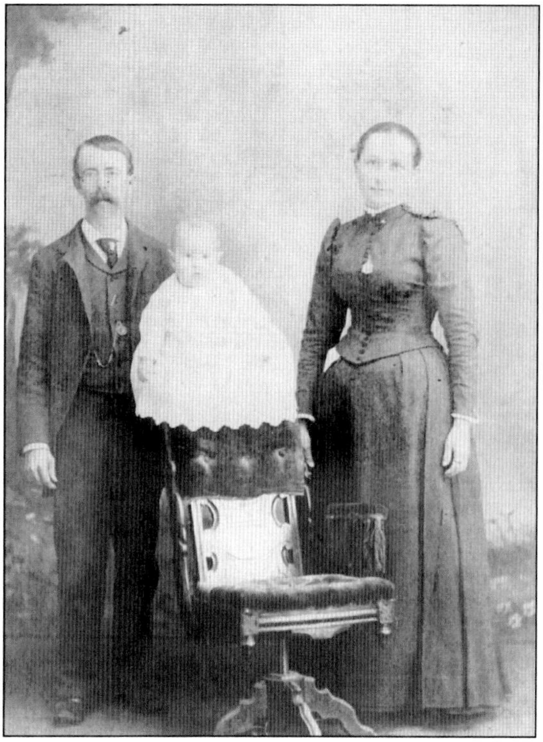

Hagy Family. Joseph E. Hagy (1884–1921) and Alice Lamar Davis (1867–1945), who were distant cousins, were married in Washington County in 1884. The Hagy Wagon Company, established in 1855, manufactured wagons, surreys, buggies, and hacks. The wagon company was originally located on Abingdon's Main Street from about 1885 to 1906 and then moved to larger facilities beside the railroad depot square. The company advertised "the original and genuine Hagy Wagon celebrated for durability, strength, and light running." (Courtesy Ken and Nellie Akers.)

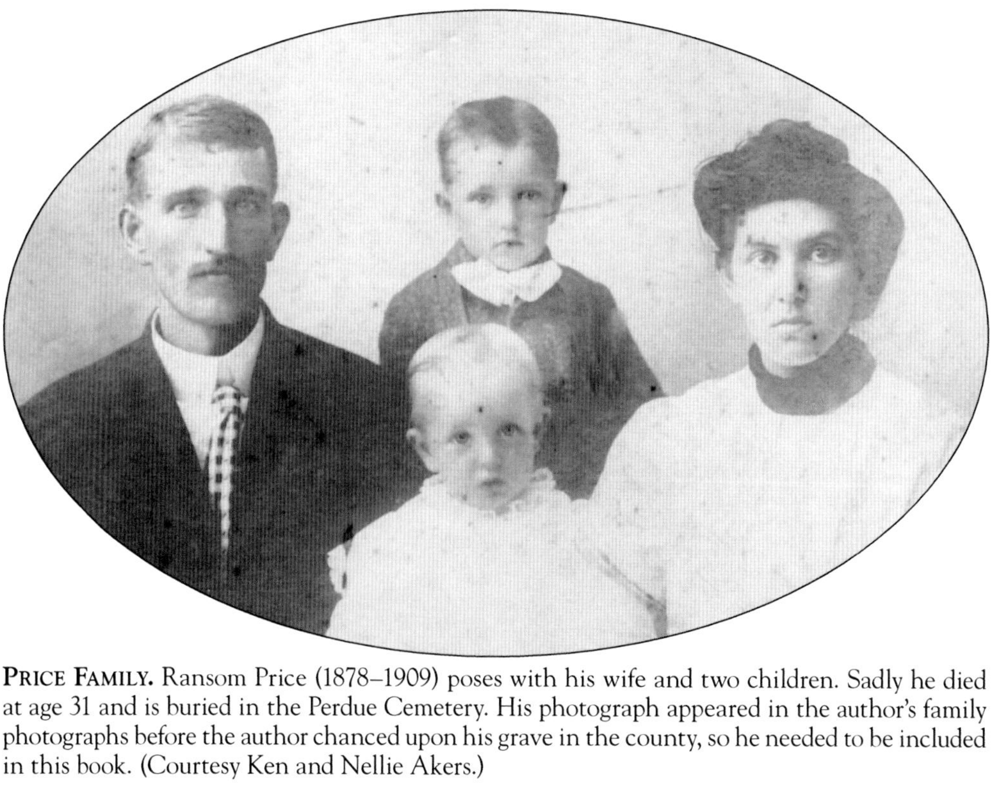

Price Family. Ransom Price (1878–1909) poses with his wife and two children. Sadly he died at age 31 and is buried in the Perdue Cemetery. His photograph appeared in the author's family photographs before the author chanced upon his grave in the county, so he needed to be included in this book. (Courtesy Ken and Nellie Akers.)

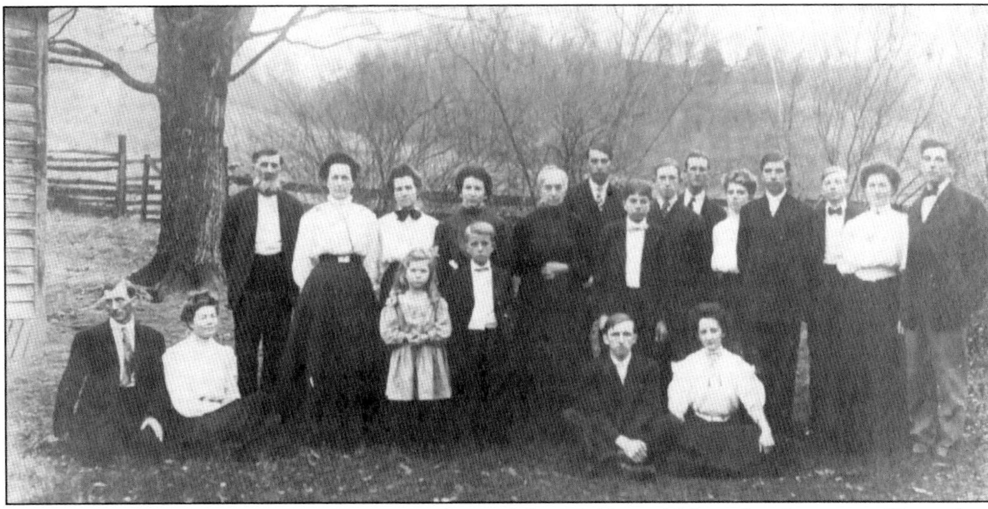

HAGY AND WEBB THANKSGIVING. Members of the Webb and Hagy families joined here for a group photograph at the home of Andrew J. Hagy (1854–1955) on a *c.* 1905 Thanksgiving. Mary Ann Elizabeth Hagy (Davis) Webb, daughter of Jacob E. Hagy Jr. and Catherine Keller, is the oldest lady in the center of the photograph. This photograph was taken by Graham Roberts, a farmer/photographer who captured images in the early 1900s. (Courtesy Ken and Nellie Akers.)

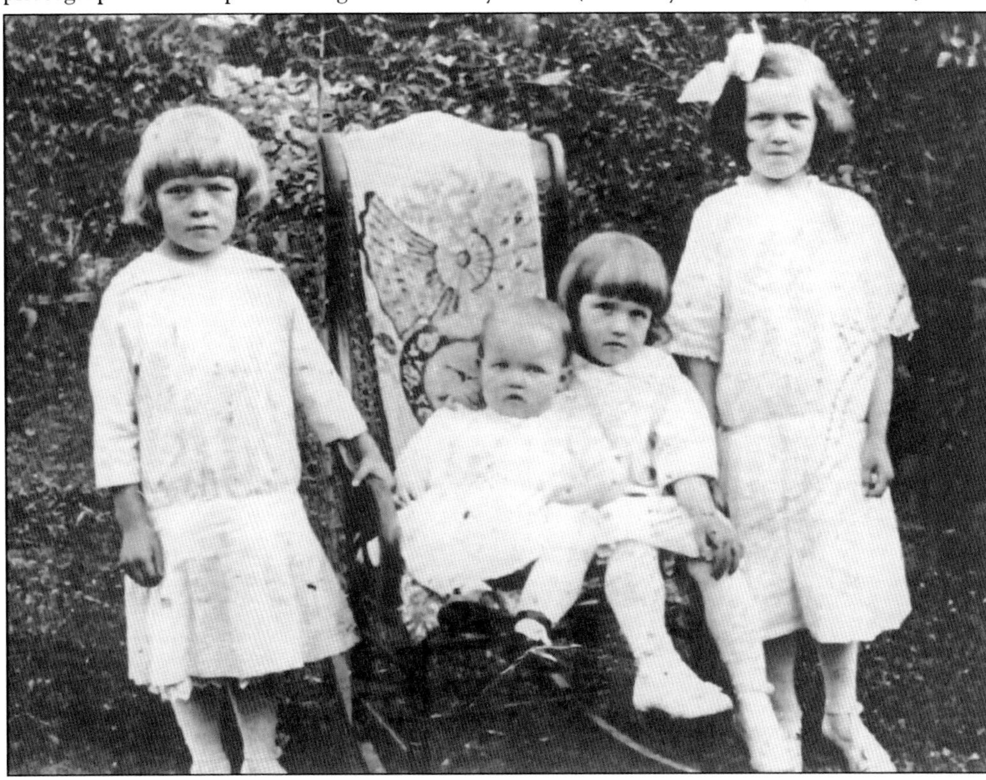

KESTNER GIRLS. Four of the five daughters of Walter J. Kestner and Lottie Annis Gilmer Kestner are shown here with the family rocking chair. Walter Kestner was a grist miller who moved his family to different mills in the Abingdon and Bristol area. From left to right are Bessie M. A., Cleo Thelma, Cora Kate, and Pearl Kestner. (Courtesy Ken and Nellie Akers.)

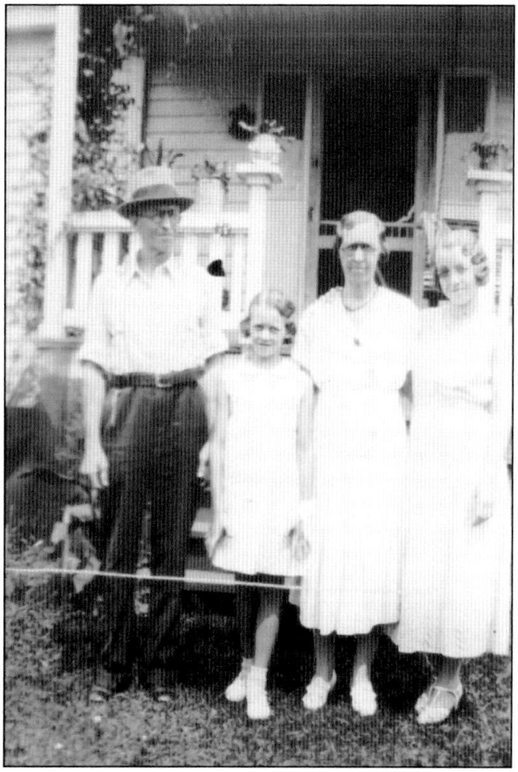

W. J. KESTNER. Walter J. Kestner (1880–1963) and Lottie Gilmer Kestner (1888–1946) pose with two of their daughters, Cleo (left) and Kate. W. J. was a miller who worked at several different mills in the region. Kate married Roy Light, and they founded Light Milling, originally a feed store and now Light's at Stone Mill, a popular retail and farm store. (Courtesy Ken and Nellie Akers.)

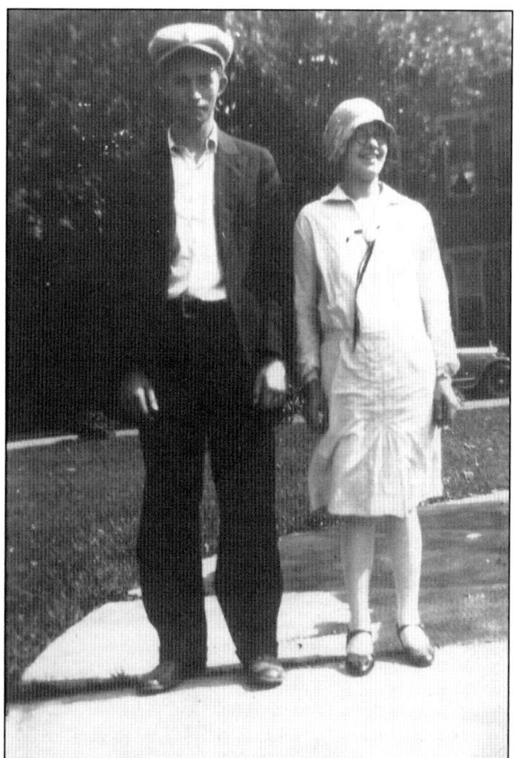

COURTING COUPLE. Charles Edward "Ed" Akers (1908–1987) and Pearl Frances Kestner (1907–1997) pose here in their courting days. They were married in 1927 and lived on the Akers/Davis family farm on S.R. 700 in Rich Valley near White's Mill. Ed was a hardworking farmer, and Pearl kept the house and was the church pianist at Lowland United Methodist Church. (Courtesy Nellie and Ken Akers.)

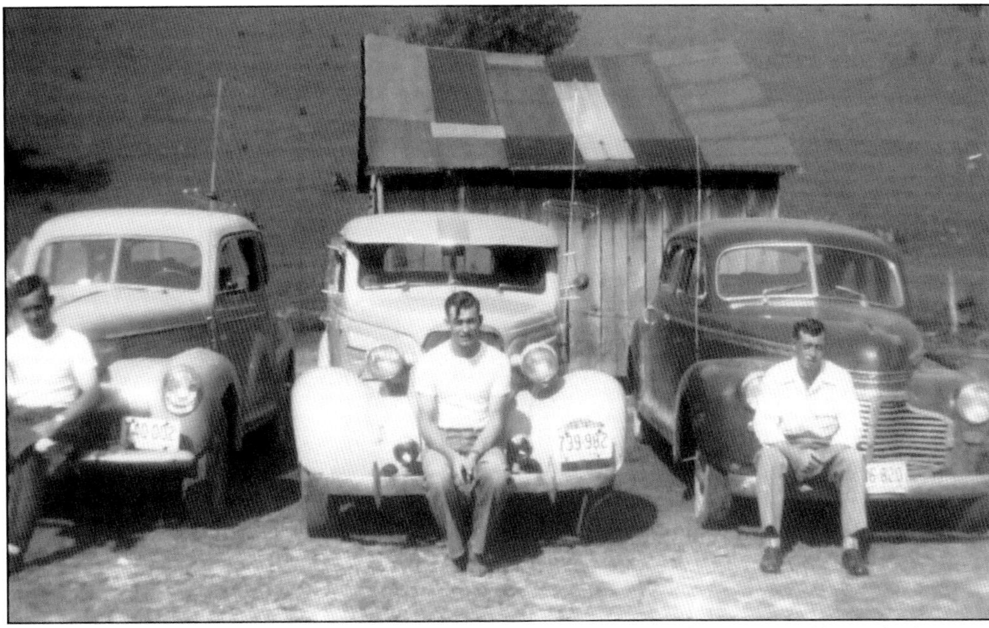

BOYS AND CARS. Brothers LeRoy (left), Gene (center), and C. E. Akers sit proudly on the bumpers of their first cars, a Studebaker, a 1939 Chevy Sedan, and a 1946 Chevy Deluxe, respectively. The boys were sons of Pearl Kestner and Charles Edward Akers and grew up on the Akers/Davis farm in Rich Valley, which is still owned by Jameson descendants—the family that has owned it since the 1820s. (Courtesy Ken and Nellie Akers.)

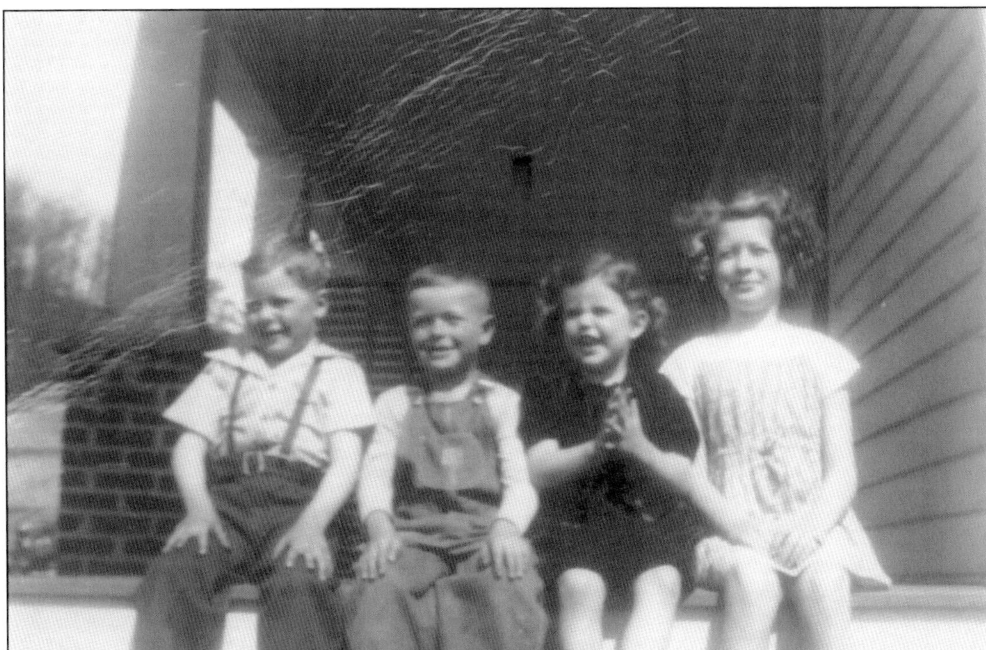

SCOTT AND AKERS CHILDREN. The Scott family lived up the hollow from the Davis/Akers farm in Rich Valley. Pictured porch, from left to right, are Danny Scott, Kenneth Akers, Charlotte Scott, and Annette Akers. (Courtesy Ken and Nellie Akers.)

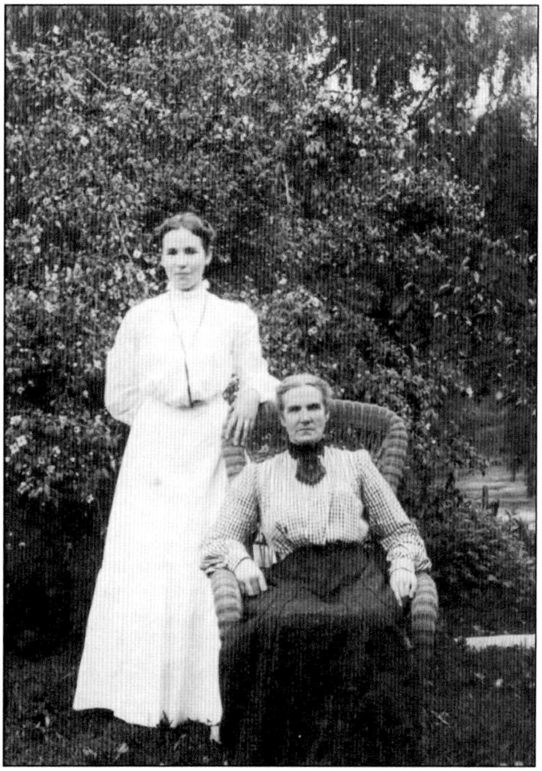

MARY AND LIZZIE WEBB. Lovely Mary Webb and her stepmother, Mary Ann Elizabeth "Lizzie" Hagy (Davis) Webb, enjoy a summer's day in the garden. In 1873, Lizzie was widowed at age 27 when her husband William M. Davis died at age 35, leaving her with three young children. She married Leonidus Webb and became an important matriarch in the Webb family of Rich Valley. (Courtesy Nellie and Ken Akers.)

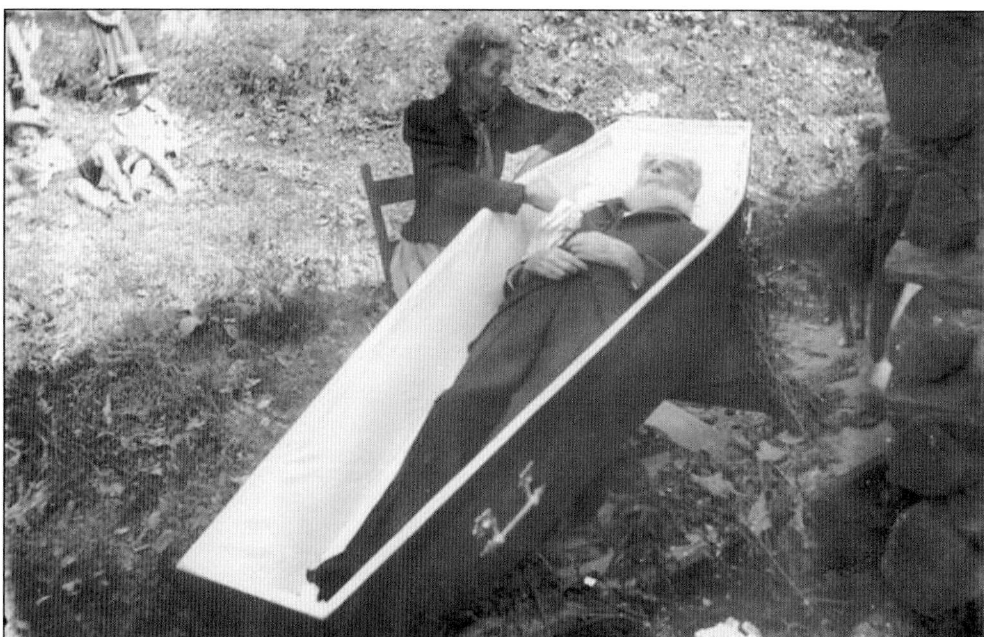

TUMBLING CREEK WAKE. A forlorn widow dressed in mourning black poses beside her deceased husband in his casket. Although slightly morbid to us today, in the past, funeral photographs were important ways to document a loved one's passing. Sometimes these funeral photographs were the only pictures taken of their loved ones. (Courtesy Jeffrey Weaver.)

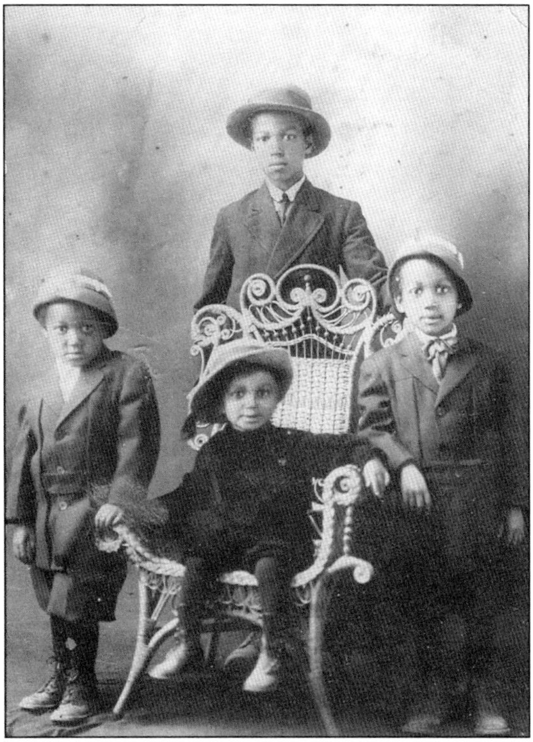

Carroll Brothers. In 1911, these handsome sons of Nathaniel Carroll posed for a studio photograph in Abingdon. From left to right are (seated) Telford, Damon, and Maceo; (standing) eldest brother Winston Carroll. Nathaniel Carroll owned an icehouse in Abingdon and was a successful self-made man. (Courtesy Damon C. Carroll Jr.)

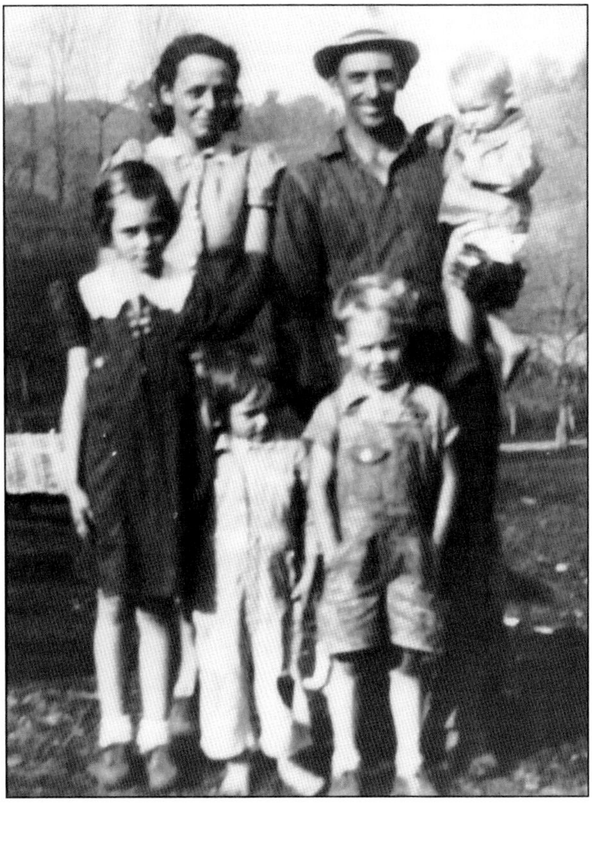

Joseph Scott Family. The Scott family of Blackwell Chapel community is pictured here. From left to right are (first row) Darlene (born 1932), Mary Catherine (born 1936), and Ralph (1934–2006); (second row) Mary Jo Steele Scott (1917–2006), Joseph Scott (1911–1986), and Charles Scott (born 1938). (Courtesy Darlene Scott Hockett.)

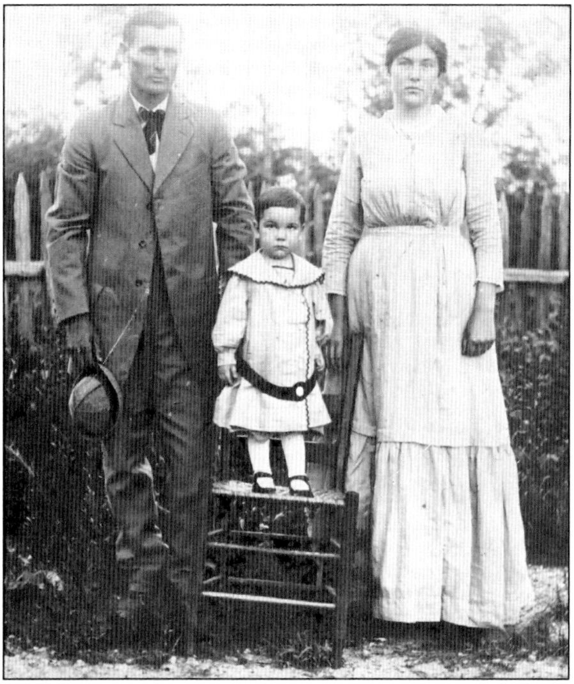

Floyd Kestner Family. Pictured here is handsome Floyd B. Kestner (1883–1970[?]), a popular local preacher; his wife, Francis E. Casey (1891–?); and their son Paul (1912–1998) in Blackwell Chapel. (Courtesy Darlene Scott Hockett.)

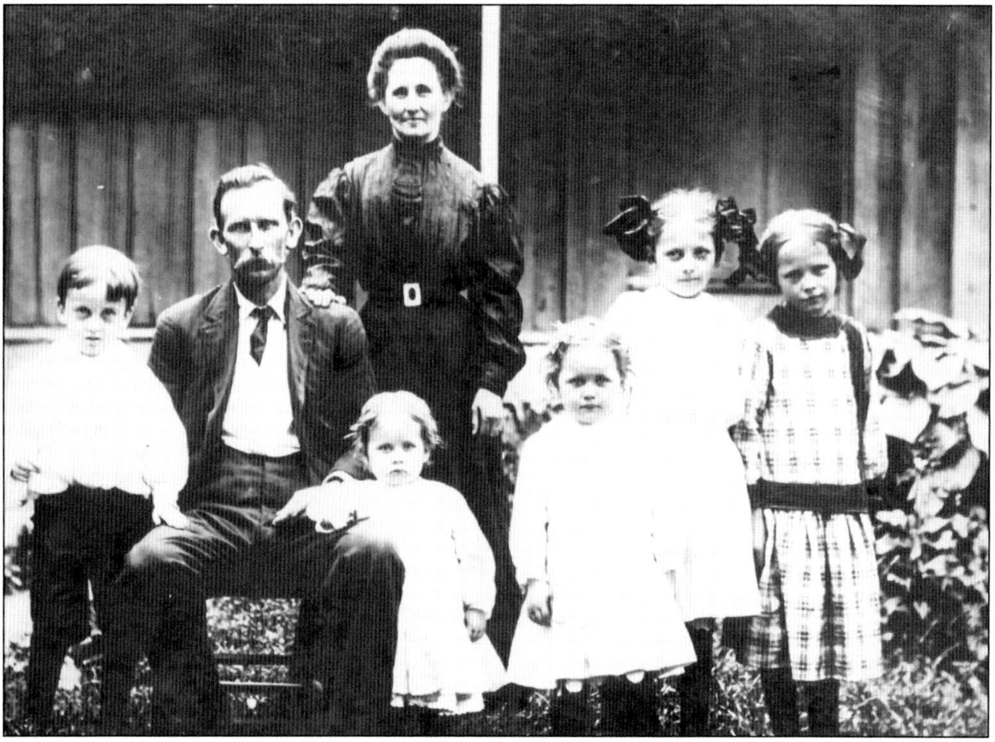

Francisco Family. Pictured around 1910 is the Edward Herbert Francisco family. From left to right are the following: (first row) Marvin, Edward H. Francisco (farmer), Delaphine, Lona, Martha, and Lela; (second row) Edward's wife and mother of the children, Nannie Dunn Francisco. (Courtesy Tammy Martin.)

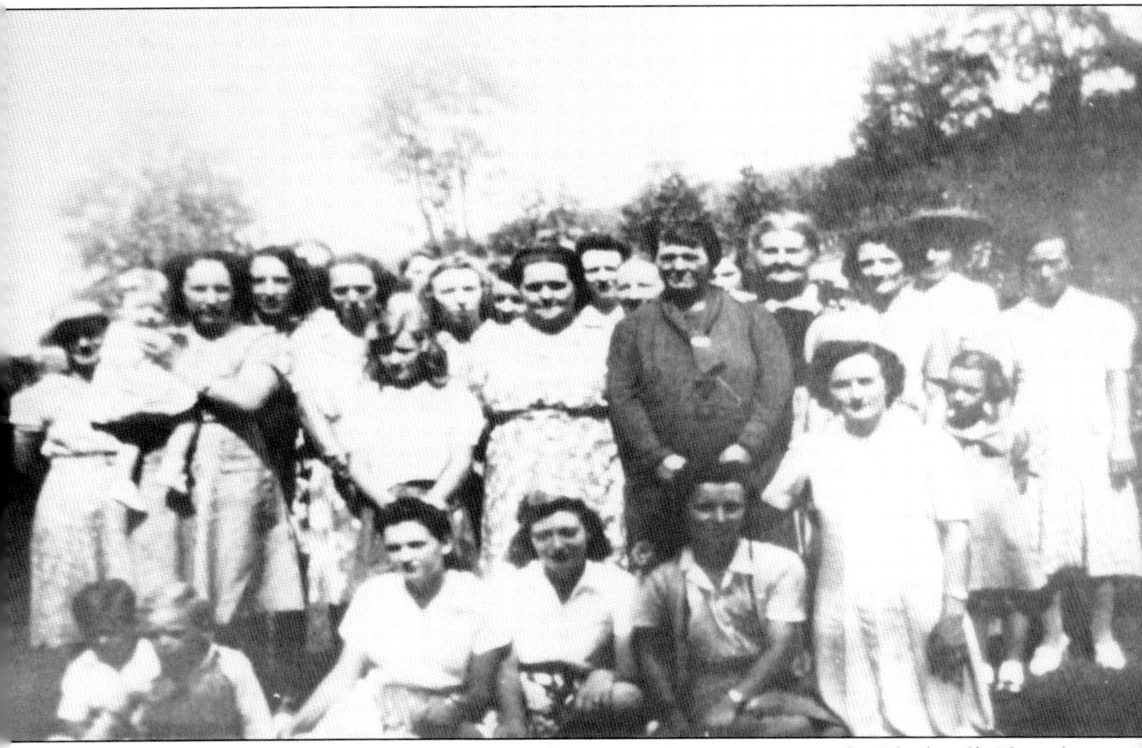

HOME DEMONSTRATION CLUB, C. 1943. This women's group met in the Blackwell Chapel community. Pictured are, from left to right, the following: (first row) Teidler Dye, Ralph Scott, Evelyn Helton, Dorothy Helton Grace, Mary Blackwell Martin, and Oma Price Colley; (second row) Jewel Counts Caudill with baby, Mary Hockett Counts, Bess Hockett Scott, Mary Jo Steele Scott, Polly Blackwell Hoback, Rose Hockett Kestner, Sally Helton Blackwell, Harriet Taylor Dye, Laura Helton Addison, Laura Parks Farris, Betty Farris Boardwine, and Charlotte Pickle Eastridge; (third row) Susie Holmes Bailey, Ethel Grace Farris, Dixie Martin Sampson, Lucille Blackwell Snodgrass, Virgie Blackwell Crabtree, C. W. Puckett, Bruce Hill Colley, and Louella Puckett Thompson. (Courtesy Tammy Martin.)

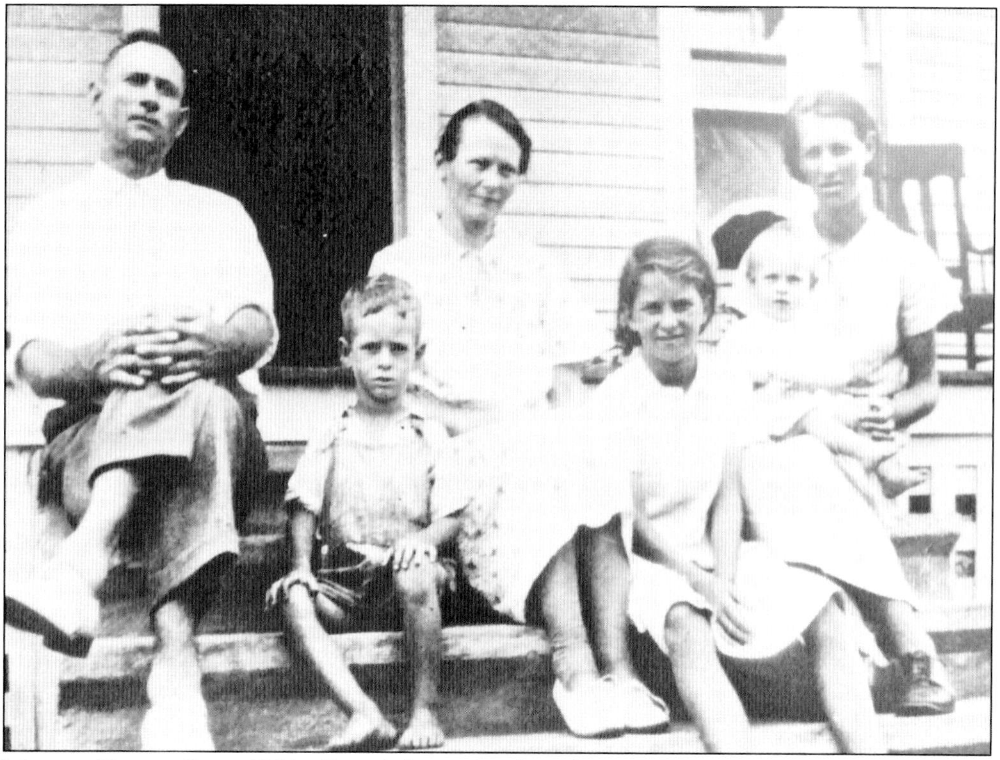

MARTIN FAMILY, LATE 1920S. From left to right, dairy farmer Austin Martin, his nephew Glenn Martin, wife Lela Francisco Martin, niece Dixie Martin, and sister Eula Martin Moore (holding Shirley Martin on her lap) are relaxing on the porch of their house on S.R. 700 in the Blackwell Chapel community. (Courtesy Nancy Moore.)

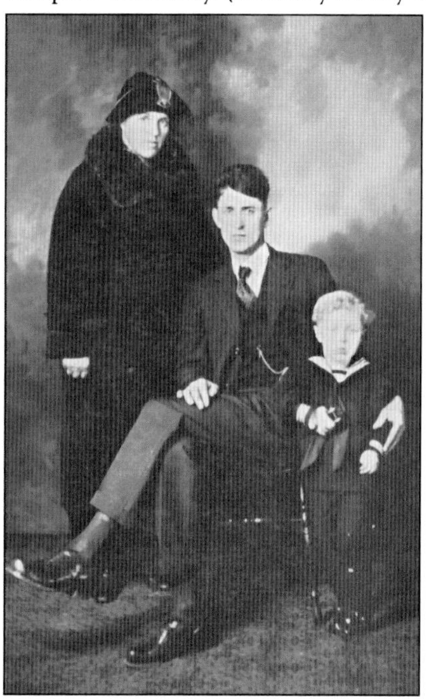

BLACKWELL FAMILY. A dapper Stonewall Jackson Blackwell of the Blackwell Chapel community is seated with his wife and son in this c. 1920 photograph. (Courtesy Eleanor Arnett Blevins.)

HELTON FAMILY. Dan Helton and Nannie McNew Helton are posed in their Sunday best in front of a scenic backdrop of mountains. These fake backdrops were in vogue for a time to represent the great outdoors. It is humorous to see a palm tree in the lower left, along with the mountains and pine trees of Appalachia. (Courtesy Eleanor Arnett Blevins.)

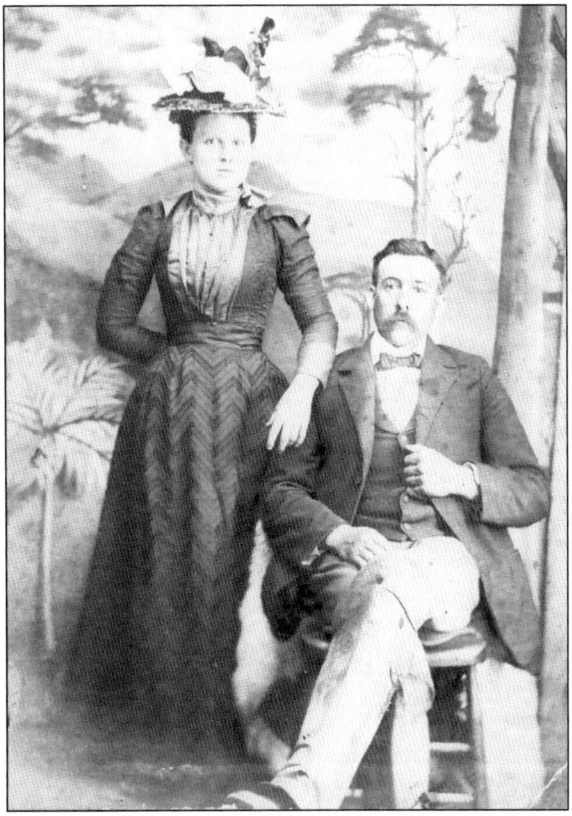

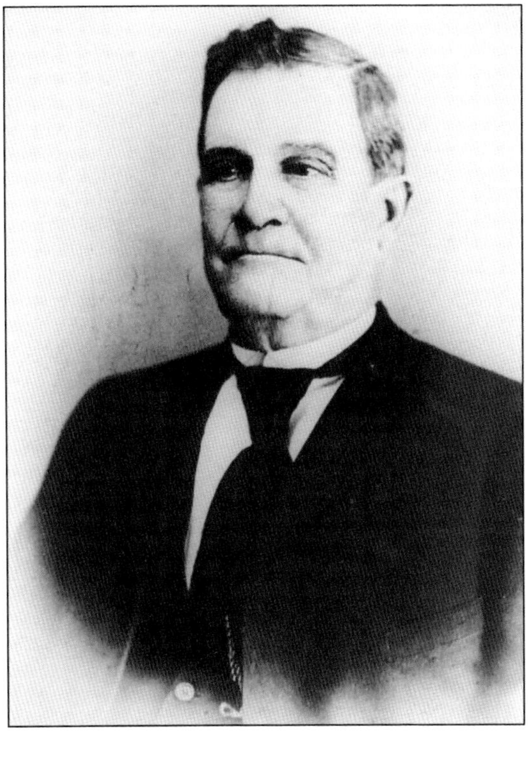

JOHN D. BLACKWELL (1822–1908). John Blackwell helped establish the Blackwell Chapel community and donated the land for the Blackwell Chapel United Methodist Church. He was a much-respected man in the community and did many good works. (Courtesy Tammy Martin and Michael Hoback.)

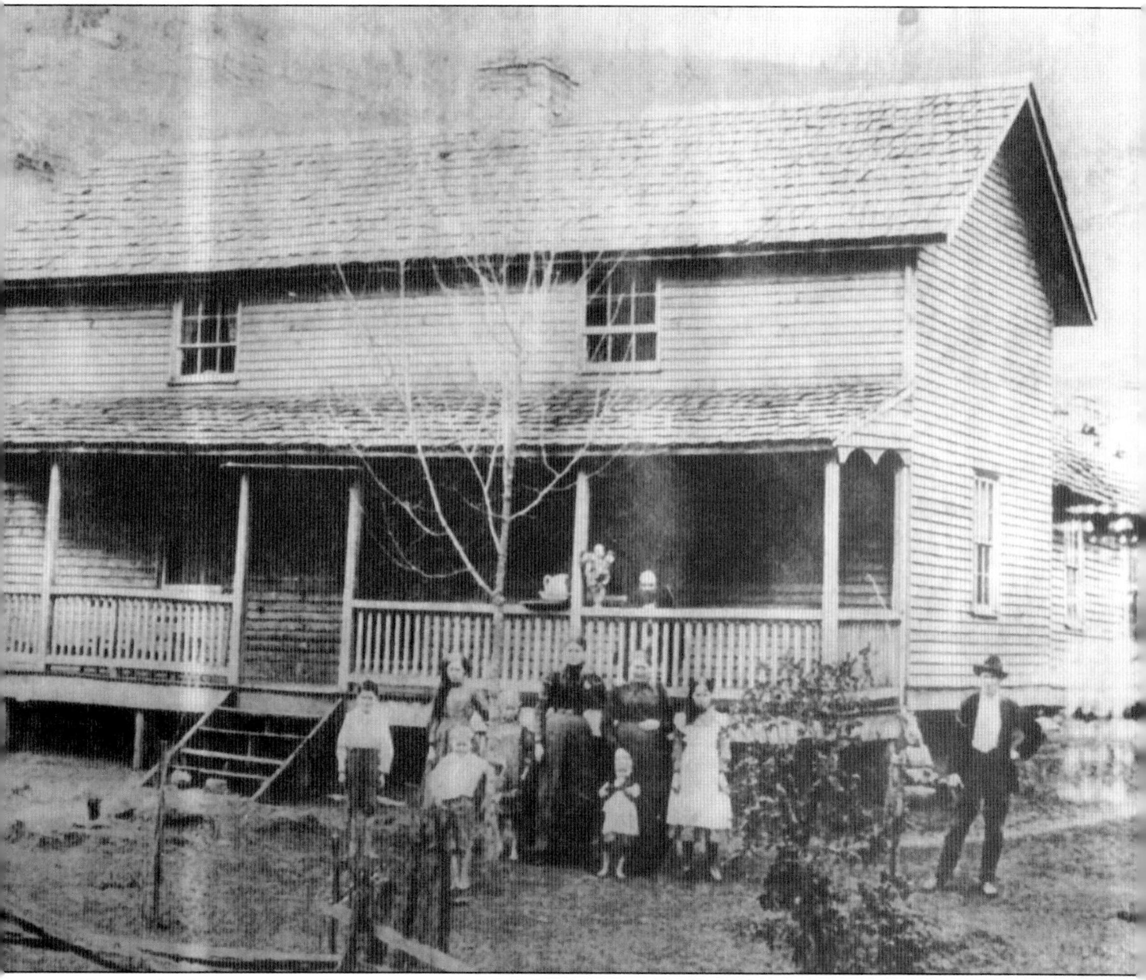

JOHN A. BLACKWELL FAMILY, C. 1898. The home of John Alexandra and Josephine Logan Blackwell is still standing one mile east of Blackwell Chapel. From left to right are (first row) Bolding Granville and George Gamon; (second row) James C. P., Alice Lake, Barbara Ella, Myrtle King, Josephine L., Hester Josephine, and John David ("Johnnie"). Seated on the porch is John Alexander Blackwell. This simple I-house style was common in this region. Decorative brackets were added on the side of the porch. The limestone foundation is visible on the bottom of the house. A washbowl is standing ready on the porch. (Courtesy Michael Hoback.)

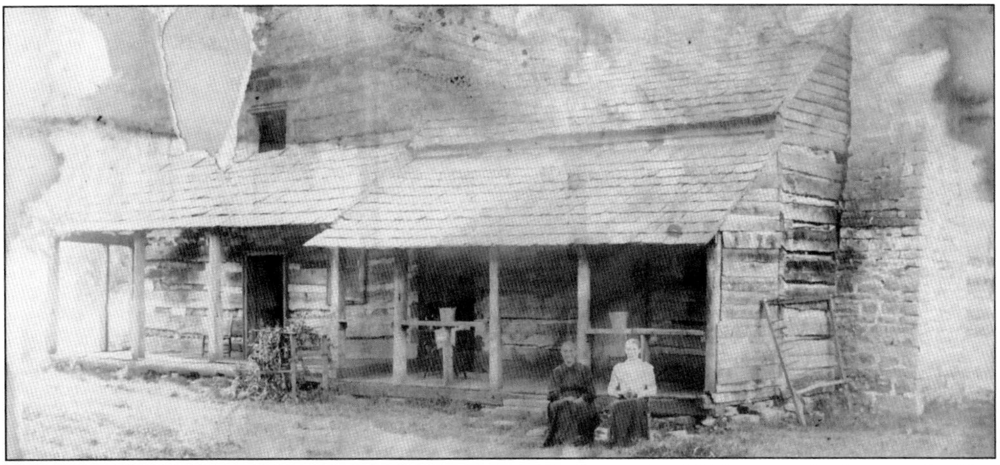

ALLEY BLACKWELL CABIN. This rustic log cabin, built in the 1800s, was the home of Alley Blackwell and was located on S.R. 700 across from Herndon's (later Crabtree) Store in Blackwell Chapel. This is a good example of the typical double-pen log cabin joined by a dogtrot in between. It is no longer standing. (Courtesy Eleanor Arnett Blevins.)

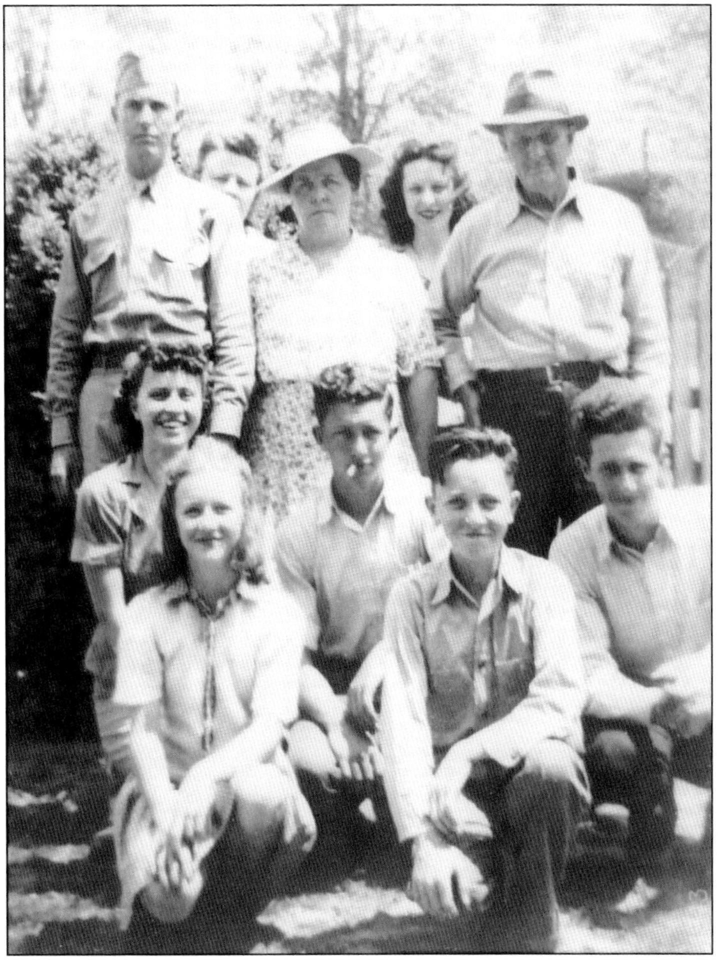

GEORGE BLACKWELL FAMILY. The Blackwell family is gathered to send their oldest son off to fight in World War II. From left to right are (kneeling) Mary Blackwell Martin, Geneva Blackwell Hoback, Ernest E. Blackwell, Roscoe E. Blackwell, and James E. Blackwell; (standing) Clarence Blackwell, Lucille Blackwell Snodgrass, Sallie Helton Blackwell, Virgie Blackwell Crabtree, and George W. Blackwell. (Courtesy Michael Hoback.)

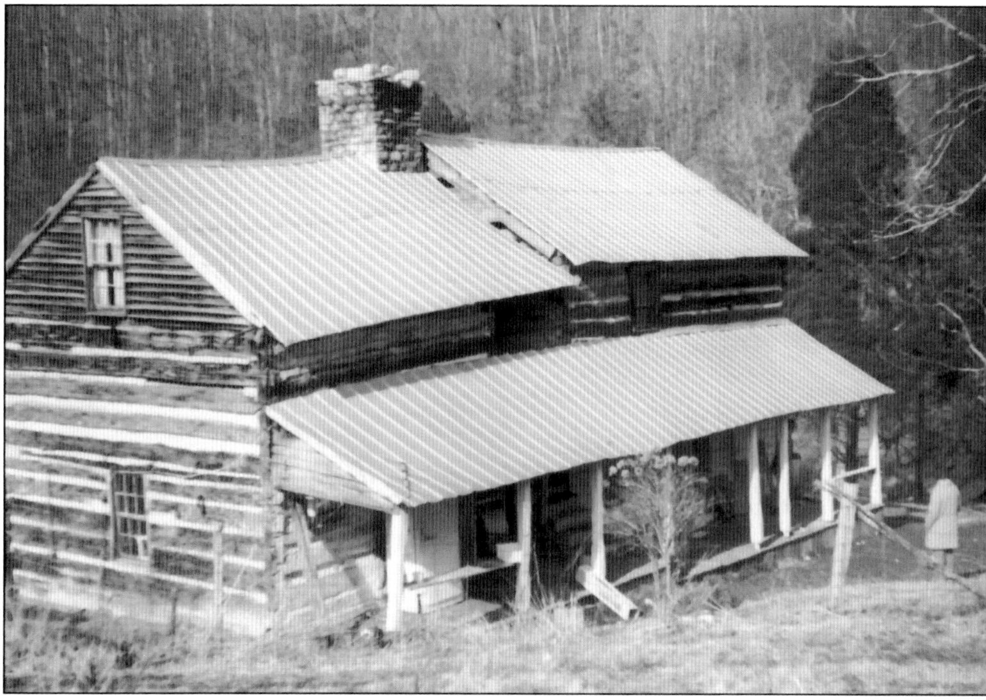

CRABTREE-BLACKWELL LOG CABIN. The Crabtree-Blackwell log cabin was built around 1849 on Moore Creek in the Blackwell Chapel community. The cabin is a double-pen structure with a loft. (Courtesy Michael Hoback.)

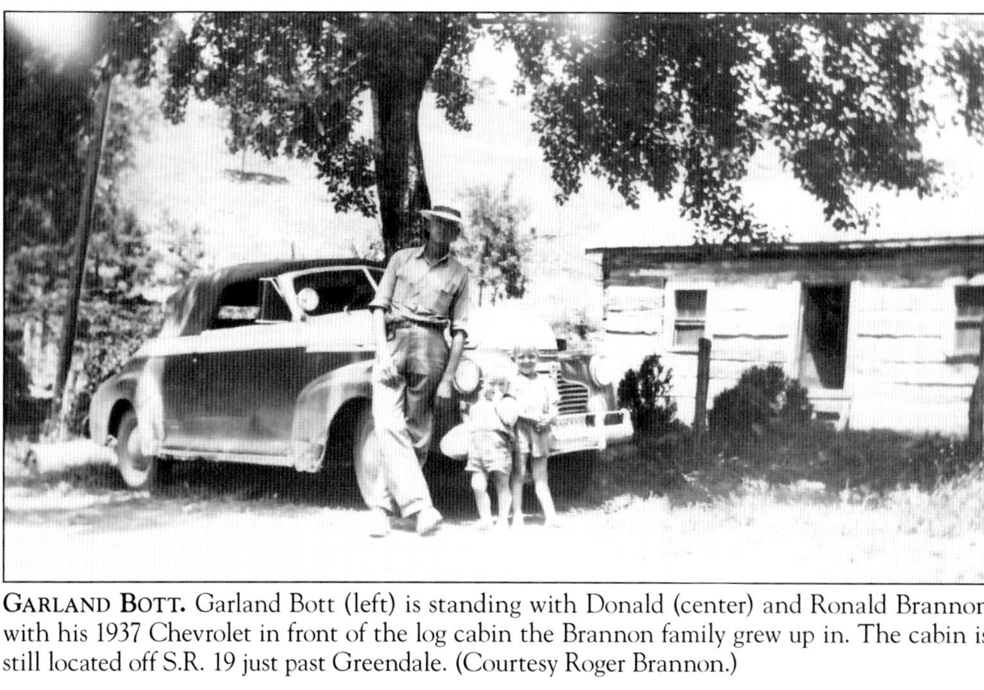

GARLAND BOTT. Garland Bott (left) is standing with Donald (center) and Ronald Brannon with his 1937 Chevrolet in front of the log cabin the Brannon family grew up in. The cabin is still located off S.R. 19 just past Greendale. (Courtesy Roger Brannon.)

EDITH BOTT BRANNON. Dressed in an early nurse's uniform around 1945, Edith Irene Bott Brannon is holding a baby. She worked at Johnston Memorial Hospital in Abingdon for many years. (Courtesy Roger Brannon.)

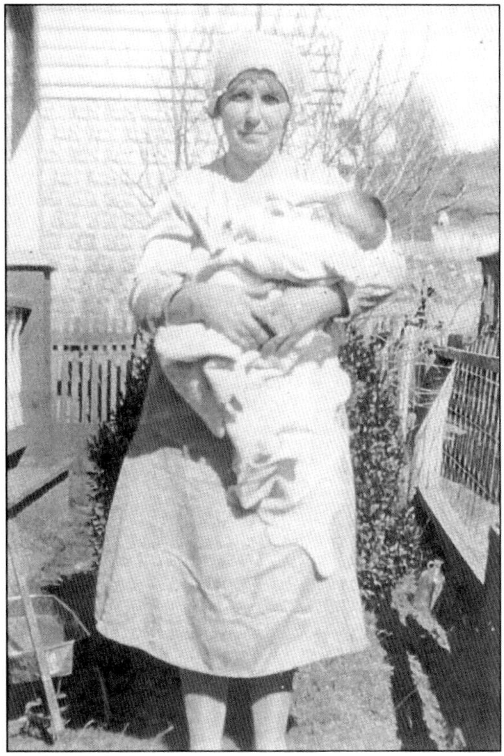

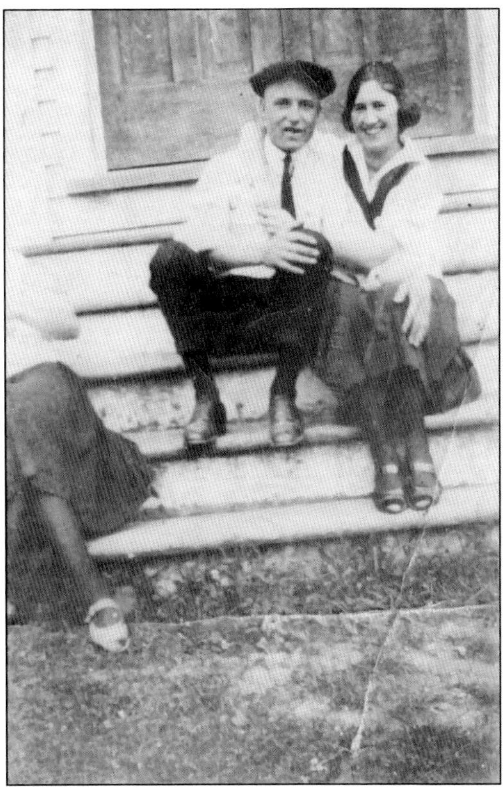

JAMES AND JOSEPHINE STOVALL. Embracing while sitting on steps are James Stovall (1901–1962) and his wife, Josephine Norris Stovall (1905–1967). Stovall was a farmer in the Prices Bridge area. (Courtesy Ruby Stovall Clark.)

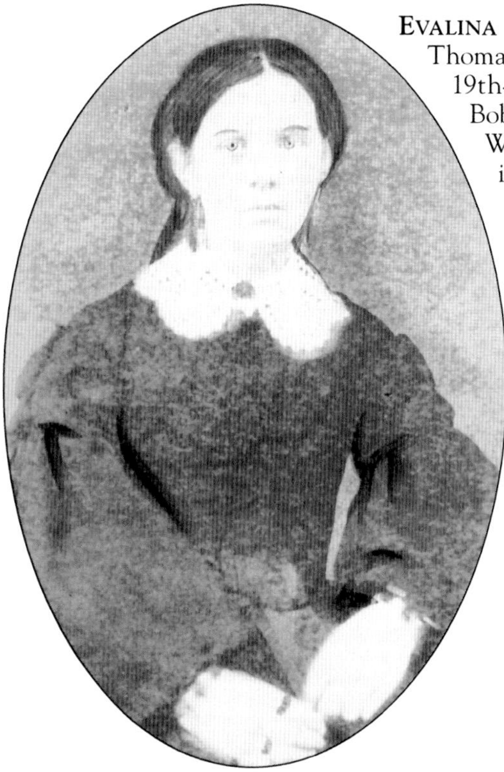

EVALINA GRAY PRESTON. Evalina Gray, who married Thomas Montgomery Preston, is shown in this mid-19th-century tintype. It was her great-grandson, Bob Preston, whose heroic efforts helped to hide Washington County records during the Union raid in Abingdon. (Courtesy Marilou Hall Preston.)

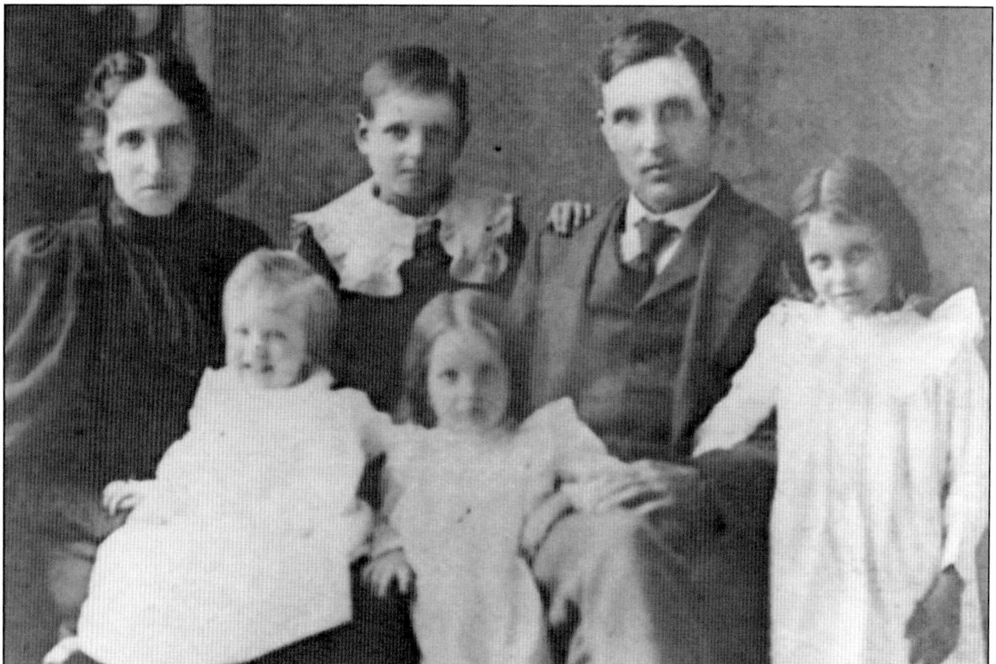

RHEA FAMILY. Pictured in about 1900 is the Joseph Felix and Florence Mock Rhea family of Damascus. Bess Rhea Preston is the young girl in the middle of the photograph. (Courtesy Marilou Hall Preston.)

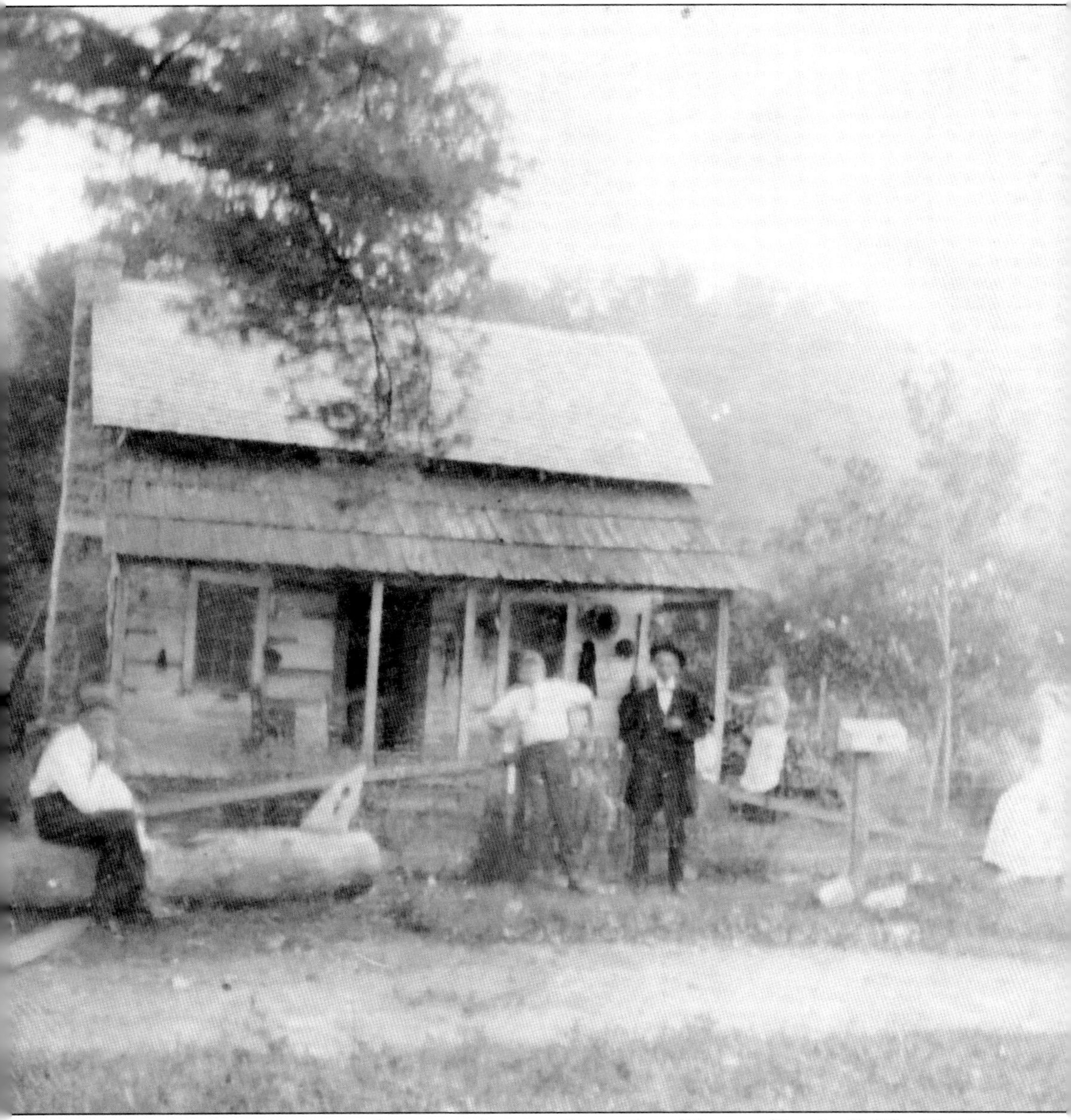

RAMSEY CABIN. The Hiram Ramsey cabin was located on Blossom Road off S.R. 58. The photograph is labeled "the honeymoon" and shows the first home for Rebecca Ramsey (far right) and Hiram Ramsey. Preacher James McChesney is the man in the long dark coat and hat. Dr. Charles Clendenen would often stop and stay overnight at the Ramseys' house on his house calls far and wide. Note the shake roof on the porch. (Courtesy Virginia Cornett Smith.)

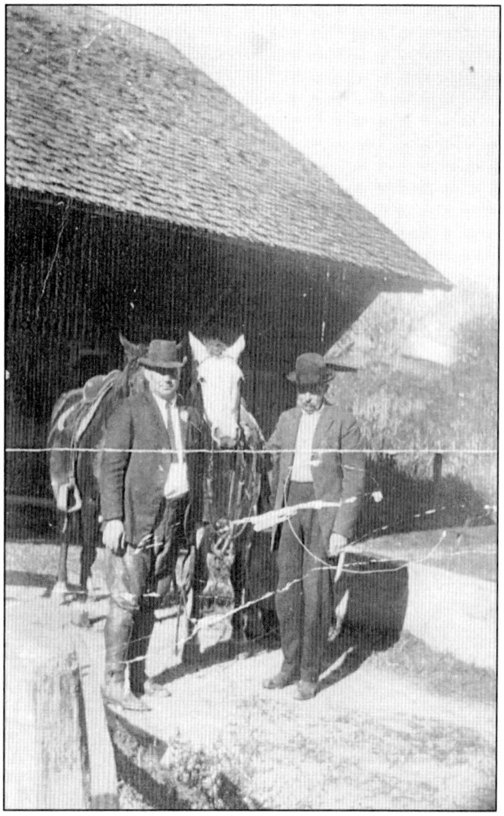

DR. C. M. CLENDENEN. Pictured here are Dr. Charles M. Clendenen (left), a local physician in the Damascus area, and John F. Ramsey. Dr. Clendenen came to Damascus in 1910 and rode horseback to pay house calls. He and Ramsey were good friends. (Courtesy Virginia Cornett Smith.)

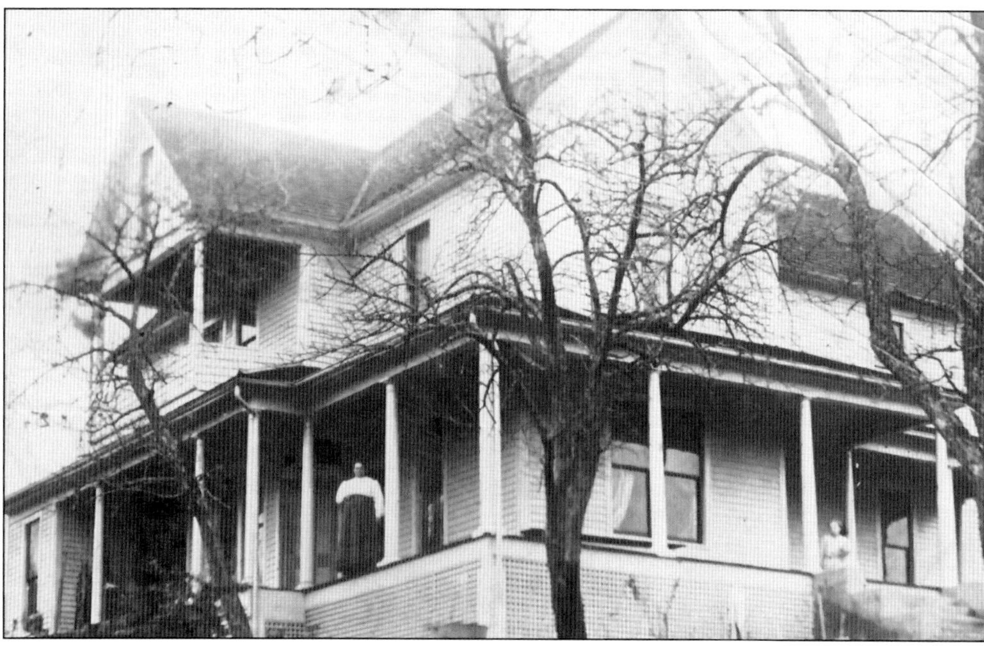

RAMSEY HOUSE. Located in Damascus, the Ramsey house was a fine dwelling for one of the older families of the town. The lady on the left is Josephine Cassandra Duff Ramsey, and Rebecca Ramsey is the child sitting on the right side of the porch. (Courtesy Virginia Cornett Smith.)

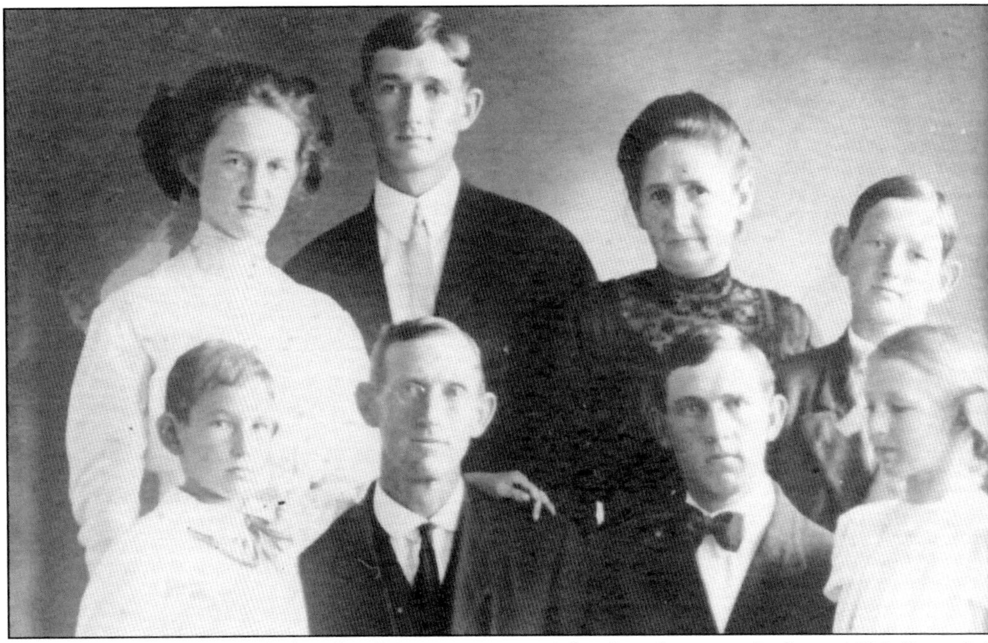

MOCK FAMILY. The Mock family of Damascus posed for this photograph about 1909. From left to right are (first row) Wilton Clement Mock, Albert Alexander Mock, Baxter Witten Mock, and Henrietta Ellen Mock; (second row) Mary Lillian Mock, James Ward Mock, Harriet Rachel Waugh Mock, and Albert Karl Mock. (Courtesy Virginia Cornett Smith.)

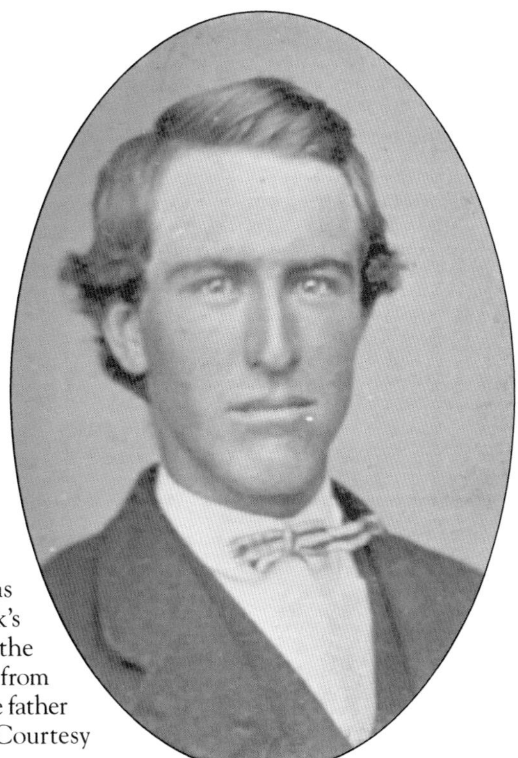

HENRY MOCK. Henry Mock (1794–1892) was a prominent businessman and owner of Mock's Mill. Mock's Mill was also the first name for the community that became Damascus. Mock was from Davie County, North Carolina, and became the father of 30 children with three different wives. (Courtesy Virginia Cornett Smith.)

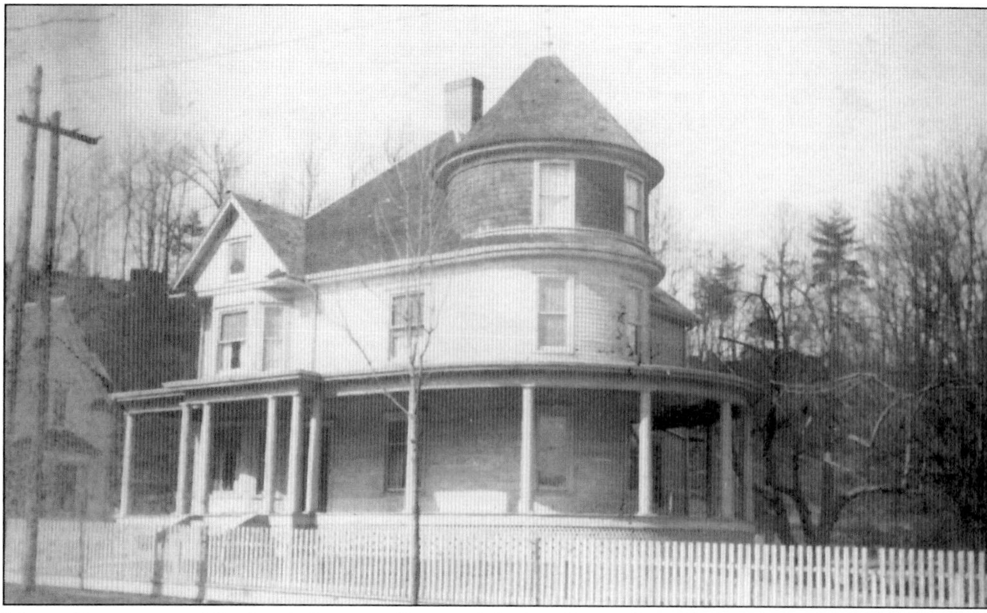

MOCK RESIDENCE. The lovely house of Baxter Mock still stands in Damascus. Many businessmen and merchants built fine houses in the late 1800s and early 1900s, a prosperous time for the community. (Courtesy Virginia Cornett Smith.)

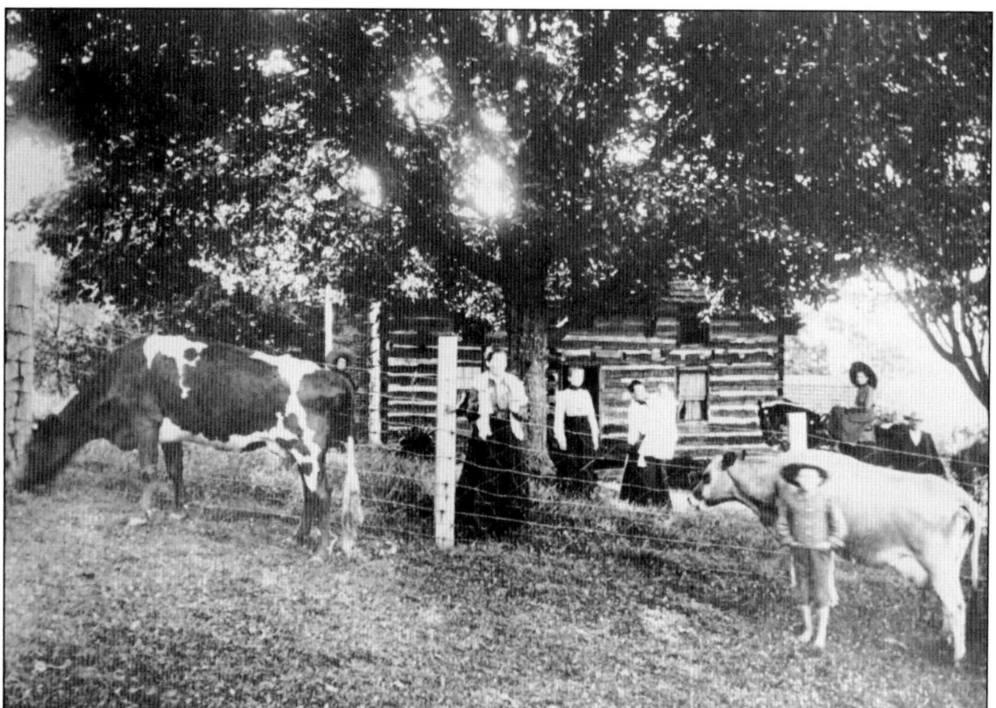

DUFF CABIN. Built in the early 1800s, the Duff log cabin once stood on the land later known as the Keller farm in the Good Hope community. The lady on the horse is using a sidesaddle. (Courtesy Walter B. "Blair" Keller Jr.)

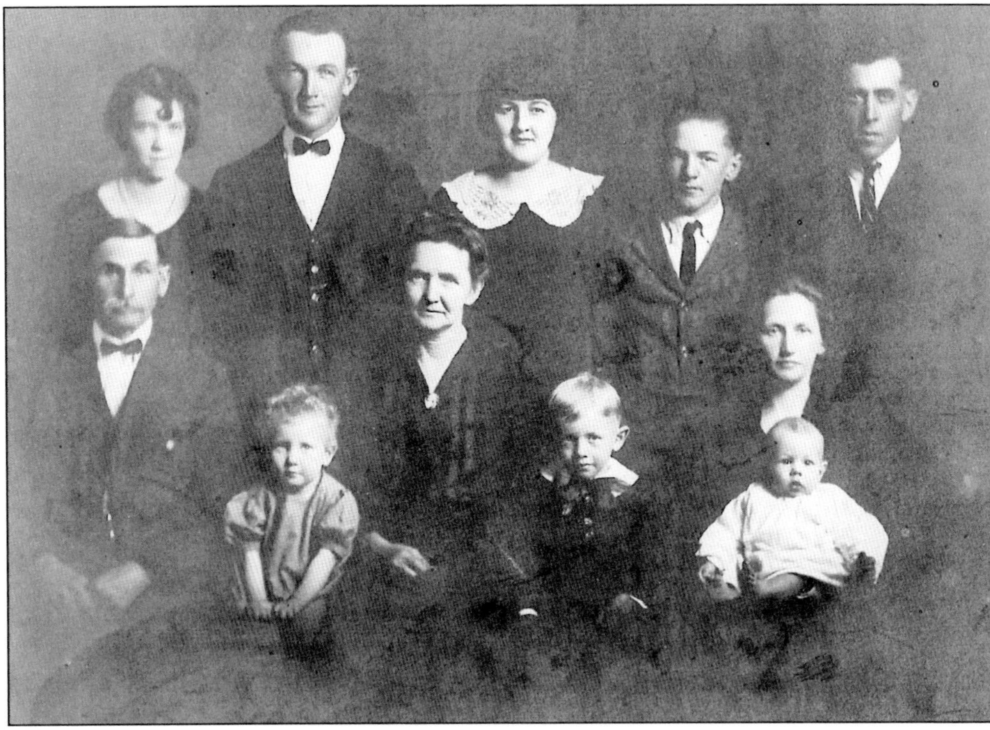

GRANTS AND KELLERS. The Grant family from Bethel and the Kellers from Watauga are shown here. From left to right are (first row) Irene Grant, Junior Grant, and Walter Grant; (second row) Walter J. Keller (1865–1958), Minnie Belle Hope Keller (1873–1927), and Naomi Keller Grant; (third row) Eula Preston Keller (1902–1995), Walter Blair Keller Sr. (1873–1927), Juanita Grant, Frank Hope Keller, and Arthur Grant. (Courtesy Walter B. "Blair" Keller Jr.)

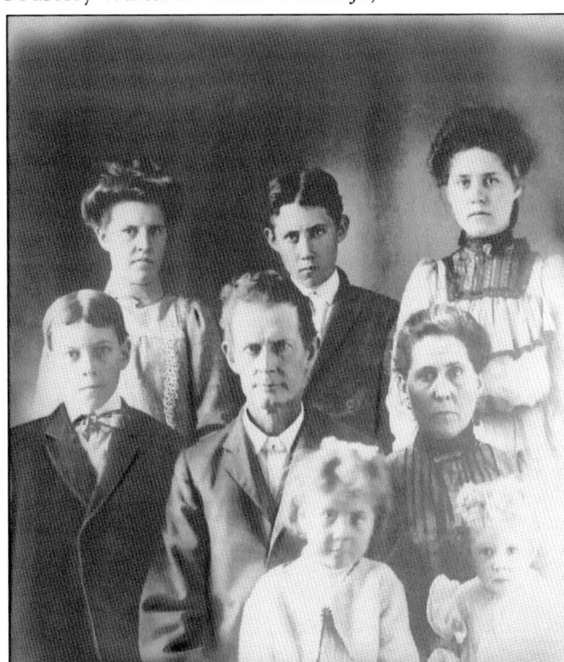

DR. JAMES GRANT FAMILY. Members of the Grant family were early landowners in the Shallow Ford area. From left to right are (first row) Eula Glenn and Grace Duff; (second row) Arthur McClure, Dr. James Lewis Grant, and Dr. Grant's wife, Molly; (third row) Ora Paxton, Robert Edwin, and Martha Jane. (Courtesy Irene Grant.)

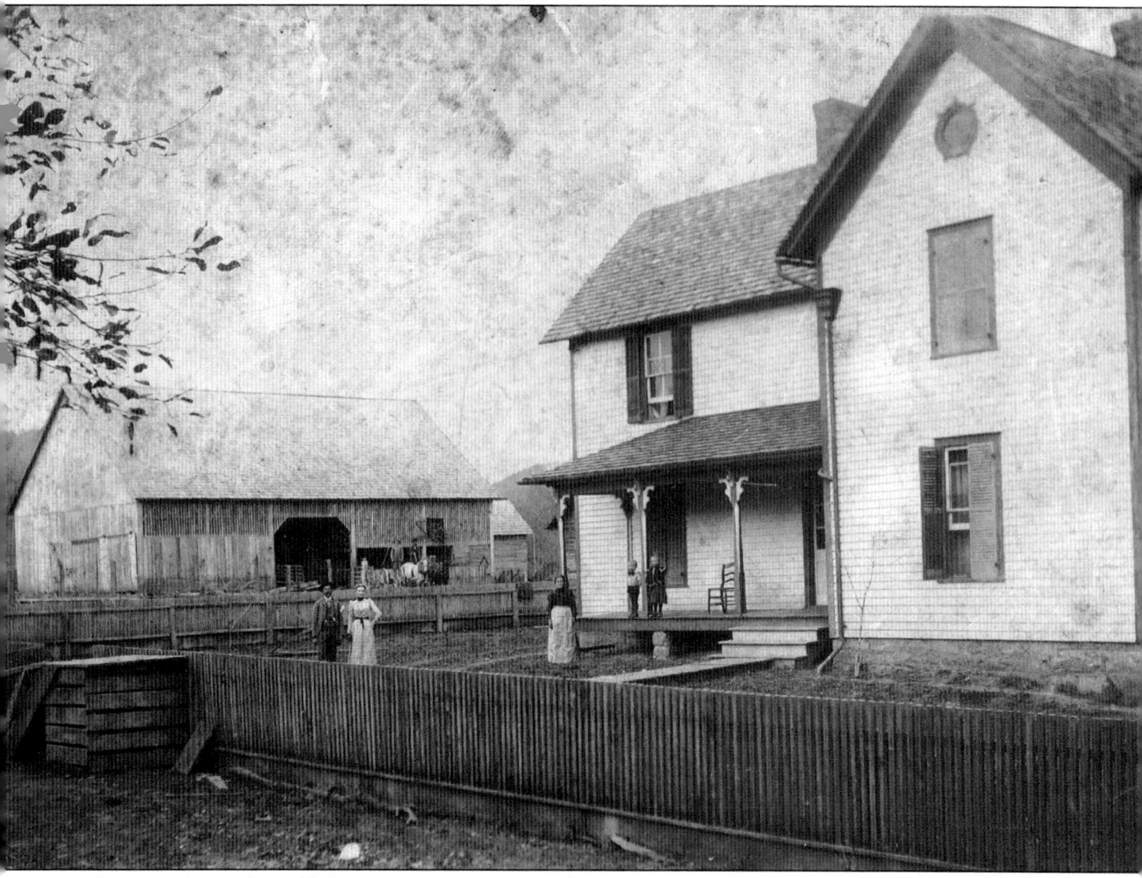

KELLER FARM. The Keller farm is a "century farm," or a farm owned by the same family for at least 100 years, is located out Good Hope Road, and is lived on by the fifth generation of Kellers. The farm once included 1,000 acres but has been reduced in size. The house was built in 1901 for $600 for Walter J. Keller, a farmer and owner of an Abingdon bank. The timber for the house and older barns was cut from the farmland, mortised, and tenoned to fit together. The timbers were cut, matched, and numbered with Roman numerals to later assemble. In this photograph, a paling fence circles the house, and a horse mounting block is positioned to enable ladies to mount the sidesaddles. Walter Joseph Keller and Minnie Belle Hope stand near the house. The children on the porch are Blair Keller Sr. and Naomi Keller. This farm serves as a tribute to the history of the Keller family, early settlers who still own the same property in Washington County. (Courtesy Irene Grant and Walter B. "Blair" Keller Jr.)

L. R. JOHNSON FAMILY. Posing with their children, Robert Lee (the baby) and Herbert, are L. R. Johnson and Susie Hockett Johnson. L. R. was a local builder and farmer. (Courtesy Helen Johnson Holliday.)

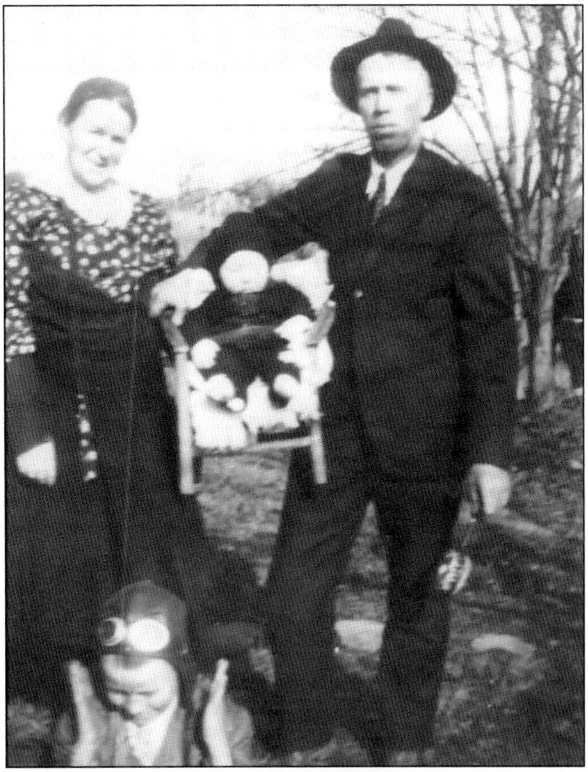

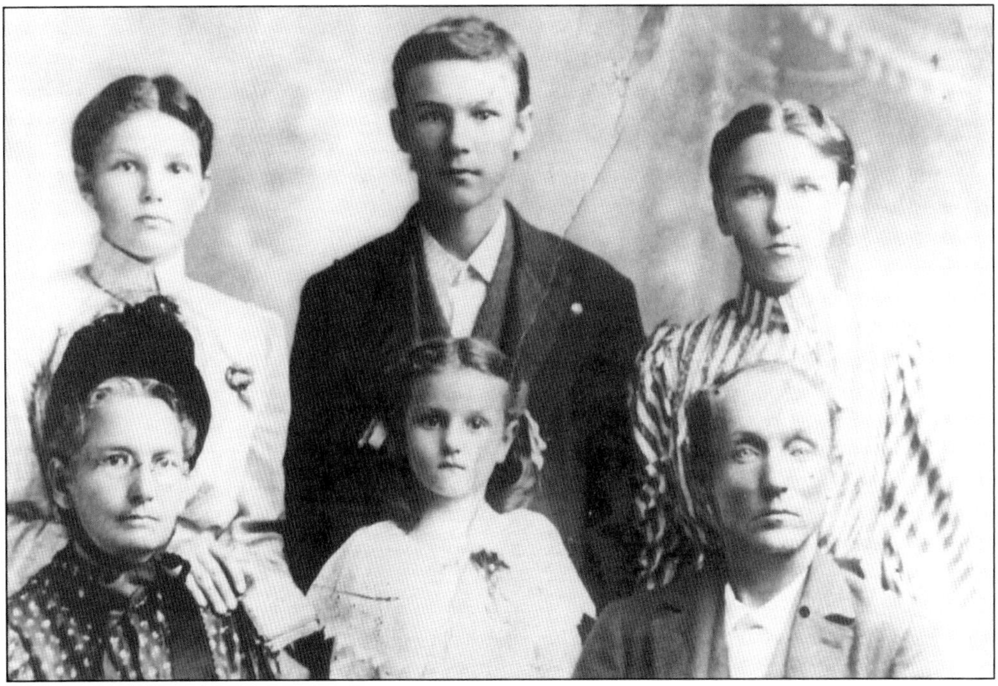

BRYAN FAMILY. The Newton and Lucy Bryan family is pictured here. From left to right are (first row) Lucy, Margaret, and Newton King Bryan; (second row) Jennie, John, and Nannie. (Courtesy Jane and Helen Bryan.)

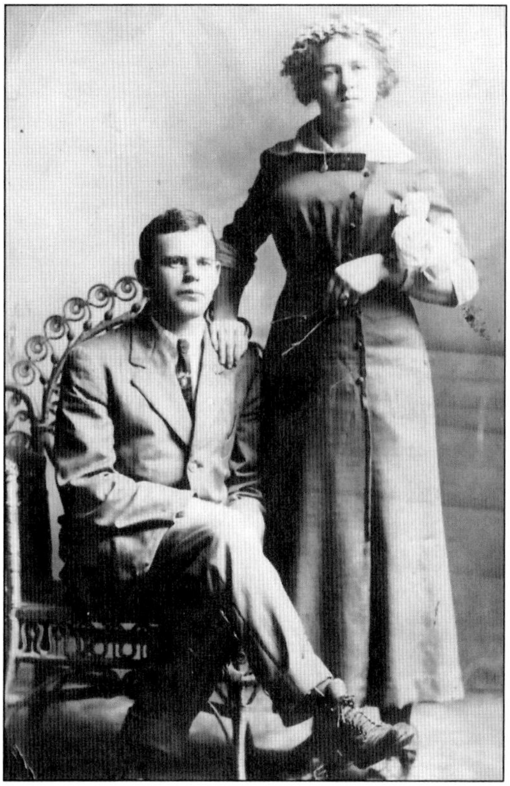

RECTORS. This postcard dated 1918 shows John Lee and Ella Viola Caldwell Rector. Lovely Ella is holding roses and wearing a wedding ring, so this may be their wedding picture. The couple lived in the Seven Springs area. (Courtesy Roy Rector.)

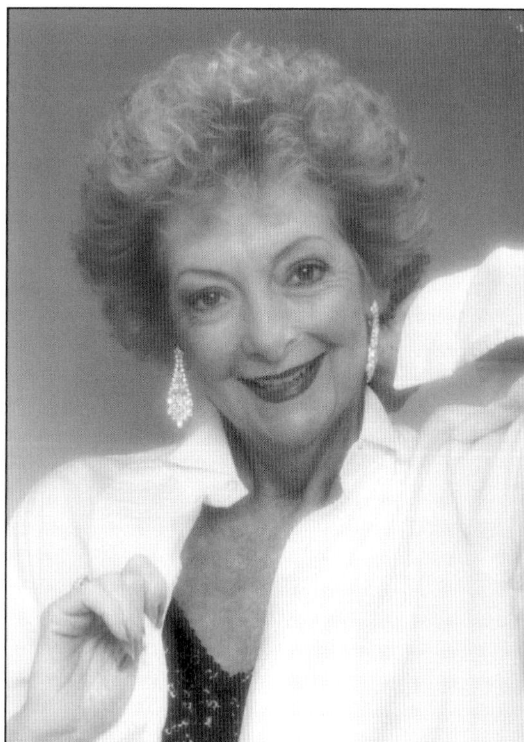

ROMA WILSON BAKER. Roma Wilson Baker (1934–1998) was a well-known, talented artist from the area. She was affiliated with the Arts Depot and the Starving Artist Restaurant and also created an art award for the local YWCA. She received a memorial people's choice award from the Depot Artist Association. Baker is still missed by many folks. (Courtesy Doris Musick.)

BIBLIOGRAPHY

Davis, Edward H., and Edward B. Morgan. *The Virginia Creeper Trail Companion*. Johnson City, TN: 1997.
Hall, Louise Fortune. *A History of Damascus 1793–1950*. Abingdon, VA: John Anderson Press, 1950.
The Historical Society of Washington County, Virginia. Miscellaneous files.
King, Nanci C. *Places in Time: Volume I, Abingdon, Virginia 1778–1880*. Abingdon, VA: self-published, 1989.
———. *Places in Time: Volume II, Abingdon, Meadowview, and Glade Spring, Virginia*. Abingdon, VA: self-published, 1994.
———. *Places in Time: Volume III, South from Abingdon to the Holston*. Abingdon, VA: self-published, 1997.
McGuinn, Doug. *The Virginia Creeper*. Boone, NC: Bamboo Books, 1998.
Neal, J. Allen. *Bicentennial History of Washington County, Virginia*. Dallas, TX: Taylor Publishing, 1977.
Summers, Lewis Preston. *History of Southwest Virginia 1746–1786, Washington County, 1777–1870*. rep., Johnson City, TN: The Overmountain Press, 1989.
Tennis, Joe. *Southwest Virginia Crossroads*. Johnson City, TN: The Overmountain Press, 2004.
Warmuth, Donna Akers. *Abingdon, Virginia*. Charleston, SC: Arcadia Publishing, 2002.
———. *Washington County*. Charleston, SC: Arcadia Publishing, 2006.
Weaver, Jeffrey C. *Saltville*. Charleston, SC: Arcadia Publishing, 2006.

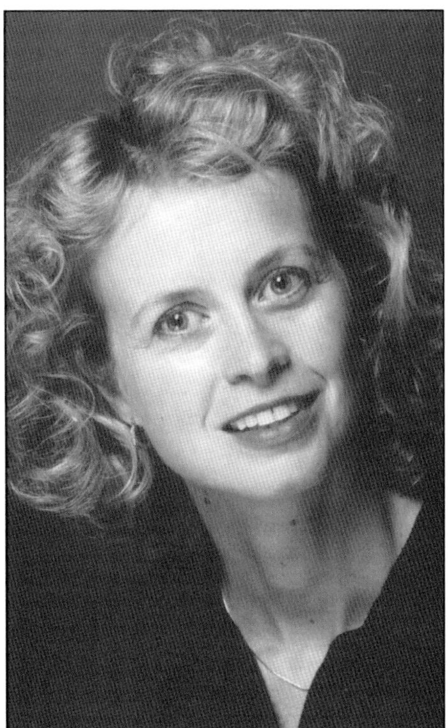

Donna Akers Warmuth is proud to be a ninth-generation Washington County native and has combined her love of local history, preservation, and people's stories by compiling several books in the Images of America series (*Washington County Revisited*, *Washington County*, *Abingdon*, *Boone*, and *Blowing Rock*), as well as an Abingdon children's book and a ghost story and legends book. This is the second Washington County Images book, necessitated by the county's geographic size, as well as the large number of photographs and stories from residents and readers.

The author has published stories and articles in *Appalachian Heritage*, *Smoky Mountain Living*, and *High Country* magazine. As well as winning several regional writing contests, Donna's works include humorous anecdotes about Boone mountain living that aired on WNCW in Spindale, North Carolina.

Today she, her husband Greg, and their two young sons, Riley and Owen, live near the Blue Ridge Parkway just outside Boone, where she writes, teaches writing workshops to children and adults, and is working on an Images of America book on Watauga County, as well as a historical fiction novel set at White's Mill near Abingdon.

Consistent with our mission to preserve history on a local level, this book was printed in South Carolina on American-made paper and manufactured entirely in the United States. Products carrying the accredited Forest Stewardship Council (FSC) label are printed on 100 percent FSC-certified paper.

MADE IN THE USA